FASCINATING RHYTHM

FASCINATING RHYTHM

READING JAZZ IN AMERICAN WRITING

David Yaffe

PRINCETON UNIVERSITY PRESS ■ *Princeton and Oxford*

Copyright © 2006 by Princeton University Press
Published by Princeton University Press, 41 William Street,
Princeton, New Jersey 08540
In the United Kingdom: Princeton University Press, 3 Market Place,
Woodstock, Oxfordshire OX20 1SY

Library of Congress Cataloging-in-Publication Data
Yaffe, David, 1973–
Fascinating rhythm : reading jazz in American writing / David Yaffe.
p. cm.
Includes bibliographical references and index.
ISBN-13:978-0-691-12357-8
ISBN-10:0-691-12357-8 (acid-free paper)
1. American literature–20th century–History and criticism.   2. Jazz in literature.
3. Jazz musicians–Biography–History and criticism.   4. Music and   .
literature–History–20th century.   5. African American musicians in literature.
6. Ellison, Ralph–Knowledge–Jazz.   7. Jazz musicians in literature.   I. Title.
PS228.J39Y34 2005
810'.9357—dc22   2005043242

British Library Cataloging-in-Publication Data is available

This book has been composed in *Adobe Caslon* and Futura

Printed on acid-free paper.

pup. princeton.edu

Printed in the United States of America

1   3   5   7   9   10   8   6   4   2

Grateful acknowledgment is made for permission to reprint excerpts
from the following poems:

"This Sick Man" by Wallace Stevens; "Dream Boogie," "Consider Me," "To a Negro
Jazz Band in a Parisian Cabaret," and "Motto" by Langston Hughes; "The Day
Lady Died" by Frank O'Hara reprinted by permission of Random House.

"Mexico City Blues," reprinted by permission by SLL/ Sterling Lord Literistic, Inc.
Copyright 1959 by Jack Kerouac.

"February in Sydney" and "Twilight Seduction" from *Neon Vernacular*.
Copyright 1993 by Yusef Komunyakaa and reprinted with permission of
Wesleyan University Press.

C O N T E N T S

FOR AMY

"Boy, am I riffin' this evening, I hope."
—Louis Armstrong

ACKNOWLEDGMENTS

I began formulating the ideas for this study the year I began graduate school, when I realized I would be allowed to write it. I started writing jazz criticism when I was an undergraduate, when Gary Giddins gave me assignments in his *Village Voice Jazz Supplement* and, when he went on a sabbatical from the *Voice*, my first push into jazz journalism. I subsequently met Stanley Crouch, and our hours of talking and arguing undoubtedly influenced some of these pages. They will each find much to disagree with here, but then, as Emerson wrote, imitation is suicide.

I discovered scholarly possibilities for my jazz scavenging when I had the good fortune to meet Krin Gabbard, who read every chapter of this book and has been a loyal confidant, mentor, and mensch. Krin showed me how current approaches to the humanities and jazz criticism could be ingeniously synthesized, and I thank him and his wife, Paula, for being my surrogate Upper West Side family. Another jazz scholar who read this entire study and gave me much needed encouragement was John Szwed, whose marathon phone calls have inspired and instructed me into the wee small hours. In the later stages, some rambling dialogues with Eric Lott regenerated my thinking about American culture. In addition to Krin and Eric, I was also fortunate to give panels with Farah Jasmine Griffin, Bob O'Meally, Brent Edwards, Arnold Rampersad, Yusef Komunyakaa, Johanna

Garvey, and Herman Beavers, and the events spurred some of the writing that ended up here. I am grateful for the collaboration.

At the CUNY Graduate Center I was fortunate to have teachers who encouraged my interdisciplinary interests and countenanced my disappearances into the wilderness of New York media. As my director, Wayne Koestenbaum has been a constant source of support, inspiration, brilliance, and fabulousness, and his comments always gave me the push I needed. Wayne combines my favorite Henry James maxims—"Be kind, be kind, be kind," and "Be one of those on whom nothing is lost"—as well as the master could have ever envisioned. And Morris Dickstein has been a steadfast polymath and nurturer of my work for years. He selected me for a 2000 Mellon seminar he directed that gave me the space to formulate some key ideas for this study, and he has continued to look out for me and provide an admirable intellectual example. I am also thankful to Marc Dolan, who dazzled me with his quick intelligence, perception, and range of cultural knowledge, asking questions that inspired and enriched the final revisions. Thanks to Luke Menand, who helped me when I was starting out, and has always provided an example of exquisite prose. A CUNY Writing Fellowship gave me the support and the time to write the final pages and allowed me to take a hiatus from the freelance grind. A wonderful benefit of that fellowship has been my friendship with John Matteson, whose kindness helped make the writing of this book possible. My hat is off to Scott Saul, who made some optimal suggestions for reshaping the book. I'm also grateful to Meridith Walters, who gave me a place to stay when I needed to do research at the Library of Congress, as well as an always sympathetic ear and good humor.

Much thanks to Hanne Winarsky at Princeton University Press, whose enthusiasm for this project accelerated what is often a glacial editorial process. It was my good fortune that she believed in this project so strongly, making sure it saw print more quickly than I had any right to expect. Jonathon Munk's judicious copyediting saved my syntax many times. Big gushy gratitude to Amy Zielinski, who gave me a professional photo shoot for nothing but pizza and a cheap carafe of Chianti, and who did what she could to make me look like a rock star. I am also grateful to Grant Orbson for his swift, smart work on the index. Michael Cogswell at the Louis Armstrong House kindly reduced his rate for a photograph, a generous gesture for a subvention-deprived author.

My parents, Martin and Connie Yaffe, supported the musical and literary curiosities that gave me the ability to write this, and I am grateful that, even in my grad school despair, they never once told me I should have gone to law school. My grandmother, Norma Stern, let me know she was proud and was enormously generous in many a difficult time.

I reserve my greatest gratitude for my wife, Amy Leal, who lived through every moment of this book with me while writing two of her own, and it would take a volume longer than this study to express my debt. She remains my most perceptive reader and most trusted editor, looking out for *le mot juste* while offering encouragement, insight, scholarly acumen, humor, love, and much more. I could not have imagined writing these words without the pleasure of sharing them with her. Amy is all for me, body and soul, and I dedicate this to her.

Brooklyn, New York

INTRODUCTION

In Donald Barthelme's short story "The King of Jazz," attempts to describe a trombone solo by Hokie Mokie demonstrate the folly of jazz writing. The story narrates a cutting contest between Mokie, the former "King of Jazz," and his Japanese contender as onlookers grasp for superlatives. The dethroned trombonist, whose playing had earlier been described as having an "epiphanic glow" with a style known as "English Sunrise," emerges with a solo so thrilling that it inspires a series of questions that build to their own absurdist crescendo:

> You mean that sound that sounds like the cutting edge of life? That sounds like polar bears crossing Arctic ice pans? That sounds like a herd of musk ox in full flight? That sounds like male walruses diving to the bottom of the sea? That sounds like fumaroles smoking on the slopes of Mount Katmai? That sounds like the wild turkey walking through the deep, soft forest? That sounds like beavers chewing trees in an Appalachian marsh? That sounds like an oyster fungus growing on an aspen trunk? That sounds like a mule deer wandering a montane of the Sierra Nevada? That sounds like prairie dogs kissing? That sounds like witch grass tumbling or a river meandering? That sounds like manatees munching seaweed at Cape Sable? That sounds like coatimundis moving in packs across the face of Arkansas?[1]

Barthelme famously observed that "the principle of collage is the central principle of all art in the twentieth century," but these descriptions, even when patched together, do not add up to much—and that is Barthelme's point. Hokie Mokie might be blowing his trombone with superb virtuosity, but the act of matching it to language is, to paraphrase Barthelme, about as elegant as a herd of musk ox in full flight. With each simile more useless than the last, Barthelme demonstrates the pomposity, hubris, and failure of language when it is applied to jazz.

Since "The King of Jazz" is a parody, Barthelme offered no alternative to a jazz writing built on ridiculously insufficient similes. In recent years, jazz and literature scholars have been attempting to do just that. Some of the most important work now being done in jazz studies engages in research that says as much about what jazz musicians thought of themselves as it does about the writers who were inspired by them. Recent examples would include John Szwed's anthropological journey into the minds of Sun Ra and Miles Davis (*Space is the Place* and *So What*); Krin Gabbard's shrewd scholarship of the cinematic, psychoanalytic, and racial terrain of the jazz canon (*Jammin' at the Margins* and his anthologies *Representing Jazz* and *Jazz Among the Discourses*); Robert O'Meally's and Farah Jasmine Griffin's demystifications of Billie Holiday (O'Meally's *Lady Day* and Griffin's *If You Can't Be Free, Be a Mystery*); Ingrid Monson and Paul Berliner's semantics of improvisation (Monson's *Saying Something* and Berliner's *Thinking in Jazz*); Scott DeVeaux's rewriting of the history of bebop (*The Birth of Bebop*); Eric Porter's account of jazz musicians as critics and activists (*What is this Thing Called Jazz?*); Fred Moten's theoretical investigations into African American Aesthetics (*In the Break*); Brent Hayes Edwards's international inquiries into improvisation's syntax ("Louis Armstrong and the Syntax of Scat," "The Literary Ellington"); Michael Jarrett's demonstrations of jazz as a pedagogical model (*Drifting on a Read*); Aldon Nielsen's limning of postmodernism and postbop aesthetics (*Black Chant*); Eric Lott's narratives about America's ongoing minstrel show and bebop's social consequences (*Love and Theft* and "Double V., Double Time"); and Scott Saul's historical narrative about how jazz musicians pressured the social upheavals of the 1960s (*Freedom is, Freedom Ain't*). These are among the many scholarly studies that have been important for this one, and the interdisciplinary work on this subject is just getting started.

Fascinating Rhythm builds on these scholarly conversations, using narrative, anecdote, and musical analysis to unravel what has often been a convoluted interaction between jazz and American writing. Throughout this study, when I describe performances by Louis Armstrong, Billie Holiday, Charles Mingus, or Miles Davis, I hope that I have used literary devices with more precision than have Barthelme's commentators. Part of what makes "The King of Jazz" funny is that the arcane similes are doled out as part of a conversation between effete jazz snobs who know all the rules. The musicians, meanwhile, are oblivious—they are too mired in a cutting contest to pay attention to prattle—and the uninitiated are left out in the cold. If mystification is inevitable, demystification is, on its own, sterilizing. The purpose of this study is not to dismiss the inspiration that jazz provided for novelists and poets, but to see if literary writing about jazz can hold up to a serious historical, aesthetic, and biographical investigation of the music and the artists who made it.

The jazz fan is such a marginal cultural figure that he—and it is, alas, often "he"—spends a considerable amount of energy identifying the places where the music is misrepresented when it does make it into cultural arenas outside clubs, festivals, and reissue packages. Sometimes, these arguments are about trivial carelessness: how could Cameron Crowe misidentify the year of the Miles Davis and John Coltrane Stockholm concert in the film *Jerry McGuire* as 1963? (It was 1960.) But getting jazz wrong can also have more troubling implications. When Norman Mailer claimed that "jazz is orgasm" in "The White Negro" (1957), he was not simply off base in his conflation; the word "jazz" has been associated with everything from an African word for "jism" to a synonym for "fuck"—a meaning upheld even by Jazz at Lincoln Center Artistic Director Wynton Marsalis.[2] And yet in the year when Mailer wrote this, Coltrane was famous for practicing so extensively that he could spend an entire day on the same scale. His regimen was so demanding, he would even practice using harp and violin books, too, insatiably reaching beyond what his instrument was designed to produce.[3]

What Coltrane produced might have sounded like ecstasy to Mailer, but it was rehearsed and thought out with a religious devotion. In the music of Thelonious Monk, Miles Davis, and other figures Mailer revered, that orgasmic sensibility was expressed with a level of harmonic and rhythmic sophistication he never recognized. Because improvisation was not notated, it was often confused with mere unrestrained id, and forty years after Mailer's essay, Allen Ginsberg still claimed of bebop that "anyone can pick up an axe and blow." Mailer's and Ginsberg's characterizations of jazz as noble savagery are not that different from a statement overheard by Miles Davis on a night when he was sharing the bandstand with Charlie Parker: comedian Milton Berle referred to the band as "headhunters," a derisive epithet reclaimed by bop musicians who spoke of "cutting heads" in jam sessions, and revised generations later as the name of Herbie Hancock's wildly successful fusion band. Getting jazz wrong in literary writing has often been a case of underestimating the complexity of jazz musicians—even in intended admiration.

I would be equally remiss if I did not take these levels of understanding into account. If this study does not offer a single unified theory that can explain representations of jazz in writing, it is because the music itself has steadfastly eluded stable definition. "Jazz is only what you are," said Louis Armstrong, and Duke Ellington, Charlie Parker, Charles Mingus, Miles Davis, Max Roach, and Anthony Braxton, to name only a few, have all expressed misgivings with the word.[4] This study will not attempt to impose order where it does not exist. Nor will it attempt to be an exhaustive account of jazz's representations in the history of American writing—a work that would necessarily span volumes.

Jazz fans are often notorious completists, but the musicians often resist the whims of collectors and requesters. I remember seeing Hancock playing a trio gig at the Blue Note in 1995, accompanied by Ron Carter on bass and Gene Jackson on drums. At one point, a white man of advanced years began calling out for a Vincent Youmans number. "More Than You Know!" the patron called out. "More Than *You* Know?" Hancock replied. "You see, we only rehearsed certain songs. If we had anticipated every song you were going to call out, that . . . would have been a *long* rehearsal." There will be readers of this book who will wonder why certain authors are not discussed at length here. This study is neither an encyclopedia nor an attempt to uncover every last reference to jazz in American letters. That would have been a long rehearsal.

And there are plenty of texts that made it into my rehearsal but not the final cut, and this is not because I am unaware of them, but because they simply did not fit into my rhetorical strategy. So while, for example, the first chapter examines the relationships between blacks and Jews in jazz and literature, there is no discussion of Mezz Mezzrow's *Really the Blues*. Why? Mezzrow was a friend of Armstrong, a hepcat, pothead, and Virgil through the jazz matrix—a Jew who actually believed he had physically turned black. All this is of tremendous interest, but since this is a book that examines writers on the level of Philip Roth or Ralph Ellison, or musicians as vital as Louis Armstrong and Charles Mingus, Mezzrow, a mediocre clarinet player and entertaining, if sentimental writer, could neither write like Ellison nor wail clarinet like Sidney Bechet. His importance, in other words, resides more in the realm of anthropological interest than aesthetic exactitude, and thus does not fit with the figures examined in depth here. Other modes will reveal much about ethnic appropriation in his wild narrative. There are many other writers that merit attention in this book but do not get it, and an entire study could be written about what is not included here—including William Carlos Williams's "Old Bunk's Band," Toni Morrison's *Jazz*, Elizabeth Bishop's "Songs for a Colored Singer," and William Melvin Kelley's *A Drop of Patience*, in which the music is never described, but the metaphor of the struggling performer is depicted with harrowing immediacy. These outtakes deserve to be polished off and appreciated, but they simply did not fit into the narrative I was weaving here. A study of equal length could certainly be written about the writers I did *not* include.

What this book *does* examine is a series of crucial moments when jazz has surfaced in the work of major American novelists, poets, and playwrights, and how, in turn, the musicians chose to represent themselves in autobiographies. The movement of this book is more thematic than it is historical or syllogistic. Jazz history is an unstable mass of recordings, liner notes, reviews, biographies, documentaries, and endless arguments. I have used that history—a history that is itself still in revision—as the basis for what Ralph Ellison would have called a "jazz-shaped" reading of some American literary texts.

This book tells a story of how Ellison's description of a Louis Armstrong record led to a jazz repertory movement labeled as "neoconservative"; how Langston Hughes and Charles Mingus's distinct aesthetics clashed in the recording studio; how a Billie Holiday performance left Frank O'Hara's muse breathless; how a Bessie Smith-inspired record saved Salinger's Holden Caulfield from phonies; and how autobiographies by Billie Holiday, Charles Mingus, and Miles Davis both reinforced and redeemed jazz's red-light district origins. I have let jazz history—more nuanced, distanced, and researched now than it was for many of the writers discussed in this study—serve as a background for the texts, often allowing it to demonstrate how literary writing can be both dated and prophetic. The distinct role jazz played in ethnic relations, the Ellisonian formation of the jazz canon, the collision between the poetics of jazz and jazz-inspired poetry, and the revelations and mystifications surfacing in jazz autobiography—all of these subjects will be given close attention in this study.

In attempting to describe jazz, writers have used the technical language of musicology, the contextual devices of history, the complex dialogue of race, or resorted to figurative language, using those very images, metaphors, and similes parodied in "The King of Jazz" to describe rhythms, chords, tones and the ephemeral drama of improvisation. When Ellison wrote about the music, he took all of these factors into account. In the prologue to *Invisible Man*, Ellison balanced literary devices, harmonic insight, and history when he used a metaphor to describe how Louis Armstrong "bent that military instrument into a beam of lyrical sound."[5] Ellison's image is as ambitious as one of Barthelme's absurdist similes. It simultaneously addresses the "bent" thirds of the blues with a reference to Armstrong's early cornet training at the Colored Waif's Home. And yet it is also steeped in Armstrong's technique, idiom, and biography, as well as a metaphysical conceit indebted to T. S. Eliot. For jazz to be a guiding principle for a major modernist novel was a remarkable achievement indeed. It was a turning point in the middle of a trajectory that this study follows from Hart Crane's 1923 attempt to "transform jazz into words" in his poem "For the Marriage of Faustus and Helen" to Richard Powers's 2003 novel *The Time of Our Singing*, in which the biracial Strom brothers discover jazz with the discipline of prodigies.

It has been difficult for writers to approach an art form that confounds Western principles of notation and empirical analysis. In the heart of the so-called Jazz Age—a term F. Scott Fitzgerald used as a generational signifier more than a specific discourse about a musical art—jazz music was either mystified by white writers like Crane or set to mellifluous verse for those already in the know by Harlem Renaissance writers like Langston Hughes. The music itself, though, remained as indeterminate as a modernist poem. What, after all, is jazz? Is it a radical rejection of popular music or is it just more popular music? Is it about improvisational audacity or structural intricacy? Does it embody racial strife or transcend it? Is jazz about being in the moment or does it make a self-conscious statement about that moment? The answer to these questions would turn out to be "all of the above," but it was midway into the music's rapid-fire development before Ellison could catch up with it.

Ethnic strife obfuscated an understanding of jazz among many writers during its most fertile moments of development, but among the musicians themselves, interethnic dialogue happened much sooner. The first chapter, "White Negroes and Native Sons," shows that the story of black-Jewish relations is one of opposition in the literary texts of Bellow, Mailer, and Baldwin, but one of collaboration in the music of George Gershwin, Thelonious Monk, Benny Goodman, and others. Ellison lamented on PBS that there was no equivalent of an Alfred Kazin of jazz, and as a Century Club member in the 1960s, he found looking for New York Intellectuals who took the music seriously to be a lonely business. The Jews who learned to read in a different way were jazz musicians like Red Rodney, Benny Goodman, and Stan Getz. If literary texts were the only evidence of black-Jewish relations, there would be J. D. Salinger admiring Bessie Smith from afar, Amiri Baraka concocting versified conspiracy theories about Israel, Saul Bellow wondering if there could be a Zulu Tolstoy, Mailer's "jazz is orgasm." The collaborations of blacks and Jews tell a different story: when George Gershwin's "I've Got Rhythm" was hermeneutically developed at Harlem's Minton's under the aegis of "rhythm changes"and by artists including Charlie Parker, Dizzy Gillespie, and Thelonious Monk, the idiom of bebop was invented partly as the result of an inter-ethnic exchange. These "rhythm changes" were flying around decades before the civil rights legislation of the 1960s, but when it came to the music that was produced, who could ask for anything more?

Ellison provided a bridge between literary modernism and the jazz canon with the publication of *Invisible Man*, which achieved instant status as a modernist classic and made people listen when Ellison argued that Louis Armstrong was as modern as T. S. Eliot. Ellison's characterization of jazz as a high modernist art was a necessary corrective to the prevailing notion that improvisation did not have its own overdetermined structure, and among literary figures, he is unique in his influence on the formation of a jazz canon—one that many critics and musicians have found to be too confining and restrictive. This study's second chapter, "Listening to Ellison," argues that, while Ellison may have failed to produce the long awaited follow-up to his 1952 masterpiece *Invisible Man*, Ellison's true second act was actually not the writing of a second novel, but the narration of jazz history from beyond the grave. Ellison was a transgressive novelist and traditionalist jazz critic whose criticism, like his poetics, was overtly indebted to T. S. Eliot. He set strict parameters for his jazz canon and anticipated many of the "jazz wars" that have divided jazz critics for the past decade.

The third chapter, "Stomping the Muse," explores how poets as disparate as Hart Crane, Langston Hughes, Wallace Stevens, Frank O'Hara, and Amiri Baraka identified themselves with jazz, engaging in a strange and paradoxical wrestling match as they vied to be what Hughes called "The Original Jazz Poet." "For the Marriage of Faustus and Helen" would ultimately reveal more about Hart Crane's desire for sonic, celestial transport than about his stated attempt to "forge an idiom for jazz into words, something clean, sparkling elusive."[6] (Crane would later characterize the results as "impotent.") In a 1950 poem by Wallace Stevens, "The Sick Man," the figure of the poem's title attempts to resolve the southern music of "thousands of black men, / Playing mouth organs in the night or, now, guitars" and the northern music of "Drifting choirs."[7] The poem concludes, "The words of winter in which these two will come together," without acknowledging that Duke Ellington and other figures in 1950 were already addressing the classical-vernacular split Stevens's poem pledges to resolve. Meanwhile, there is no split at all in the poetry of Langston Hughes, who, in poems such as "Jazzonia," "The Weary Blues," and "Morning After," did not merely write about the blues, but actually *wrote* the blues. Manifesting the music itself, Hughes avoided the high-low problem posed by other poets by acting as a participant rather than an observer, but when he teamed up with Charles Mingus in 1957, their contrasting sensibilities were documented on record. This chapter explores whether jazz-inspired poems can sufficiently address the poetics of jazz.

The final chapter, "Love for Sale," finds jazz autobiography to be the red-light district of African American narrative, with Billie Holiday, Charles Mingus, and Miles Davis telling tales of the oldest profession while selling their wares to editors and ghostwriters, and turning narrative tricks of their own. Holiday and Davis, submitting their stories to ghostwriters, and Mingus, working under financial pressures and an aggressive editor, were well aware that doing the hustle told a more lucrative story than practicing scales. Holiday's harrowing tales of childhood prostitution, Davis's unrepentant tales of pimping, and Mingus's anguished account of the same profession (the dominant subject of his memoir) anticipated the hip hop fascination with the hustle. One would have thought that jazz autobiography would be the medium where writers could finally tell the story of jazz accurately, where the subaltern, as Gayatri Chakravorty Spivak put it, could speak. But the textual histories of these memoirs are as seedy as the tales of the streets they tell, with publishers and editors manipulating the stories of these artists for maximum titillation and profit.

"Instead of the swift and imperceptible flowing of time, you are aware of its nodes, those points where time stands still or from which it leaps ahead. And you slip into the breaks and look around" (*IM*, 8). This is Ellison's Invisible Man listening to Louis Armstrong's trumpet, and while he is describing a feeling of displacement—and this is right after he describes smoking a "reefer," Armstrong's medicine of choice—he is also demonstrating how a serious contemplation of Armstrong's music can leave a writer to slip into the breaks and look around, often without a compass. The writers in this study struggled to find language for a music that defied empirical explanation. The word "jazz," of course, comes up in writing more often than the music is actually confronted. F. Scott Fitzgerald coined the term the "jazz age" without offering his views on Ellington and Armstrong, but as Fitzgerald himself noted, the word's meaning in the 1920s was multivalenced: "The word jazz in its progress toward respectability," he wrote, "has meant first sex, then dancing, then music." Add "drinking" to the list, and Fitzgerald would have been concerned with music the very least.[8] By 1992, Toni Morrison had titled a novel *Jazz* without directly writing about the music; like Fitzgerald, her use of the word described a feeling— an aura, an attitude—but not an inscribed and historicized musical art.[9]

In this study, I have looked beyond the auras to examine what was actually happening with the music these writers described. All art may aspire to the condition of music, but jazz has presented particular challenges to the American writer. When Ellison had Armstrong score his hero's "music of invisibility," Frank O'Hara privileged Billie Holiday for a sublime moment in a prosaic day, J. D. Salinger looked to Bessie Smith for authenticity in a fraudulent world, and Norman Mailer mythologized jazz as the apocalyptic orgasm itself, I have listened for the music beneath the writing, slipped into the breaks and looked around. This book measures jazz music against the writing it inspired: how Billie Holiday the artist can be understood within Frank O'Hara's gaze, how Thelonious Monk rewrote Gershwin and Berlin in collaborations that could have made Mailer rethink his ethnic allegories, and how Duke Ellington found a synthesis between classical music and the blues that Wallace Stevens only wrote about as an imaginative conceit. After surveying these novelists, playwrights, poets, and critics, this study concludes with jazz autobiography in which the musicians are given an opportunity to speak for themselves, taking the music's mythology back to the whorehouses where, according to the legends of Storyville, the music began.

This book begins with understanding the jazz process itself as an antithesis to an ethnic divide in the literary world and ends with ghostwritten accounts of jazz legends as streetwalkers and pimps, with modernist poets, hipster essayists, and transgressive novelists giving their accounts in between. Somewhere between Mailer's "jazz is orgasm" provocation and Ellison's conflation of Louis Armstrong with T. S. Eliot resides the poetics of jazz, on the threshold of spontaneity and precision.

You ain't heard nothing yet!
—AL JOLSON, *The Jazz Singer*, 1920

How do we know who copied what?
—LOUIS ARMSTRONG, 1960

I

WHITE NEGROES AND NATIVE SONS

BLACKS AND JEWS IN WORDS AND MUSIC

Literature has not completely told the story of relations between African Americans and Jews in America. Irving Howe famously thought he could tell Ralph Ellison how to be black, and Saul Bellow contributed a footnote to the culture wars by asking a newspaper interviewer where he could find the Zulu Tolstoy.[1] Ellison and Richard Wright, meanwhile, had their own stories to get out, relegating their complex relations with Jewish communists in the 1930s to the sidelines, and Langston Hughes did not exactly achieve a Tikkun with a 1926 volume called *Fine Clothes to the Jew*. Seventy years later, Amiri Baraka refused to step down from his post as Poet Laureate of New Jersey for implying, in his poem "Somebody Blew Up America," that Israeli forces were somehow complicit in the terrorist attacks of September 11, 2001; knowing "the World Trade Center was gonna get bombed" beforehand and warning "4000 Israeli workers at the Twin Towers / To stay home that day."[2]

It is unfortunate that Baraka is now better known as the conspiracy theorist who wrote these lines than he is as the music critic who called for "standards of judgment and aesthetic standards that depend on our native knowledge and understanding of the underlying philosophies and local cultural references that produced blues and jazz in order to produce valid critical writing and commentary about it."[3] Such a mode would have to acknowledge collaboration as much as it castigates exploitation. "I got the extermination blues, jewboys," Jones wrote in 1965. "I got the hitler syndrome figured." The Jones of 1963 was arguing that to understand jazz one had to understand the culture it came from. Baraka sang his "extermination blues" while casting off his Jewish wife, Hettie Jones, as a "fat jew girl," and while he could cut himself loose from Jews in his life—and, with such writings, offend as many Jewish readers as possible—the cultural background of the music he loved could not be separated into discrete ethnic strands so easily. Novels, poems, and hostile letters to the editor are usually written in isolation. Musicals, songs, and bop lines are usually crafted in collaboration. The literary exchanges between blacks and Jews often reinforced their differences: Irving Howe versus Ralph Ellison, Norman Mailer versus James Baldwin, Amiri Baraka versus the states of Israel and New Jersey. Black-Jewish musical exchanges—from Thelonious Monk's troping of Berlin's "Blue Skies" and Gershwin's "I've Got Rhythm," to the call and response of Artie Shaw's clarinet and Roy Eldridge's trumpet—often demonstrate an aesthetic symbiosis.

If anyone could have been in a position to understand how crucial the black-Jewish collaboration was for jazz, it would have been the author of "Jazz and the White Critic" (before he became the author of "Somebody Blew Up America"), and if one were to follow the former LeRoi Jones's assertion in 1963 that a true understanding of jazz required an examination of the "local cultural references" of the music, casting off Jews from the narrative is not only bad politics, it is bad scholarship. To sever the ties between blacks and Jews is to miss the collaboration that transformed George Gershwin's "I've Got Rhythm" from a 1930 showcase for Ethel Merman to the "rhythm changes" used as a basis for Duke Ellington's "Cottontail," Charlie Christian's "Seven Come Eleven," Charlie Parker's "Salt Peanuts," Thelonious Monk's "Rhythm-a-Ning," and much more. Gershwin's 1-6-2-5 chord structure served as a guiding theme for the birth of bebop, and even if he was a Jew who was overt in his indebtedness to black music, the exchange worked both ways. Dizzy Gillespie's Minton's sessions would often start with playing the chords to "I've Got Rhythm"—known as "Rhythm" changes—and survival on the bandstand depended on adapting those changes to the heat and structural innovations of the moment. To this day, calling for "Rhythm" changes is a universally understood directive on the bandstand; it is a common language of bop, and while Gershwin came up with his chord sequence borrowing from the swing and stride he heard from black musicians in Harlem, the beboppers returned the favor. Many "Rhythm" changes were flying around on 52nd Street, and listening to Parker and Gillespie trade choruses on Gershwin's tune did not mean that their musical dialogue should have given way to political complacency—that at the dawn of the civil rights era it was not also necessary to, as Ira Gershwin's lyrics put it, ask for anything more. But because blacks lived in segregated America, the music was an avenue for a genuine collaboration with Jews that was documented in records but largely unacknowledged by the literati.

Indeed, the least understood yet most thoroughly developed dialectic between blacks and Jews was achieved not through literature but music, where song provided a haven for two marginalized ethnic groups before integration became the law of the land. By the time Jewish immigrants first arrived in the United States around the turn of the century, African Americans, though a despised and segregated minority, provided the most appealing identity to trope. As Eileen Southern's work has shown, African Americans were a central force in this country's music as early as 1790.[4] By 1927, music was decidedly the dominant path to cultural assimilation—certainly for Eastern European Jews—as the hugely successful film *The Jazz Singer* famously demonstrates, even before Al Jolson gets blacked up for the film's "Mammy" finale.[5] It is impossible to unravel the ethnic DNA of American music without examining the intertwining paths from ghetto to ghetto. Louis Armstrong got his first trumpet from the Karnofsky family, Jews who hired him to deliver coal to the whores of Storyville, his first joint from Mezz Mezzrow, a mediocre Jewish clarinet player, pledged allegiance to Joe Glaser, a Jewish gangster manager, and wore a star of David around his neck for most of his life. (So, by the way, did Elvis Presley, who, according to the website *www.schmelvis.com*, had a Jewish great-grandmother.) Irving Mills helped Duke Ellington negotiate New York show business and was an early champion of his talent, pressuring record companies to let him write his first extended pieces. Charlie Parker shared bop lines (and a heroin habit) with the Jewish trumpeter Red Rodney and died in the arms of the Baroness Nica de Koenigswarter, a Jewish patroness. Benny Goodman led Billie Holiday's first recording session, and saxophonist Stan Getz, a disciple of Lester Young, liked to say that, for a Bronx Jew, he swung pretty hard. The stories of Armstrong, Ellington, and Parker—arguably the central figures of American music—would be incomplete without acknowledging these Jewish alliances. George Gershwin, Benny Goodman, and Stan Getz were New York Jewish intellectuals who learned to read in a way that Howe, Alfred Kazin, Susan Sontag, and Lionel Trilling could not. They absorbed the language of black artists and transfigured the American vernacular forever.

Twenty years earlier, Benny Goodman, the Jewish clarinetist

from Chicago's South Side, initially resisted including black musicians in his touring band, but, at the prodding of producer John Hammond, made history by going into the studio with a band that included Lionel Hampton on vibes, Billie Holiday on vocals, Charlie Christian on guitar, and Teddy Wilson on piano. Goodman did not integrate his band to be a civil rights activist. He nevertheless made history with that multiethnic recording, and did so because, fixated on music and little else, Holiday, Hampton, Christian, and Wilson were simply the best collaborators he could find. When Goodman first played with Wilson in 1935, he recalled, "Teddy and I began to play as though we were thinking with the same brain." Stan Getz, alluding to Charlie Parker's famous statement about Dizzy Gillespie, similarly described the pianist Kenny Barron as "the other half of my heart." Blacks and Jews have thought and felt together in the world of music, but this fact has not been recorded in literature until recently: Richard Powers's novel *The Time of Our Singing* follows musical prodigies that are neither black nor Jewish, but both, and the outside world has trouble with this proposition.

But when competing versions of jazz appeared in the works of J. D. Salinger, Norman Mailer, and James Baldwin, the story was often similar. For Salinger jazz offered an alternative to bourgeois ennui, for Mailer, an orgasmic release from his existential dread, and for Baldwin, an underground, transgressive alternative to a somber algebra teacher. This is a far cry from the interethnic ideal exemplified in the Goodman-Wilson and Getz-Barron collaborations. Beyond the appropriation and transgression, jazz has offered a mode of expression that has brought blacks and Jews together in ways that the literature has largely kept separate, but even when literature visits jazz as a subject, African Americans and Jews are often relegated to limited roles. Max Roach has said that records are the textbooks of jazz, and when

it comes to black-Jewish relations in America, records are much
better textbooks than conventional literary writing. The recent
historical fiction of Richard Powers may be revising that story,
but it remains a work in progress.[6] Jazz inspired the prose of the
Jewish writers J. D. Salinger and Norman Mailer, and a James
Baldwin short story answered back. The music they were writing
about was making a different kind of call and response than the
one they heard, an ethnic hybrid that was stranger than fiction.

HOLDEN CAULFIELD'S BLUES

"A lot of jazz is outright Fraud. Charming, even richly evocative
fraud on occasion. But don't kid yourself that these jazz musicians are in possession of some wonderful and otherworldly
power beyond anything you and I can comprehend." This invective against jazz comes from J. D. Salinger, according to Joyce
Maynard's memoir about her 1972 affair with the author. Salinger, who was said to enjoy listening to Blossom Dearie, Glenn
Miller, and the Andrews Sisters, dismissed jazz musicians as
merely "serving up a meal of old chestnuts from some other set
they've played some other night, in front of some adoring audience of marvelous, thrillingly cool fans." Salinger's complaint, it
seems, was that jazz improvisation was essentially scripted, disin-
genuous, warmed over, or, to use the term favored by *The Catcher
in the Rye*'s Holden Caufield, "phony."

The Salinger of 1972 apparently knew the drill of a jazz solo,
and he found the spontaneity predictable. In his disappointment
that jazz is like any other art, with its own structures, styles, and
genres, Salinger echoes Adorno's notorious dismissal of jazz improvisations as "mere frills. Any precocious American teenager
knows that the routine today scarcely leaves any room for improvisation, and that what appears as spontaneity is in fact care-

fully planned out in advance with machinelike precision." Adorno concludes that jazz is the "false liquidization of art."[7] In his stolen moment with Joyce Maynard, Salinger made a point similar to the Frankfurt School philosopher, yearning for an authentic expression that would somehow be spared the condemnation of phoniness Salinger applied to English teachers, history lessons, and prep school kids. When Phoebe Caufield accuses her brother, Holden, of complete misanthropy—"You don't like anything that's happening," she tells him—she is nearly right, but he does spare a few things from his line of attack. In addition to Isak Dinesen's *Out of Africa*, Thomas Hardy's *The Return of the Native*, and the image of his sleeping sister, Holden singles out a record by the fictitious African American singer Estelle Fletcher called "Little Shirley Beans."

With this record, Salinger did not write about the white jazz musicians for whom he claimed preference. Instead, the voice of an African American singer and her legend serves as a contrast to the world of privilege he held up for contempt in a best-selling novel. The black jazz musicians of Salinger's fiction, like Phoebe Caulfield and the precocious Glass children, are marginal figures who are both valorized and infantilized. Salinger's novel has been obsessively scrutinized, but his peculiar relationship to jazz has not.[8] The music may have played a seemingly marginal role in Salinger's already slim output, but it was a crucial fetish object for Holden Caulfield—and apparently for Salinger, as well. *The Catcher in the Rye*'s title refers to both a misreading of—or, indeed, an improvisation upon—a Burns ballad and a fantasy about saving children. Salinger's jazz fantasies arise out of his dissatisfaction with traditional language but lead him to a sentimental paternalism that recalls Josephine Baker's famous observation that "the white imagination sure is something when it comes to blacks."

Salinger's musings on jazz are significant not because he was in any way an authority on the subject, but rather because *The Catcher in the Rye*, which has sold over sixty million copies since its publication in July 1951, has been a widely influential account of what was missing from the life of a white, privileged American teenager during the greatest period of economic prosperity the United States would ever know. The music of a historically despised minority would somehow fill such a gap for many of the first teenagers who read *The Catcher in the Rye* in the 1950s. Salinger, who was raised Jewish (his mother, it turned out, was passing to appease her chosen in-laws), had the same contempt for the prep school WASPs he encountered at Valley Forge, a military prep school, that Holden Caulfield had for the WASPs he encountered at Pencey. Like Holden, Salinger was a dropout, and both were interested in the not-yet-codified discourse of jazz. Salinger mentions jazz only briefly in *The Catcher in the Rye*, but explores it at length in the never anthologized story "Blue Melody" about a black singer named Lida Louise—a thinly veiled approximation of Bessie Smith, or at least her legend. Although there are no openly Jewish characters in this story, it is set against the backdrop of World War II and implies a correlation between damaged black and Jewish bodies. The action of the story turns on Smith's mystique and the myths surrounding her death as told to a soldier on the German battlefront. As he faces death at the hands of the Nazis, the narrator finds in her story the authenticity that eludes Holden Caulfield.

In *The Catcher in the Rye*, Holden spends more time on things he considers to be "outright fraud" than things he considers to be authentic, and this, of course, is part of the book's perennial contrarian appeal. Since Holden has flunked every subject at Pencey but English and managed to alienate himself from all of his peers, it is not surprising that he holds most people, artifacts, and modes of communication—from the history of the Egyptians to Laurence Olivier's performance in *Hamlet*—in contempt for one reason or another. Holden searches for underground obsessions, and Salinger is not necessarily subtle with his imagery when he has his hero repeatedly badger cab drivers about the fate of the ducks when the Central Park pond freezes. But it is exactly such a mysterious underworld that fascinates Holden. A record by an African American singer named Estelle Fletcher also provides Holden with access to such a secret underground. Assuming the connoisseurship of the collector, Holden is proud of acquiring something outside of the mainstream:

> There was this record I wanted to get for Phoebe, called "Little Shirley Beans." It was a very hard record to get. It was about a little kid that wouldn't go out of the house because two of her front teeth were out and she was ashamed to. I heard it at Pencey. A boy that lived on the next floor had it, and I knew it would knock old Phoebe out, but he wouldn't sell it. It was a very old, terrific record that this colored girl singer, Estelle Fletcher, made about twenty years ago. She sings it very Dixieland and whorehouse, and it doesn't sound at all mushy. If a white girl was singing it, she'd make it sound cute as hell, but old Estelle Fletcher knew what the hell she was doing, and it was one of the best records I ever heard.[9]

There is no such singer as Estelle Fletcher and there is no such song as "Little Shirley Beans," but the combination of childhood loss and a "Dixieland-and-whorehouse" sound combine Salinger's twin obsessions, if Joyce Maynard's account of her affair with the author—when the memoirist was eighteen and the author was a Humbert Humbertesque fifty-two—is to be believed. A few pages before the description of "Little Shirley

Beans," Holden holds Sally Hayes of Mary Woodruff Prep in contempt for her use of the word "grand." ("If it's one word I really hate, it's grand.") Although Holden's slang sometimes feels dated, his casual profanities sound closer to contemporary speech than the official language from which he dissents. And the sounds of segregated speakeasies from the twenties—what he calls "Dixieland and whorehouse"—is more contemporary to Holden Caulfield than the haughty language of anyone in his social stratosphere. He also responds to the narrative about the young girl's shame, not from a white girl who would make it sound "cute as hell," but a "colored singer" whose "whorehouse" rendition would prove that Estelle Fletcher "knew what the hell she was doing." In his *Interpretation of Dreams*, Freud observed that the losing of teeth can symbolize the losing of virginity, but Estelle Fletcher's voice sounds like a nymph who is also a whore.

The nymph version of "Little Shirley Beans" could have been sung by Ella Fitzgerald, whose 1938 version of "A Tisket-A-Tasket" may have conflated a children's rhyme with coy allusions to lost girlhood similar to "Little Shirley Beans" with a lament for a lost "brown and yellow basket" similar to the loss of the two front teeth in "Little Shirley Beans." If Salinger had a children's rhyme set to a jazz record sung by an African American woman as an inspiration, Fitzgerald's recording, which sold a million copies, would have been the likeliest prototype. The record had a novelty quality to it, taking a familiar rhyme and setting it not to Dixieland accompaniment, with overlapping contrapuntal lines and loose arrangements, but rather to a tightly wound arrangement typical of late thirties commercial swing. But Fitzgerald—who actually worked at a whorehouse as a teenager in Yonkers—conveyed the opposite of the "whorehouse" quality Holden so admires. Although Fitzgerald was only eighteen when she made the recording, and her voice was not yet at its most mature, she was not exactly a child, either, but a young adult with a rhythmic and harmonic mastery in contrast to what the rhyme's theme of childish carelessness would suggest. Frank Sinatra would later praise Fitzgerald by saying "never have such innocent sounds been set to music," and the combination of playfulness and sophistication—a precocity not unlike Salinger's Phoebe—was part of the record's appeal. In a 1938 film—a testimony to the record's great reach—Fitzgerald is seen gallivanting across a train aisle singing her tale of loss to random passengers, who regard her with entertained concern, but without a hint of lasciviousness.

Although "A Tisket-A-Tasket" is the closest actual record to Salinger's fictional one, Ella Fitzgerald is not Estelle Fletcher, even though they shared initials. She did not sing in a "Dixieland-and-Whorehouse" style; in fact, one thing that is notable about her style is that she avoided the blues. Holden, looking for a jargon of authenticity beyond the prep school argot he so precisely skewers, is in search of a blues sensibility without quite articulating it. Right after his account of "Little Shirley Beans," Holden overhears a six-year-old boy singing, "If a body catch a body coming through the rye" and hearing the song makes him feel "not so depressed any more." As Phoebe will later point out to him, he has just misheard a Robert Burns lyric, or fetishized a child's misquoting of it. But Holden prefers it, and Salinger apparently does, too, using it for the title of his book. A Scottish ballad lyric mangled in the syntax of a six year old has more authenticity—is less "phony"—than an appropriate rendering of the Burns lyric, and so, apparently, is a child's song refashioned as a "Dixieland and whorehouse" tune by a "colored girl singer" who "knew what the hell she was doing."

Salinger never connects this misreading of Burns with the "Dixieland-and-whorehouse" style Holden fetishizes in Estelle Fletcher, but the short story "Blue Melody" not only provides a clue to Salinger's blues predilections, but also illustrates the problematic connections Salinger draws between blackness and authenticity, particularly in contrast with the world of WASP privilege for which Holden is unable to provide an alternative. The story, dismissed as a "soggy bagel" by John F. Szwed, was originally titled "Scratchy Needle on a Phonograph Record" before editor A. E. Hotchner infuriated the author by changing the title for *Cosmopolitan* in September 1948. It would be the last time Salinger would publish short fiction in a venue other than the *New Yorker*, and, as such, the last time he would publish in a "slick" that would do less to temper his more melodramatic impulses. Although the story may have benefited from more editorial intervention, Salinger's chagrin at seeing his title changed was justified, for the mediation between jazz as consumer object and jazz as lived experience is central to what his story attempts to express.

The racial imagery of "Blue Melody" has not aged well, but Salinger's framing device and somewhat obvious uses of irony do maintain an ambiguity about his own endorsement of this imagery—and they certainly render Holden Caulfield's relationship to "Little Shirley Beans" even more problematic than it already would be on its own. On the opening page, there is an illustration of a fresh scrubbed young white couple sitting on the floor in a state of rapture, and only the bottom half of a pianist's body is visible. "Every day after school they would go to the dingy café, to listen entranced as Black Charles made the old piano talk," reads the caption. But Salinger's message to *Cosmopolitan* readers is a complicated one: "Blue Melody" is a story of the South, of segregation, of violently exploited musicians, and well-intentioned children who realize their abuse of black musicians only when it is too late. The unnamed narrator serving in an infantry division in Germany in World War II speaks like a grown up Holden Caulfield, that is, with slang-laden non-chalance and evasive bitterness. Like Norman Mailer, who opens "The White Negro" with a reference to the Holocaust, Salinger begins his story of mistreated black artists with a scene from a German battlefield. Benny Goodman and Duke Ellington's orchestras were sent to entertain troops during that war, but the black-Jewish alliance represented by the music had not found its ethnic footing in literature. In "The White Negro," Mailer went from the Holocaust to "jazz is orgasm." Salinger went from the front at Halzhoffen, Germany, to a story about young southern white kids in love and the black musicians who entertain them. The narrator of "Blue Melody" learns about the pianist Black Charles and the blues singer Lida Louise from a southern gentleman named Rudford while two soldiers fight against ethnic cleansing abroad, and he cautions the readers that it should not be read as "a slam against one section of the country. It's not a slam against anybody or anything. It's just a simple little story of Mom's apple pie, ice-cold beer, the Brooklyn Dodgers, and the Lux Theater of the Air—the things we fought for, in short. You can't miss it, really."[10]

The narrator should not be trusted. "Blue Melody" is, in fact, a resounding slam not only against that "one section of the country," but against the white fetishization of black performance held to be as contemptible—indeed, as "phony"—as the Norman Rockwell-like images the narrator lists as the things he and his fellow soldiers fought for. (The overtly Rockwell-like *Cosmopolitan* illustration is an unintentional irony.) Rudford comes from the town of Agersberg, Tennessee, which includes a street named for a woman who took down five Union soldiers, and is the son of an author of textbooks with titles like "Science for Americans." Like the Glass children, Rudford is quizzed, trained, and grilled to be a prodigy, and by the age of eleven, he has, according to the narrator, acquired more knowledge than the average high school freshman. But the narrator learns something essential about Rudford that could never be measured in the official histories of intelligence tests or the lore of the antebellum South: Rudford's moment of a schoolboy crush, shattered innocence, and musical worship comes out when he and the narrator narrowly escape freezing to death in the back of a GI truck.

Rudford recalls his visits to Black Charles's café, a "hole in the wall" known as "unsanitary"—all the more reason to be appealing to a young man in search of one final taste of transgression before he is sent off to boarding school. Rudford appreciates Black Charles's piano playing, but what he appreciates even more is Black Charles himself. He was "something few white piano players are. He was kind and interested when young people came up to the piano to play the piano to ask him to play something, or just to talk to him" (*BM*, 111). Because Black Charles "slept like a dead man," he often needed to be woken up, and Rudford's preferred method was kicking him in the stomach. When Rudford strikes up a schoolboy romance with Peggy Moore, a crucial part of their courtship is not only listening to Black Charles's music, but beating him into consciousness. The act of kicking a black body becomes a substitution for sexual interaction as the kids are still in the presexual stage fetishized by Salinger, whose conflations of childhood and sexuality resonated in his own work and in the tell-all memoirs about him:

> "Well, go ahead and *do* it," Rudford said.
> "I'm fixin' to; I'm fixin' to. Go away."
> Rudford watched her a little smugly.
> "Naa. You can't just shove him around and get any-

where. You've seen me," he said. "You gotta really haul off. Get him right under the kidneys. You've seen me."

"Here?" said Peggy. She had her finger on the little island of nerves set off by the dorsal fork of Charles's lavender suspenders.

"Go ahead."

Peggy wound up and delivered.

Black Charles stirred slightly, but slept on without even seriously changing his position.

"You missed. You gotta hit him harder than that anyway."   (*BM*, 112–13)

When Black Charles finally is woken up, he never complains about this treatment or even shows any signs of pain. With his lavender suspenders providing a gay signifier, there is even a hint of queer bashing as Black Charles is all too happy to take Peggy's request for "Lady, Lady." When he is informed that these nice, white kids are on summer vacation and will be coming to the café for a performance (and, according to the ritual, to deliver a beating), Black Charles's response is "My, my! Ain't that fine!" (*BM*, 113) Salinger's fiction tends to be forgiving of children and unrelentingly hostile toward adults, yet Rudford and Peggy's innocence is unsettling in the Jim Crow South: they practice their (literally) heavy-handed exploitation without any consciousness of its consequences. The violence inflicted on Black Charles is a familiar part of the master-slave performance, which Saidiya Hartman identifies as "the diffusion of terror and the violence perpetrated under the rubric of pleasure, paternalism and property."[11] In Rudford and Peggy's Edenic paradise, they can kick a black musician to perpetuate their pleasure and initiate their romance.

It is a long way from beating Black Charles into playing

"Lady, Lady" to recording an iconic singer for a major label, but in "Blue Melody," they are linked in the same exploitation. Salinger makes this point with the introduction of Lida Louise, Black Charles's niece. The children do not beat her, but the white adults of the segregated South ultimately bring her down. Lida Louise is a singer described as having a "powerful, soft voice. Every note she sang was detonated with individuality." Nevertheless, her real function in the story is only to stimulate the romance of Rudford and Peggy, who, when they first meet the singer, introduce themselves as Black Charles's "best friends." Lida Louise writes a song for the young couple, "Soupy Peggy," and they have a moment of weepy passion while they watch her debut at Black Charles's café: "I love you good, Peggy!" Rudford exclaims. Violence and black music whet their passion. Rudford first kisses Peggy after she falls on her head, both still giddy from a spitting contest and the dizzying piano-playing of Black Charles, whom they have beaten into inspiration. Rudford's concern for Peggy's white body underlines the abuse and neglect of black bodies in the story, even as Jewish bodies pile up in the concentration camps of the framing story: Black Charles never plays without a kick-start, Lida Louise will soon receive a fatal blow from the segregated South, and the reader of Salinger's story is left wondering how much irony there is in the statement that these are "the things we fought for."

Lida Louise's debut causes a stir in the small town, and soon enough, college students are rhapsodizing about her in their papers, leading to gigs on Beale Street and a record contract where she records with Louis Armstrong, Benny Goodman, and "all the boys." But as Lida Louise ascends to power, it is she who beats the body of a black man when she whacks a "well-dressed colored man"—presumably, her manager—with her handbag, flees a gig, and makes her way back to Agersberg. By this violence, she escapes the exploitation of the music industry and arrives famous but hardly rich, only to succumb to a crueller blow in the segregated South. During a farewell picnic seeing Rudford off to boarding school, Lida Louise is suddenly struck with an agonizing pain in her side—the very place where Black Charles was hit—and Rudford, remembering his father's "Science for Americans," identifies the cause as acute appendicitis. In a moribund fit of delirium, she mistakes Rudford for a former lover whom she earlier referred to as a "colored guy named Endicott." Right before going off to boarding school, Rudford gets to engage in an act of passing, replying: "I'm right here, baby." They drive frantically through Agersberg, and after being turned away from two segregated hospitals, Lida Louise dies.

Salinger's source for the death of Lida Louise was surely an article by John Hammond for *Down Beat* magazine in 1937 titled, "Did Bessie Smith Bleed to Death While Waiting for Medical Aid?" Smith, like Lida Louise, was a legendary blues singer from Tennessee, and like Salinger's singer, had her ups and downs in the music business. Smith died from wounds sustained in a car accident, not of untreated appendicitis, but Hammond's narrative of martyrdom provided a convenient hook for Salinger's narrative of injustice and hypocrisy, as it would a decade later for Edward Albee, another upper-class dropout malcontent, in his play *The Death of Bessie Smith*. Hammond's story used Smith's fame to point out an injustice of segregation to an audience that might have otherwise been indifferent: "Some time elapsed before a doctor was summoned to the scene, but finally she was picked up by a medico and driven to a leading Memphis hospital. On the way, this car was involved in some minor mishap, which further delayed medical attention. When finally she did arrive at the hospital, she was refused treatment because of her color and bled to death while waiting for attention."[12] This account spread the word about a cause that was hardly

popular in 1937, but it was, like "Blue Melody," a work of fiction. In Chris Albertson's 1972 biography of Smith, testimonies
from the attending physician, the ambulance driver, and witnesses debunk the account, and John Hammond's memoir, published in 1980, is apologetic about it, assuring readers that he
had every reason to believe the story that he had received as
hearsay.

Of course, there is no reason why Salinger would have been
aware that this account of Smith's death was, as he attacked much
of jazz performance, "outright fraud." But it was also easier for
Salinger to place Smith in an infantilized victimhood rather
than fully confront the ferocious figure she was. Smith exuded a
raunchy, confident exuberance that was precisely the opposite of
the precocious nymphettes of *The Catcher and the Rye*'s Phoebe
Caulfield and Estelle Fletcher or, for that matter, *At Home in the
World*'s Joyce Maynard. Rudford and the narrator of "Blue
Melody" agreed that Lida Louise's voice "couldn't be described,"
but part of their difficulty with coming up with a language for
her music is not just the difficulty of synaesthesia, but rather
comprehending a woman who acts as the sexual predator, judge,
and jury. It is no wonder that feminist scholars including Hazel
Carby and Angela Davis have claimed Smith as an icon. When
Smith sings, "You've been a good old wagon, honey, but you
done broke down" or, in "Empty Bed Blues," loads a trombone-
driven blues with erotic allusions and metaphors—among them,
"He's a deep sea diver with a stroke that can't go wrong / He can
touch the bottom, and his wind holds out so long"—the lyrics
she sings were not written by her, but she owns them with her
performance nevertheless. Unlike the jazz singers she influenced, Smith's singing is not distinguished by her flexibility, but
her persistent rhythmic throttle. Smith does not sing off the

beat; she zeroes in on it and makes her presence unmistakably felt.

The most memorable retort to the type of Bessie Smith fandom exhibited by Salinger was in LeRoi Jones's *Dutchman*, the play that gave Jones an Obie Award and his first taste of fame. Toward the end, the white femme fatale Lula is interrogating Clay, accused of being the "Black Baudelaire," and Clay responds in a monologue that sounds more like Huey Newton (or the latter-day Baraka). Clay rebuffs Lula's advances to do the "belly rub" and imagines the repressed rage of Bessie Smith at the worship of a million Holden Caulfield types: "Old bald headed four eyed ofays popping their fingers . . . and don't know yet what they're doing. They say, 'I love Bessie Smith.' And don't even understand that Bessie Smith is saying, 'Kiss my ass. Kiss my black unruly ass.' Before love, suffering, desire, anything you can explain, she's saying, and very plainly, 'Kiss my black ass.' "[13] Clay's monologue would be fair enough if it were directed at Salinger, who can only enshrine Smith as a martyr and fetish object, not as someone who could convey adult suffering with greater depth and nuance than Holden Caulfield's "Sorrow King." But not all Jewish guys were mere "ofays popping there fingers." On "Gimme a Pigfoot," a raunchy tune from Smith's last session in 1933, when Smith expresses her desire to follow her "pigfoot with a bottle of beer" with a "reefer with a gang o' gin," Benny Goodman can be heard in the background blowing soulful clarinet lines that merge effortlessly with her growls. Like Mezz Mezzrow, another Jewish clarinet player who "spent weeks studying Bessie Smith's slaughter of the white man's dictionary, analyzing all her glides and slippery elisions,"[14] Goodman internalized Smith's approach to rhythm and phrasing, and even though he did not, like Mezzrow, actually believe he had physically become black, he had adopted a blues-based approach to rhythm and diction that even came out in his speech. There is a recording of Goodman introducing a 1937 radio feed where a bluesy cadence is detectable not only in his clarinet lines, but in his introduction as well. "This is Benny Goodman, and I think I've heard that one before," Goodman intones with phrasing more akin to Duke Ellington's than any other midwestern Jew. There was nothing self-conscious about this adoption: it was the world in which he walked. Goodman is welcome at Smith's rent party, too, and, unlike Lida Louise's death scene, in which Rudford's parting line for her is more like minstrelsy without blackface, his absorption of her rhythm, cadence, and articulation is no mere mask.

The producer of that session was John Hammond, the Columbia Records talent scout who was also responsible for promulgating the Bessie Smith fable that inspired Salinger. Like Salinger, Hammond was a blue-blood dropout in search of an alternative discourse to prep school banter, and his memoir, *John Hammond on Record*, tells a fascinating story about a Vanderbilt heir who rebelled against his family by bringing blacks and Jews—two ethnic groups restricted from his family's country clubs—together in recording studios, and while his narrative often smacks of a self-serving paternalism, his achievement in this arena was undeniable. Three days after producing that Smith-Goodman session, he would bring Goodman back into the same studio for Billie Holiday's recording debut, and a few years later, Goodman would integrate his band with Charlie Christian, Teddy Wilson, and Lionel Hampton. By 1961, when *The Catcher in the Rye* had been a cultural phenomenon for a decade, Hammond would discover the Jewish performer who would provide an entire generation of Holden Caulfields with a cross-ethnic icon. Young, ambitious Robert Zimmerman was evasive about his origins. He contrived a name from a famous Welsh poet, told reporters and publicists that he learned guitar from Leadbelly, and concocted the phenomenon of Bob Dylan. Dylan's appeal is often explained in generational terms, but his crossover of the styles of white and black folk musicians is no less significant.

For the 1960s generation of dropouts, Bob Dylan was a Holden Caulfield with an outlet, and the language of prep school kids and Ivy League dropouts would find a voice that could complain, as Dylan does in "It's Alright Ma, I'm Only Bleeding," that "all is phony" to the twang of a blues guitar riff. In Salinger's fiction, the records are collectors' items, but they don't find their way into the frustrated voices of privilege. In *The Catcher in the Rye*, Holden breaks that Estelle Fletcher record shortly after buying it, and in "Blue Melody," when Rudford runs into Peggy in the Palm Room of the Biltmore Hotel, they are both sophisticated grownups, and their memory of Lida Louise is as inaccessible as childhood itself. Peggy begs to hear Rudford's rare copy of "Soupy Peggy," since hers was stepped on by a drunk college boy. Rudford promises to let Peggy hear it, but, Salinger writes, "he almost never played the record for *anybody* in 1942. It was terribly scratchy now. It didn't even sound like Lida Louise anymore." Like Vinteuil's "little phrase" in Proust's *À La Recherche du Temps Perdu*, which grows increasingly faint the more Swann's passion for Odette fades, Salinger uses the obscurity of a dead blues singer as a poignant coda to a buried past—in this case, of simultaneous racial exploitation and fetish. John Hammond supplied the mythological Bessie Smith for "Blue Melody," but he also brought the reconstructed Benny Goodman and Robert Zimmerman to the world. Frustrated young professionals in posh hotels would never have to look far for the blues again.

CRISS CROSS: BEBOP'S MIXED MARRIAGE

In "Blue Melody," Rudford had only a brief moment of passing, when he is mistaken for the black musician Endicott. If he had been able to extend a life of saying things like, "I'm right here, baby," America beyond the wartime trenches might not have seemed so grim. The denouement in the Biltmore lobby is filled with the kinds of bourgeois utterances that drive Holden Caulfield to homicidal rage before turning to the "Dixieland-and-Whorehouse" "Little Shirley Beans" for solace. Six years after the publication of *The Catcher in the Rye*, Norman Mailer's "The White Negro" found a way to extend the trope of passing that Salinger entertains only briefly, and when it first appeared in the pages of *Dissent* in 1957, it caused as much of a stir for a certain set of grownups as did *The Catcher in the Rye*—and does still— for adolescents of all ages. Mailer's intended audience in *Dissent* was a more rarefied set than the readers for his short-lived column in the *Village Voice*, where he delineated the difference between the "Hip and the Square." Explaining to *Village Voice* readers that Thelonious Monk was to Dave Brubeck what orgasms were to cancer was to delineate an obvious analogy for hipsters of 1956. "The White Negro" was another matter. It was written for Irving Howe and served as a wake-up call for New York Intellectuals.

And to write for New York Intellectuals was to write for New York *Jewish* Intellectuals, and this was not a crowd that had figured out what to make of jazz. *Commentary* ran two essays on bebop in 1950 and 1951 by an essayist who at the time claimed first-hand knowledge of Negro culture, an assertion he subsequently retracted when he rose up the ranks of New York's literati. That author was Anatole Broyard, the future *New York Times* daily book reviewer, who described the new phenomenon

as "an increasingly miscegenated ritual which was gradually losing its original identity[15] and cathartic quality."[14] Broyard's words
turned out to be prophetic: he lost his original identity himself
as a black man passing as white.[16] As a "White Negro" in reverse, Broyard's quest for a "pure" blackness—something like the
"blackness of blackness" parodied by Ellison in the prologue to
Invisible Man—would turn out to be the very thing he tried to
erase from his biography. Mailer departed from Broyard and all
other conventional wisdom about bebop by treating it not as
"miscegenated," but as a phenomenon of unreconstructed black
masculinity that white hipsters desperately wanted to trope. In
doing so, he identified a cultural phenomenon that startled
Howe and subsequently drew ire from Norman Podhoretz (in
public, in *Commentary*) and Ralph Ellison (in private, in a letter
to Albert Murray).[17] Coming from Broyard, "miscegenated" was
meant to be a dismissal, in a moment when a black literary critic
was compelled to pass for white, and when the Supreme Court
still allowed for states to keep miscegenation laws on the books.
The Supreme Court would not strike down miscegenation laws
until 1967, a decade after the publication of "The White Negro,"
but the music that inspired Mailer's influential account of appropriation was a more covertly mixed marriage than Mailer himself realized.

A detailed investigation into what was actually happening on
and around the bandstand would have complicated his argument, and the nuance could have cooled the fire of his prose.
Mailer needed jazz musicians to be tough, black, hypersexual
men, and the last thing he wanted was for bop to be the "miscegenated" phenomenon identified by Broyard, particularly if it
meant that Jews would be thrown into the mix. He preferred being known as tough guy who served in World War II as opposed
to a Brooklyn Jew who went to Harvard, and, for him, black

masculinity represented the ultimate triumph over his existential dread. While Mailer was taking notes on "The Hip and the Square" in 1956 and working on "The White Negro" in the spring of 1957, he spent a considerable amount of time obsessively taking in Thelonious Monk's quartet.[18] By the time "The White Negro" appeared in the pages of *Dissent* that summer, Mailer had left his *Voice* column and looked on to new novelistic and pugilistic territory, and the tenor saxophonist John Coltrane had taken involuntary leave from Miles Davis's quartet, kicked heroin, and looked on to new harmonic and rhythmic territory. Monk's quartet provided the setting for Coltrane to make this conversion, and when "The White Negro" came out, Monk's quartet with Coltrane was in residence at the Five Spot.[19] Mailer was transfixed by Monk's music, but he did not understand it; he remained on the outside. On the CD *Live at the Five Spot: Discovery!*, Coltrane can be heard under the sway of Monk and Islam, developing what the critic Ira Gitler called "sheets of sound" in which Coltrane wrapped rococo patterns around a harmonic idea, in double, triple, even quadruple time. Mailer was entranced by Monk's eccentric pounding and twirling, but he was not really listening. For Mailer, Monk was hip in the way that homicide and rape were hip: the music was transgressive, dangerous, linked to drugs and outlaw behavior. To demystify its origins, or complicate it or subject it to analytical scrutiny, would have made it less hip.

Those who knew Mailer well said he never did have an ear for music, and, according to Carl Rollyson's biography, he rented a saxophone to play along with Monk's music despite his complete inability to play the instrument. Indiscriminately honking along with Monk's music was "hip" to Mailer, who thought he was witnessing black masculinity in its purest, unadulterated form. Without actually analyzing the music, he probably did not realize that he was witnessing Monk rewriting the compositions of Jews, most notably George Gershwin and Irving Berlin. Mailer's notes for "The Hip and the Square" explained that "Negro" was hip and "white" was square, but what he did not fathom was that on the bandstand, such distinctions had nothing to do with race in the biological sense, but rather with a musical formulation. Being able to play the changes of "I've Got Rhythm" was how you made the cut at Minton's Playhouse. It didn't matter that the changes were drafted by a Jew, and, by the time of Mailer's writing in 1956, the Jewish saxophonists Stan Getz and Lee Konitz had as much of a chance to be hip as the black popularizer Ramsey Lewis had to be a square. The greatest insult a jazz musician could lodge against another one was, "He sounds white," but the judgment has nothing to do with appearance and everything to do with sound.[20] Getz was a Jew who was able to internalize the language and style of Lester Young, and to the undiscerning Mailer, he might have seemed like just another White Negro, but to those on the bandstand that could hear the difference, there was nothing white about his sound.

Mailer's readers in *Dissent* never got the news, but when he heard Monk playing "In Walked Bud," he was not only hearing a tribute to the great Harlem bebop pianist Bud Powell but, using the same chords and structure, a variation on Irving Berlin's "Blue Skies." It was not the first time Berlin's tune was the occasion for a black-Jewish crossover. Thirty years earlier, in 1927's *The Jazz Singer*, Al Jolson's Jacob Rabinowitz—who, like the former LeRoi Jones, would change his name—serenades his mother with "Blue Skies," following it with a stage patter that sounds as much like Louis Armstrong's comic routines on "Chinatown, My Chinatown" and "Laughin' Louie" as it does like the vaudeville stage. "You ain't heard nothin', yet," the artist, now known as Jack Robin, tells his mother in a famous refrain, an improvised aside by Jolson that would inadvertently become the first words spoken in the history of cinema. "I'm gonna play it jazzy." Jolson then does something with "Blue Skies" that may strike contemporary viewers as relentless mugging and grandstanding, but, with his rhythmic variations, aggressive pounding, and melodic fill-ins, also anticipates Monk's "In Walked Bud." Robin's Oedipal paradise is shattered by the entrance of his cantor father. "You dare to bring your jazz songs into this house!" read the titles while a bearded Jew rants and raves. "I taught you to sing the songs of Israel to take my place in the synagogue!" Monk took the changes of "Blue Skies" back and imposed his own inimitable melodic and rhythmic attack on it, showing that the racial interplay could go both ways.

Mailer has so many of his own riffs to get out in "The White Negro" that he did not have time to pay attention to specific compositions and their origins. One can only imagine what Mailer would have come up with if he had investigated the complexities and contradiction of Monk's music and mystique. When Mailer's intended farewell column was originally published in the *Village Voice*—he quit over a typesetting error—it was a vicious attack on *Waiting for Godot*. But then Mailer saw Beckett's play on Broadway the following week and felt compelled to make a final public notice. No such addendum on jazz ever appeared after the publication of "The White Negro," but the collaboration between Irving Berlin and Thelonious Monk that was really responsible for Mailer's improvised orgasms might not have taken away from their intensity. As it is, though, there are no specific references to Monk or any other jazz musicians in "The White Negro." Instead, jazz is an attitude, an alternative way of approaching sex, death, and ennui in 1957, in which orgasms can be apocalyptic and subjects ranging from the atom bomb to the death of God can be greeted from the hipsters

Mailer calls "really cool cats" with the response of "Crazy, man!" The bad things in life for Mailer are the things that get in the way of phallic sex and Reichian orgasms. Jazz itself is the best route to take for these pursuits for, as he noted in a notorious passage,

> jazz is orgasm, it is the music of orgasm, good orgasm and bad, and so it spoke across a nation, it had the communication of art even where it was watered, perverted, corrupted, and almost killed, it spoke in no matter what laundered popular way of instantaneous existential states to which some whites could respond, it was indeed a communication by art because it said, "I feel this, and now you do too."[21]

Jazz was always linked to blackness and phallic sex for Mailer, and, in typical self-hating fashion, Jewishness was characterized as an obstacle to these lofty goals. At the end of his story "The Time of Her Time," the bullfighter Sergius O'Shaugnessy finally brings the Jewish NYU student Denise to orgasm, and just in case the point is not made through anal sex and the triumph of what he calls his phallic "avenger," he also whispers in her ear, "You dirty little Jew." Arthur, Denise's Jewish boyfriend, is able to satisfy her through cunnilingus, which O'Shaugnessy dismisses as "Jewish bonanzas of mouth love." But the purest orgasm for Mailer is a retreat from Jewishness to blackness, and with Monk he thought he was seeing it in its purest, undiluted form. Mailer practiced what he preached: in addition to growing a goatee and sometimes affecting black dialect, Mailer married Beverly Bently, a former lover of Miles Davis. According to Mary Dearborn, Mailer's biographer, part of Mailer's fascination with Bently was her history with Davis, and he always felt himself to be an inferior follow-up act, an anxiety that apparently haunted him all the way to their divorce proceedings. The homosocial relations between Mailer and Davis are blatant in this triangulation, only confirmed when, accused of repressed homosexuality, Mailer responded, "Of course I'm a latent homosexual, but I choose, as Sartre puts it, to be heterosexual."[22]

Mailer offended many with his reading of jazz in "The White Negro," but this was really part of his plan. James Baldwin published his most venerated fictional account of jazz in "Sonny's Blues" in 1958, a year after the publication of Mailer's essay, and the literary feud that was occasioned by Baldwin's reaction to "The White Negro" was so sweeping that an entire book was devoted to the subject.[23] "Sonny's Blues" has become the most anthologized short story on the subject of jazz, and while Baldwin's first-hand knowledge of the music was surely greater than Mailer's—as his finest essays have shown—the divide in Mailer's essay is similar to that in Baldwin's story, and if the racial dynamic is yet more nuanced, the reading of jazz is also similar. Compared to Mailer, who introduced himself to Diana Trilling at a party by asking, "Now, how about you, smart cunt?"[24] Baldwin was more diplomatic with the group, although he may have harbored a similar hostility. Baldwin looked back somewhat bitterly on his period as an essayist for the *New Leader*. "Most of the books I reviewed were Be Kind to Niggers, Be Kind to Jews, while American was going through one of its liberal convulsions."[25] Mailer could not have been accused of dispensing such empty platitudes, and "The White Negro" was written to make them seize all the more. Baldwin responded to the essay by claiming to know "more about that periphery [Mailer] so helplessly maligns in 'The White Negro' than he could ever hope to know,"[26] and that Mailer was himself a failed hipster. Baldwin describes hanging out with Mailer and a group of unnamed jazz musicians in Paris, and Mailer was outcooled:

And matters were not helped at all by the fact that the Negro jazz musicians, among whom we sometimes found ourselves, who really liked Norman, did not for an instant consider him as being even remotely "hip" and Norman did not know this and I could not tell him. He never broke through to them, at least not as far as I know; and they were far too "hip," if that is the word I want, even to consider breaking through to him. They thought he was a real sweet ofay cat, but a little frantic.[27]

It was the ultimate swipe to his erstwhile literary adversary for Baldwin to describe Mailer as an interloper in the hipster underground, just another "frantic," schvitzing Jewish nebbish. But Mailer and Baldwin both characterized jazz as the lingua franca of hip, and while "Sonny's Blues" varies up the racial template, like "The White Negro" it is at heart about a divide between instinct and intellect.

Baldwin sets up the divide between an unnamed narrator, a math teacher, and his brother, Sonny, a bebop pianist. On the first page of "Sonny's Blues," we learn about a tabloid report that Sonny has been picked up for using and peddling heroin, and the further we are drawn into the narrative, the more we are presented with a familiar study in contrast. Most of the story is then a trip backward to find out what went wrong. If the narrator is not exactly a "White Negro in Reverse" like the passing Anatole Broyard, he certainly would have fit Mailer's definition of a "square." Baldwin sets this up by putting Sonny in a perpetual state of mourning, for his daughter, Gracie, for his mother, and, metaphorically, for the brownstone Harlem community (also, although he does not realize it, the Swing Era) as he sees drifters languishing in the Urban Renewal chaos of the postwar era. For most of "Sonny's Blues," the narrator casts Sonny's music in the same dour light, as his descent into jazz is chronicled like a descent into addiction itself. The narrator is disturbed to learn that his brother has become a musician, recalling an uncle he never knew who was murdered by a group of southern white men. In hipster New York, the lynch mob is replaced by the drug-saturated subculture of bebop—a place where the narrator fears he cannot watch over him. When Sonny tells his brother, "I want to play jazz," it is treated as a statement of transgression, as if he were saying, "I want to be a junkie." For Mailer, jazz is orgasm, but for Baldwin, jazz, or at least bebop, is transgression.

Baldwin, like Mailer, was explaining jazz for a New York Intellectual venue. As one of the few black writers who could get into the pages of the *Partisan Review* in 1957, Baldwin was acting as the native informant, but the way he sets it up, it is really told from a perspective nearly as outside of the world of Minton's and 52nd Street as would have been that of *Partisan Review* editor, William Phillips. Like so many ambitious young Jewish writers of the fifties, Baldwin's path to literary assimilation included falling under the tortuous spell of Henry James. Philip Roth recalled taking the Jamesian path of literary assimilation as a graduate student at the University of Chicago. "I'd be in class with all those Jew boys and we'd have our hands up. Hey ya! Heeyyaaaaa! I know the answer! *Whaddyamean a Jew knows Henry James?*"[28] If Roth felt incongruous as a Jew who knew Henry James, Baldwin was aspiring to be among the aspirants. Baldwin kept a portrait of James over his desk, and like *Portrait of a Lady*'s Ralph Touchett and *The Ambassadors*' Lambert Strether, the narrator of "Sonny's Blues" hovers outside the gates of experience hiding in image and semicolon. It's not just that he cannot get to the thing itself. It is the very mystery of the music that enhances its eros. The narrator of "Sonny's Blues" is less of an outsider to the music than is the author of "The White Negro," but he is still not completely inside it, either. "All I know about music is that people never really hear it," the narrator says. When the narrator finally hears the music, it is during a performance of "Am I Blue?" by the Jewish Tin Pan Alley tunesmith Harry Aks, a song made famous by Ethel Waters. It was not a tune bebop musicians tended to play, and in addition to Waters, the most well-known version was Louis Armstrong's, dismissed by Sonny as "that down home crap." What Baldwin shrewdly identifies as the connection between the "down home" Armstrong and the revolutionary, postwar harmonics of Parker is the cadence of the blues. They provide the title of the story and the metaphor of suffering that Sonny, the self-destructive junkie, must endure to be Baldwin's idea of a true bebop artist. And Harry Aks's tune provides an occasion for a horn player named Creole to "let out the reins," for a "dry, low, black man" to "say something awful on the drums."

The blues were central to bebop, as Parker's 1948 "Parker's Mood," just to give one example, would demonstrate. But there are other modes of communication going on with the musicians Baldwin describes, too. When the narrator finally "gets" Sonny's music, it inspires prose as rapturous and eloquent as anything Baldwin ever produced. His epiphany is not about how jazz musicians actually formulate their ideas or communicate with each other, but how an outsider might view them and impose a narrative on them. There are brief descriptions earlier in the story of Sonny practicing, but what he is practicing is too perplexing for the narrator to fathom. What the narrator witnesses is a catharsis, but he cannot imagine how the labyrinthine language of bebop would have a logic as complex as the high school algebra he teaches.

Baldwin does not necessarily think that jazz is orgasm, but he does not present it as a learned discourse, either. In Ken Burns's *Jazz*, the Mailerian perspective of jazz as a spontaneous, orgasmic cry of expression is given by Allen Ginsberg in a somewhat dismissive but not inaccurate take on the Beat fascination with jazz: "Jazz gives us a way of expressing the spontaneous motions of the heart. It's like a fountain of instantaneous inspiration that's available to everybody. All you have to do is turn on the radio or put on a record or pick up an axe yourself and blow."[29] The image of Ginsberg picking up an "axe" and blowing the choruses of "Ko Ko" is about as comical as Mailer blowing untrained saxophone lines to "Epistrophy." Moments later in Burns's documentary, Wynton Marsalis offers an alternative reading of bop, by saying of the pianist dubbed the music's "high priest," "What I like about Monk is that he's so logical." Marsalis then walks the audience through Monk's "Epistrophy," delineating the call and response between the two phrases in the tune's A section—one a half step higher than the other—as a masterful display of that logic, referring to Monk's ingenious use of the blues and categories like "gutbucket" as if he were coming up with a new theorem or equation.[30] Ginsberg, who was nearly expelled from Columbia for writing "Fuck the Jews" on a campus window, saw the music as the ultimate form of the transgressive embrace of one ethnicity over another. But the more bebop is studied beyond its cultural moment, the more it becomes codified, resembling the "college algebra" of "Sonny's Blues"'s narrator more every day. It would take a few generations of historical perspective before jazz was written about beyond its context; that is, when the process of acquiring the language and technique of the music could be written about with as much detail as the things around it.

When it comes to race, "Sonny's Blues" certainly offers more variation than "The White Negro." In the apocalyptic realm of

Mailer's essay, there is only one kind of black man, and jazz is his orgasmic soundtrack. In "Sonny's Blues," Baldwin offers more choices for black men in 1957, and suggests that one does not have to join the lotus eaters to make the gig at the Five Spot (although given the rate of recidivism among heroin addicts, one wonders at the end of the story how long Sonny will be saved). But bebop itself was not treated as a complex path. Its central figures were black, and many of them were junkies, but the path was more multifaceted than that. Charlie Parker, of course, not only revolutionized the harmonic language of jazz, but was, as he put it, "the world's most famous junkie." By the time "Sonny's Blues" was published though, Charlie Parker's 1955 overdose had inspired Sonny Rollins and Miles Davis to kick heroin; Dizzy Gillespie, Clifford Brown, and others avoided the drug altogether. But whether Mailer was reporting on orgasmic bop and racial appropriation for Irving Howe or Baldwin was crafting Jamesian prose about a narcotic-driven Icarus myth for William Phillips, there was neither the distance nor the perspective for a more nuanced reading of the music.

There is no acknowledgment in "The White Negro" or "Sonny's Blues" of the diversity of the bop material their authors' mined for their writings, and that what was going on in the music was itself a black-Jewish dialogue. For Monk to lift Berlin's "Blue Skies"—or for Baldwin's Sonny to transform Harry Aks's "Am I Blue" into some sort of bop reverie—is to reset the cultural paradigm of the source material. Mailer's White Negroes found something appealing to appropriate at the Five Spot, but Monk found something more subtle in the chord sequence of Irving Berlin and made it his. "In Walked Bud" began with Monk riffing on Berlin's chord changes for "Blue Skies," and its title came after Jon Hendricks sat in with Monk's band and invented vocalese lyrics for Monk's melody. "In walked Bud, and then we got into something," sang Hendricks. Powell did time in Bellevue and would have been celebrated by Mailer for his madness more than for his harmonics. But Monk used a tune by a Jewish composer to teach a jazz history lesson. One can imagine Mailer and Baldwin sitting in the Five Spot in 1957 taking notes. Only part of the story came out in what they ultimately produced.

"A SUBTLER MUSIC"

Like many Philip Roth novels, his *The Human Stain* (2000) began as a story of revenge. The intended recipient was Anatole Broyard, who, in his unfinished memoir about postwar Greenwich Village, remarked, "In *Portnoy's Complaint*, Portnoy says that underneath their skirts all girls have cunts. What he didn't say—and this was his trouble, his real complaint—was that under their skirts, they also had souls."[31] Roth was aware that Broyard had something to hide, too, and his own narrative of passing inspired Roth's rancid tale of deception, revenge, and guilt. Yet in a Rothian twist, his Broyard-inspired hero does not pass, as Broyard did, as a Connecticut WASP, but as a New York Jew, and there is a brief moment in the novel in which there is a cease-fire in the ethnic strife and sexual warfare that dominates most of the book. This moment of detente occurs when Coleman Silk has a memory of 1948, right before he makes the decision to pass. With his dual ethnic status, Silk gets to play out both sides of the culture wars—as a black victim of racism in the forties and a Jewish casualty of campus politics in the nineties—when ironically, he is brought down after being accused of being racist himself. But there is one scene in which Silk is able to have the erotic highlight of a life with no shortage of sexual rigor—this is a Roth novel, after all—and his given and assumed ethnic identities are able to merge effortlessly. Silk, on a GI-funded tour of Greenwich Village bohemia, has his pick of sexual conquests and has found the woman the future classics professor calls his "Voluptuas," the Nordic Steena Palsson, who fascinates him with her enigmatic poetry, her headstrong stoicism, and, most importantly, her insatiable libido. They have one encounter that becomes a dominant motif for Coleman's sexual memories, and the soundtrack plays a crucial role:

> She was getting undressed, and the radio was on—Symphony Sid—and first, to get her moving and in the mood, there was Count Basie and a bunch of jazz musicians jamming on "Lady Be Good," a wild live recording, and following that, more Gershwin, the Artie Shaw rendition of "The Man I Love" that featured Roy Eldridge steaming everything up. Coleman was lying semi-upright on the bed, doing what he most loved to do on a Saturday night after they'd returned from their five bucks' worth of Chianti and spaghetti and cannoli in their favorite Fourteenth Street basement restaurant: watch her take her clothes off. All at once, with no prompting from him—seemingly only prompted by Eldridge's trumpet—she began what Coleman liked to describe as the single most slithery dance ever performed by a Fergus Falls girl after little more than a year in New York City. She could have raised Gershwin himself from the grave with that dance, and with the way she sang the song. Prompted by a colored trumpet player playing it like a black torch song, there to see, plain as day, was all the power of her whiteness.[32]

There is nothing arbitrary about the musical cues of this carnal respite from the ethnic psychodrama that will follow. In 1948, Coleman Silk had to escape from blackness to Jewishness, and in 1998, he would have avoided his downfall if he had decided to embrace his blackness. But the performance of a composition by a blues-inflected son of Russian Jewish immigrants by a Jewish clarinetist and black trumpeter is a three-minute fantasy of ethnic and erotic utopia. "Lady Be Good" began as a number from a musical revue that became a staple for the Jazz at the Philharmonic jam sessions that Symphony Sid Torin would have broadcast in 1948, most memorably with an early recording of Ella Fitzgerald scatting her way around Gershwin's changes accompanied by the honking polyphony of Charlie Parker, Dizzy Gillespie, and a roaring crowd. But the centerpiece of the scene is the Artie Shaw-Roy Eldridge version of "The Man I Love," a crucial composition for the Gershwins that, like *Rhapsody in Blue*, leaned heavily on the contrast between major and minor. ("Someday he'll come" begins in a major key, until "along" brings it to a bluesy minor.) On the 1945 recording Coleman hears on the radio in 1948 (and subsequently plays in septuagenarian encounters on a CD), Artie Shaw uses the major/minor shift to ingenious effect, sliding in and out of both through the language of the blue notes that are the distinguishing harmonic features of both klezmer and the blues. The Roy Eldridge trumpet fanfare that follows—only on a single A section—is brassy and affirmative, less cagey than Shaw's solo and more percussive.

The former Arthur Arshawsky toured the country—and had a brief affair—with Billie Holiday, much to the chagrin of many of his 1930s booking agents; Roy Eldridge performed a 1946 duet of "Drop Me off Uptown" with the white singer Anita O'Day, playing a solo after being encouraged by the singer to "blow, Roy, blow." (In that unprecedented interracial pairing, it is O'Day, not Eldridge, who is the sexual initiator.) The eros performed by Shaw and Eldridge is replicated in Coleman Silk's bedroom, but cannot be sustained outside of it. In the closed doors of Roth's encounter, the cultural divide between Coleman and Steena was not in any way diminished: if anything, it is turned into high drama, but it is drama used for a sexual power-play. Roy Eldridge is described as a "colored trumpet player" who spurs on Steena's body, fetishized as a Melvillian "big white thing." But that big white thing can never be harpooned, certainly not after Steena meets Coleman's proud, black family in East Orange, New Jersey, and subsequently runs away, telling Coleman "I can't do it!" (*HS*, 125). What worked on the band-stand and in the bedroom did not work when the last chorus ran out and the dance was over. Race is something Coleman Silk wants to move beyond, but it is only in this musical inter-lude that ethnicity can be troped and transcended at the same time. When Silk is buried as a Jew fifty years later to the strains of the Kaddish, then to a devastating performance of Mahler's Third Symphony (by a Jew who passed as a Catholic), Nathan Zuckerman—the doppelganger who has narrated seven previ-ous Roth novels—observes that the only music that could have affected him even more would have been "Steena Palsson's ren-dition of 'The Man I Love' as she'd sung it from the foot of Coleman's Sullivan Street bed in 1948" (*HS*, 312). The memory of all that is particularly poignant, a recollection of a privileged moment when ethnicity could be forgotten for the duration of a song.

"The Man I Love" also finds its way into the bedroom in Richard Powers's *The Time of Our Singing* (2003), and it inspires a private language where the cultural pollenation can be under-stood in the confines of ephemeral postcoital bliss. Here, Powers, the author of notoriously intellectual fiction treating such techni-cal and scientific esoterica as molecular genetics (*The Gold Bug Variations*), artificial intelligence (*Galetea 2.2*), and virtual reality (*Plowing the Dark*), applies his scientific precision and meticulous research to America's literary conversation on race. Although he wrote on the classic American theme of corporate ascent in *Gain*, and in *Plowing the Dark* even produced a prophetic book about militant Islam a year before the attacks of September 11, 2001, the WASP author may seem perhaps the least likely candidate among contemporary literary writers to cross the color line and reopen the question of what it means to be black in America. As with his earlier novels, *The Time of Our Singing* also yokes together heterogeneous cultural elements, including Einstein's theory of relativity, Miles Davis's *Sketches of Spain*, the politics of the Metropolitan Opera, and the aesthetics of the March on Washington. Unlike *The Human Stain*, which visits music only briefly, Powers's novel is a sustained meditation on musical collaboration and political apocalypse modeled after Thomas Mann's *Doctor Faustus*,[33] and Gershwin has as much cultural resonance for Powers as Schoenberg did for Mann. "The Man I Love" makes its appearance when Joseph Strom, the son of a Jewish physicist and African American mezzo, is having his first affair with the Polish-American Teresa Wierzbicki, who catches his eye while he applies his Juilliard-trained piano skills to playing Top 40 in an Atlantic City lounge, keeping himself amused with sophisticated voicings. Although Joseph is told by his boss, "Nix the Gershwin. Gershwin's for people dying of shuffleboard injuries at the Nevele,"[34] in 1970, when the cultural dynamics of Tin Pan Alley are deemed irrelevant and anemic by a geriatric Jewish club owner, Joseph and Teresa still find the lyrics to be the ideal private language of their sexual banter:

"Ah, Sunday."
"Maybe Monday," I sang.
Teresa segued: "Maybe not." She turned toward me, pulling her feet up on the sofa underneath her. She looked

down at her thighs, a little askew, the color of fine bone china. Her lips moved silently, as they had for so long in the darkness of the club, keeping me company each night. The warmth of the recording came out of her soundless mouth. *Still I'm sure to meet him one day, maybe Tuesday will be my good news day.* My right hand lowered itself onto her leg and began accompanying. I closed my eyes and improvised. I moved from chords to free imitation, careful to keep a decent range, between her knee and hiked-up hemline.

(*TS*, 443–44)

This is Joseph's first sexual encounter, and the Gershwin lyrics serves as a mode of communication for a working-class, white Jersey girl who learned about Waller, Vaughan, and Monk from her father and a biracial prodigy who spent most of his life on stage and in the practice room. Joseph represents a particular phenomenon that has never found its way into American fiction: the black (or at least part black) classical music prodigy. Unlike Mailer's phallic bopper, Baldwin's junkie bopper, or Salinger's martyred blues empress, Joseph Strom gravitates to music like no other fictive creation, and the intersection between blacks and Jews that makes Gershwin's tune so perfect for interracial private erotics is, as in *The Human Stain*, embattled outside its musical or erotic occasion.

Like Roth, Powers subverts ethnic sterotypes and their musical associations by mixing them up. He brings together a black-Jewish couple to produce three extraordinary children at a turning point in American politics and music. On an auspicious Easter in 1939, when the great contralto Marian Anderson, banished from Constitution Hall by the Daughters of the American Revolution, gives a stirring outdoor performance, the largest solo recital in American history, David Strom, a Jewish émigré physicist just barely escaped from Hitler's Europe, meets Delia Dailey, a promising black singer whose family is the embodiment of Du Bois's "Talented Tenth." Their union produces a trio of gifted children who go beyond the fractional bar set by Du Bois in 1903, including the eldest, Jonah, whose "voice was so pure, it could make heads of state repent" (8), the middle child Joseph, everyone's accompanist, and Ruth, the youngest, a deadly mimic as child and an angry activist as an adult. With a tenured appointment at Columbia and an apartment in the liminal ethnic threshold of Hamilton Heights, Professor Strom attempts to raise his prodigies in a controlled experiment "beyond race." At first, their realm is familial paradise. Life is filled with Schubert lieder, mathematical puzzles, and literary games. What could go wrong? The answer, of course, is America, with its collision between the ideal world of artistic shelter and the brutal world of racial politics. In 1950s New York, these black-Jewish children excel at everything they do, and they are instructed to refuse racial classification. Delia tells Jonah and Joseph, "You two boys can be anything you want" (*TS*, 208).

It is not hard to imagine the obstacles they confront from there. Jonah shows unlimited promise as a tenor, but halts his musical ascent when he refuses to accept a *New York Times* critic's assertion that he may become one of the "great Negro tenors" of his generation. The more passive Joseph—who serves as our anxious narrator—is less Promethean than his brother (who is memorably described in his performances as Faust), and more indeterminate in his racial identity, a Hans Castorp–like blank slate unsure whether he should fill his canvas with a postracial self-portrait or conform to his era's idea of blackness. Ruth, the youngest and darkest, passionately adopts those racial signifiers, abandons her musical talent and uses her considerable rhetorical gifts in the service of 1960s radical politics. As Jonah and Joseph barnstorm the country on the classical music circuit—while Ruth goes into hiding with the Black Panthers—they collide with history at every stop, watching Birmingham's water cannons on hotel television, and recording "The Erl-King" in Los Angeles while Watts burns.

And it is in such cloistered circumstances that they make their discoveries of jazz. Like Ellison's Invisible Man, the Strom brothers might even be said to possess minds. Coming to jazz from a classical background, they confront the music not through instinct but rather intense and rigorous study, and Joseph is baffled by the emotional response he has to improvisation. While jazz was having one of its most fertile decades in the fifties, it was mostly ignored in the halls of Juilliard, where music students still looked to the avant-garde of Roger Sessions and Elliot Carter to point the way to the next paradigm shift—assuming that such a shift could only take place in modernized versions of the sonata form. It takes Wilson Hart, one of the few black students at Juilliard, to show Jonah otherwise when he encourages him to depart from the score of Joaquin Rodrigo's 1939 *Concierto de Aranjuez*, dismissed by Jonah, under the spell of the avant-garde, as a "total throwback." But when Jonah sees Wilson take liberties with Rodrigo's themes and improvise on them, it is a revelation for Joseph, who could not have fathomed that deviating from the score could produce serious music. Suddenly confronting the blues, swing, and all of the other music going on around him while he was locked up in a practice room, Joseph blurts out, "What you just made? That was better than the stuff you made it from" (*TS*, 189). In 1961, Rodrigo's *Concierto* would be adapted for Miles Davis's *Sketches of Spain*, and when Joseph hears the theme again on the Davis record, realizing that a concerto for guitar could be transcribed and improvised upon for piano, he internalizes the mystique of Miles Davis, realizing that American music is as ad hoc as American identity. "There's not a horse alive that's purebread," Wilson tells Joseph, who has to confront the music and image of Miles Davis to understand his own ambiguous relationship to his blackness. He brushes off a knowing White Negro at a party who says "That's my man, Miles," and cathects with the music in solitude, realizing that the mixed up, pluralistic identity Wilson had so badly wanted Joseph to bring out was coming through on those speakers.

Davis was first introduced to the idea of playing Spanish music by Beverly Bently, before she became Mrs. Norman Mailer. *Sketches of Spain* is one of Davis's three crucial collaborations with Gil Evans, the white arranger who was able to bring Davis's music to a larger public, drawing from an orchestral pallette that was as indebted to French Impressionism as it was to Duke Ellington. But while Davis's recording was widely celebrated, in his autobiography he remembered his frustration with the classical musicians on the session:

> Like most other classical players, they play only what you put in front of them. That's what classical music is; the musicians only play what's there and nothing else. They can remember, and have the ability of robots. In classical music, if one musician isn't like the other, isn't all the way a robot, like all the rest, then the other robots make fun of him or her, especially if they're black. That's all that is, that's all the classical music is in terms of the musicians who play it—robot shit.[35]

Davis, in typically hyperbolic fashion, is overstating the case to demonstrate the superiority of his own idiom—really, of being Miles Davis—over any other form of expression. But Davis, a Juilliard dropout himself, was also acknowledging what Joseph Strom was figuring out in the practice room and would later have to confront in his life, torn as he was between a Jewish ancestry he never knew and a black identity to which he will make a belated gravitation. As a conservatory student, Joseph is like one of the "robot" classical musicians Davis dismisses, and it is only when he learns that music can depart from a single score that he embraces an aesthetic of diversity. The tumult that surrounds the Stroms indicates that the world is unable to accept this diversity. Only in the music can this cultural crossing truly be accepted. When Joseph hears Davis's ice-blue variations on Rodrigo's Spanish flamenco, he describes Davis as "a man so dark, I'd cross the street if I saw him coming" (261). But it is Joseph who runs back to blackness at the book's end to imagine what new sounds could be awaiting him. As a musician, Joseph can veer from varying shades until he finds the hue that fits his own idiosyncratic identity, and Powers, veering from song to history to the written page, shows how music provides a key in understanding the entwined, multiethnic collaborations of American culture.

Powers himself crossed over when he took it upon himself as a WASP intellectual author to narrate the story of a black-Jewish family in order to reopen the question of what it means to be black in America, and many of the book's reviewers were critical of the result. The resistance Powers's characters meet with was recapitulated in many of the book's reviews, suggesting that, even at the pinnacle of the literary world, stereotypes remain surprisingly fixed. John Homans, in a diatribe in *New York*, admitted that "Powers does manage, as few have, to get down in words the excitement of making music," but he is then taken aback by the Stroms's musical talent, claiming that Powers "has taken a shortcut to making them singular—he's made them gifted."[36] In his debut *New Yorker* review, Sven Birkerts, while praising the book's ingenuity and lauding Powers for capturing "what feels like the innermost sanctum of the singer's art," faulted him for failing to provide characters worthy of a racial theme, and pronounces that "Richard Wright's Bigger Thomas, though much blunter as a character, managed to leave the print of his pain, the pounding echo of his blues. Powers achieves a subtler music, but, for all its fascination, it tends to fade as the pages are turned."[37] "A subtler music": astonishingly, this is meant as a dismissal. As daring as Bigger Thomas was when Richard Wright created him in 1940, the murderous black man has since become a familiar figure in our movies and television, and the world of hip hop has rewarded such personae—from The Notorious B.I.G. to Tupac Shakur—with celebrity and notoriety. But who has ever put Marian Anderson in a novel, or imagined in narrative what Jessye Norman or Kathleen Battle must have encountered as they climbed the long stairway up to the Kennedy Center? "Richard Wright imagined Bigger Thomas, but Bigger Thomas could not have imagined Richard Wright," observed Ralph Ellison over thirty years ago. Ellison was calling for fiction to realize a black consciousness that could envision success as much as it laments victimhood. But apparently, many of today's most visible reviewers feel no need for fiction that can imagine black genius.

Indeed, it is the "subtler music" that has been missing in the hyperbolic sentimentality of Salinger's Black Charles and Lida Louise, and in the junkie beboppers represented by Mailer and Baldwin, their literary feud notwithstanding. Powers, a trained oboe player and cellist, was able to do something Salinger, Mailer, and Baldwin could not: describe with learned precision exactly how music is made. That he did so by bringing blacks and Jews together only underscores exactly how crucial this relationship has been in American music, drawing a contrast between its artistic gestation and its political resistance. *The*

Time of our Singing renders explicit what has been implicit in the work of Salinger, Mailer, and Baldwin. It should go without saying that there is more to the life of a black musician than Salinger's representation of entertaining and being beaten, Mailer's phallic fantasies, or Baldwin's searing tale of shooting up, getting arrested, and providing a blues-based epiphany on the bandstand. There have been many black-Jewish collaborations in music, but until Richard Powers's novel came along, no American writer has taken that collaboration and revealed how the range of its music could find its way into prose. To account fully for the subtleties, contradictions, and nuances that could bring together the charts of Irving Berlin and Thelonious Monk, the clarinet and trumpet call and response of Artie Shaw and Roy Eldridge, or the pairing of Powers's Delia Daley and David Strom does indeed require a subtler music.[38] The less attached authors are to conventional notions of identity, and the more American music can be understood beyond its immediate context, the more contradictions and nuances can be found in the cadence that has woven so many improbable collaborations in the music and the culture it inflects.

The black-Jewish collaboration has reached a point in American music where acknowledging its symbiosis has found its way not only into the literary fiction of Powers, but into the popular music that wears its mongrel roots like a badge of honor. On September 11, 2001, the day that inspired Baraka to contemplate an Israeli-led terrorist conspiracy in "Somebody Blew Up America," Columbia Records released Bob Dylan's *Love and Theft*,[39] the forty-third album by the former Robert Zimmerman, whose title was unashamedly lifted from Eric Lott's 1993 study of blackface minstrelsy and its integral relationship to American culture of the nineteenth century. Dylan's use of the title acknowledged that Lott's thesis was as true in 2001 as ever, confirming that a form of blackface, conscious or unconscious, was inseparable from understanding the rich, twisted history of American song. The entire album is a contemplation of the twelve-bar blues, with an acknowledged homage to Charley Patton on the apocalyptic "High Water" and plenty of hidden appropriations, including the wistful "Bye and Bye," where Dylan uses the chord changes from Leo Robin and Ralph Rainger's "Having Myself a Time" under a raspy croon that draws from Billie Holiday's 1938 recording of the tune. For the Jewish Dylan to lift the phrasing of a black icon's version of a song by Jewish Tin Pan Alley tunesmiths leaves listeners aswirl in wondering, as Louis Armstrong put it, "How do we know who copied what?" Dylan's album was an acknowledgment of blatant stealing and unabashed affection, arguing in song what Lott's book argues in scholarship: all American culture is borrowed and appropriated. "Some of these bootleggers / They've got pretty good stuff," Dylan sings on the album's "Sugar Baby." These bootleggers, of course, often operated from a privileged position and enjoyed the fruits of somebody else's blues, taking on what Greg Tate has called, in a book of the same name, "Everything but the Burden."

It would be inconceivable to imagine American music without the perpetual interplay from Harlem to Tin Pan Alley and back again. Most of the reviewers of Powers's novel have not yet caught up to it, but it is only a matter of time before more literary figures acknowledge what the musicians have known all along. Salinger's blues martyr, Mailer's White Negro, and Baldwin's junkie bebopper were all actually producing a music that was itself the result of mixing and lifting, admiring and coopting, loving and thieving. We are all lovers and thieves now, and better off for admitting it.

Invisibility, let me explain, gives one a slightly different sense of time. Sometimes you're ahead, sometimes behind. Instead of the swift and imperceptible flowing of time, you are aware of its nodes, those points where time stands still or from which it leaps ahead. And you slip into the breaks and look around.

—Ralph Ellison, *Invisible Man*

2

LISTENING TO ELLISON

TRANSGRESSION AND TRADITION IN ELLISON'S JAZZ WRITINGS

In 1963, Irving Howe and Ralph Ellison engaged in a literary sparring match that was called, by most onlookers, for Ellison. It was not a congenial moment in black-Jewish relations—a long way, certainly from Count Basie riffing on Gershwin's "Oh! Lady Be Good" with a rhythmic attack wholly distinct from its source material. Ellison and Howe's exchange was more like the battle royales alluded to in Ellison's *Invisible Man*, a literary cutting contest. Unlike a musical cutting contest, however, in which two improvisers, usually horn players, go head-to-head with styles that are as distinctive as they are complementary, this one was about the bitter divides of race and politics. The Ellison-Howe match may not have been good for black-Jewish relations, but it was ultimately good for Ellison, inspiring his most vivid piece of writing after *Invisible Man*. Howe hit Ellison with "Black Boys and Native Sons" in 1963, telling him how to write about blackness. Ellison hit back later that year with his essay "The World and the Jug," letting Howe know that he had ideas of his own about how that should be done, thank you very much. Howe might not have agreed with those ideas, but they would take on a life of their own nonetheless.

Back in 1952, Ellison was a first-time novelist who besotted much of the literary establishment. One of these exegetes was Howe, who expressed sufficient adulation in his review of *Invisible Man* in *The Nation* that his praise was chosen for a jacket blurb; he also sat on the National Book Award committee that bestowed their honor upon Ellison. Eleven years later, though, the massive success and almost instant canonization of *Invisible Man* had elevated Ellison, rather against his will, to the role of spokesperson, and Howe was no longer endorsing an up and comer but criticizing a literary celebrity. Ellison's response in "The World and the Jug" riffed on Lovie Austin and Alberta Hunter's "Downhearted Blues": "I got the world in a jug, and the stopper's in my hand, / I'm gonna hold it, baby, until you come under my command." Although Bessie Smith recorded a celebrated version of the song in 1923, the voice Ellison probably had in mind with his title was that of Jimmy Rushing, his fellow Oklahoman thanked in the acknowledgments of his 1964 collection *Shadow and Act*, where "The World and the Jug" was reprinted. The singer of "Downhearted Blues" is disgusted, heartbroken, too, but at the song's climax, makes sure you know that it is she (or, in Rushing's version, he) who is ultimately in control, and Ellison certainly intended to hold that stopper until the critics came under his command.[1] Ellison, who would lecture on the connections between Louis Armstrong and T. S. Eliot that year, could have also been paying his respects to Eliot's description of a nightingale from "The Waste Land": "And still she cried, and still the world pursues, / 'Jug Jug' to dirty ears." Howe's ears, not exactly attuned to Ellison's music, were guided by ideology, insisting that Ellison should have defined his heroes by way of his oppressors, that his hero's journey down that manhole was one of defeat. But Invisible Man is not completely alone in that basement. He has his sloe gin and he has his Louis Armstrong. "My strength comes from Louis Armstrong," said Ellison in an interview. In his own introverted way, Ellison had the world in a jug and the stopper in his hands.

Their debate became a defining moment in Ellison's life, one in which he railed against one form of an institution without realizing he would influence another one. His reading of Armstrong, that provider of strength for *Invisible Man* and its author, would play a crucial role in how that would take place. Everyone who tells Ellison's story points to his debate with Howe as one of his genuine triumphs, a time when Ellison took on the Goliath of the New York Intellectual establishment, even though much of that establishment—if his Century Club membership was any indication—had already embraced him. From Right to Left, critics as divergent as Norman Podhoretz and Cornel West have believed that Ellison emerged the victor of their duel. "Oooooh, he cut him," West recalled of Ellison's signifying "Brother Irving."[2] Meanwhile, there were some, like Jerry Watts, who offered a Marxist critique: that Ellison was merely heaping praise on Louis Armstrong, Duke Ellington, and Charlie Christian while ignoring the masses, recalling Anatole Broyard's comment, in a rather different context, that "the Negro fiddles while Rome burns." Watts, like the young Black Panther representative who drove Ellison to tears by calling him an Uncle Tom at Grinnell College in 1967, thought that Ellison's hero should not have hid in the basement, but crawled out of it to lead a revolution.[3] Instead, Ellison staged a revolution from the confines of that basement and helped to shape the institutionalization of jazz to come.

Marxists, it may be noted, did not take kindly to Ellison's novel. In *Invisible Man*, he skewered the Marxists he knew when he was a fledgling editor at *New Masses* through his creation of the hypocritical organization called The Brotherhood, and his hero runs from them, along with the black nationalist Ras the Destroyer, the mackdaddy pimp Rinehart, and mobs of Harlem rioters, and escapes into a basement. It is this retreat that Howe and many of the novel's other critics dub a cop out.[4] But, as Ellison quickly points out, even when he tries to shut out the world and the groups that have led him to retreat, "In going underground, I whipped it all except the mind, the *mind*" (*IM*, 580). In the spirit of his namesake Ralph Waldo Emerson's dictum, "Nothing is at last sacred but the integrity of your own mind," Ellison knew that his hero could not escape his own predilections, his own sense of self, in spite of all his attackers who were doing everything they could to define that self for him. Howe rejects this ending as drivel, low-rent existentialism without a solution for the struggling masses looking to the anointed Ellison for The Answer, when all Ellison could propose were what Howe derides as "infinite possibilities." Howe praised Ellison's ability to capture, among other things, "jazz chatter," and with a precision unimaginable for a white writer, but he does not address it as a jazz discourse, or what Jerry Watts, Howe's heir in the Ellison interrogation, dismisses as Ellison's "blues ontology."[5]

In that epilogue, Ellison writes that he is aware that "gin, jazz, and dreams were not enough. Books were not enough" (*IM*, 573). Books and jazz, though, would be the best weapons for the narrator's silence, exile, and cunning. How could sitting in the dark listening to Armstrong possibly have any consequences beyond the pleasures of hiding from the outside world? It is not just that one of the benefits of a freedom fought for is the freedom to reflect, the freedom to criticize, and the freedom to demonstrate why listening to Louis Armstrong is more satisfying to his hero than any group activity. Rather, his way of listening to Armstrong would prove to be so compelling, and his descriptions so influential, it would actually have institutional consequences way beyond anything even Ellison could have imagined.

THE BASEMENT TAPES

Ellison may have won the cutting contest against Howe, but the accusation that he had merely fiddled with his typewriter while Harlem burned stayed with him, as did the Black Panther member's accusation that he was an Uncle Tom. Ellison was in no emotional state to tell him that *Invisible Man* was itself a civil rights statement. "For me," Ellison wrote in 1953, "the writing of this particular book was an act of social responsibility as well as an attempt at an artistic projection."[6] Likewise, the muse of its prologue, Louis Armstrong, was no more an Uncle Tom than Ellison was—even when, as in the 1938 film *Goin' Places*, Armstrong played a character named Gabriel, frequently referred to derisively as "Uncle Tom." The Invisible Man's retreat from the world proved prophetic for his creator, as well, who—perhaps in part because of such scathing attacks—spent the next forty-two years writing and unwriting a never completed novel. And yet "Hibernation," the Invisible Man assures us, "is a covert operation for more action" (*IM*, 13). It is unfortunate that Ellison did not march on Washington or at Selma. Yet his Invisible Man was staging his own covert operation alone in his basement. In his novel, Ellison ridicules political figures ranging from Booker T. Washington ("The Founder" of the college Ellison based on Tuskegee) to Marcus Garvey (an inspiration for the rabble-rousing Ras the Destroyer). Only Armstrong survives his satire, the sole African American icon the narrator could imagine canonizing. Ellison's descriptions of Armstrong would not only inspire his narrator, but also transfigure jazz discourse forever, finding its way into institutional versions of jazz history, including the heroic narrative of Ken Burns's documentary and the mission statements of Jazz at Lincoln Center.

Ellison did not feel comfortable as a civil rights spokesman; rather, he intended to give voice to a silenced past. In his original draft of *Invisible Man*, Ellison wanted to reach even further back than Armstrong in his novel's jazz allusions. Initially, he had his narrator listening to Charles "Buddy" Bolden in the basement, invoking a history that was not only invisible, but unheard. A standard legend in jazz history is that Buddy Bolden was the first great jazz improviser, but, since he ceased performing in 1907 (demonstrating the syphilis-induced symptoms of dementia that would put him in a New Orleans sanitarium until his death in 1931) and never recorded, his reputation is purely the stuff of myth. Jelly Roll Morton's achievements are well documented through recorded performances and scores, but these scores led Morton to assert another myth: that he was the inventor of jazz. Both of these propositions are dubious at best, but they also reveal jazz's complicated relationship to writing: Morton felt justified in his claim because he was the first jazz composer—in the logocentric sense of written scores, as opposed to the oral and improvised traditions that are more central to the jazz aesthetic as conceived by Ellison—and Bolden's accomplishments were, to a certain extent, codified through the rumor mill of New Orleans folklore. Ellison deftly integrates the written myth with the oral legend in the name of "dancing and diversity." The use of Bolden, as opposed to Armstrong, suggests that Ellison originally had a jazz icon in mind who was not only more obscure, but more of a symbol of an abstract idea of jazz's origins, to which he intended to give life. Though Ellison later altered the soundtrack of invisibility in his prologue, the sense of recording the unrecorded remains in the novel and appears in its epilogue. "Old bad air is up there with his dancing and diversity and I'll be up there with mine," says the narrator on the final page of the novel, referring to the line, "Open up the window and let the bad air out," from Jelly Roll Morton's "Buddy Bolden's Blues" (*IM*, 581).

When Ellison was revising his prologue to *Invisible Man*, his editor Albert Erskine suggested he insert references to Louis Armstrong to make it more topical. Erskine apparently believed that Ellison's newly added descriptions of alienation accompanied by a Louis Armstrong soundtrack and a fog of reefer would be the epitome of hip, even though Ellison's narrator makes it clear in that prologue that he is no hipster. Unlike Armstrong, who believed "gage" to have medicinal purposes, the narrator assures his readers he has sworn off marijuana ever since the drug—along with Armstrong's recording of Fats Waller and Andy Razaf's "(What Did I Do to Be So) Black and Blue?"— propelled him into a Dantesque hallucination and Joycean nightmare of history. He swears off the "reefer" not because it is illegal, but because "it inhibits action" (*IM*, 13).

For the Invisible Man, Armstrong inspires anything but indolence, and certainly inspired a counterintuitve critical turn for Ellison. In seven years of writing the novel, Ellison saw the world changing around his Harlem apartment. Armstrong was seen as a figure from a bygone era of accommodation, someone who, after all, was actually willing to play Uncle Tom for Hollywood. Ellison saw this as an opportunity to rescue the already dated figure of Armstrong from the beboppers' condemnations. Jazz may have been a name for an "age" in the 1920s, a title for popular dance music in the 1930s, and a label hoisted on reluctant beboppers in the 1940s, but by the time Ellison was inserting his Armstrong references into the revision of his novel (following Hughes Panassie's *The Real Jazz* in 1942 and Rudi Blesh's *Shining Trumpets* in 1946), jazz was a subject that was just beginning to be historicized. Ellison's observations on Armstrong were so contrary to standard judgments that his revision to his novel was also a revision to jazz history. By the late 1940s, Armstrong had been lauded by jazz purists for his earlier work: his pioneering use of scat singing on the 1926 "Heebie Jeebies," his labyrinthine cadenza on the 1928 "West End Blues," and his brash tone and ingeniously crafted solos were among the achievements venerated by the jazz critics of the day. But many of the critics objected to Armstrong's appropriation of banal Tin Pan Alley tunes like the 1933 "Sweethearts on Parade," recordings with Hawaiian bands and The Mills Brothers, and seemingly demeaning appearances. Charlie Parker never appeared in a Hollywood movie or recorded for a major label. Breaking into the mainstream required absurd compromises; when Armstrong played that obsequious character in 1938, he gleefully sang "Jeepers Creepers" to a horse. Without Ellison, such moments of cultural embarrassment could not have begun to be reclaimed.

Ellison was writing about Armstrong in the moment of bebop, and in an essay for *Esquire* called "Golden Age, Time Past," he would reveal himself as an author out of time, never quite on the beat. Ellison described how, by the 1940s, the private language developed by bebop musicians at Minton's retreated from the public mask so ingeniously donned by Armstrong. The musical language of bebop was more overtly theoretical than swing, based on long extended riffs, solos built not merely on short eighth-note swing lines, but rather longer, more complex statements based on scales and modes. Ellison had the ears and the technical vocabulary to comprehend the revolution that was taking place at Minton's—he even wrote glowingly about their house guitarist, Charlie Christian. But the beboppers also violated his childhood memories of Oklahoma City, his Proustian reveries of Louis Armstrong. Most significantly, though, they punctured his metaphor, and he wanted it back.

Ellison described the beboppers' strictly policed boundaries between art and entertainment (and they placed themselves in the former category), bitterly observing that they were particularly "resentful of Louis Armstrong, whom (confusing the spirit of his music with his clowning) they considered an Uncle Tom."[7] It was fashionable for 1950s icons to define themselves against Armstrong. In his autobiography, Dizzy Gillespie recalled, "If anybody asked me about a certain public image of [Armstrong], handkerchief over his head, grinning in the face of white racism, I never hesitated to say I didn't like it,"[8] and in his memoir, Miles Davis concurred, writing, "I loved Louis, but I couldn't stand all that grinning he did."[9] Bebop was a radical assault on the swing era, transforming what had been perceived to be a dance music to a form of aural dialectics in which solos were supposed to be studied with hermeneutical precision. Dizzy Gillespie and Charlie Parker may have wisecracked on the bandstand, but there was no Tomming at Minton's. With a world war breaking up the big bands abroad and a recording ban barring musicians from recording opportunities, bebop, ironically, would seem to have been a kind of "music of invisibility." One would expect that this would be the kind of music that *Invisible Man*'s narrator, frustrated with the roles he is expected to play, would want to hear. The surviving recordings of those Minton's jam sessions reveal a private language being developed without any apparent thought of accessibility or commerce—basement tapes seemingly analogous to Invisible Man's underground musings.

Yet the narrator of *Invisible Man* did not look to bebop for inspiration, but rather to a figure who was criticized, much as Ellison was, for entertaining too eagerly a white, establishment audience. Ellison, however, was no more an Uncle Tom than

Armstrong was. His essay on Minton's chronicles the development of bebop while also criticizing the music itself, favoring as
it does so the less obvious transgressions more congenial to his
own sense of performativity. Charlie Parker's transformation of
"How High the Moon" into "Ornithology" seemed more obviously radical than Louis Armstrong singing "(What Did I Do
To Be So) Black and Blue," much as Richard Wright's Bigger
Thomas chopping off Mary Dalton's head and throwing it into
the furnace might seem a more obvious statement of protest than
Invisible Man stealing electricity in a basement. The critique of
cultural memory and emergence of a seemingly subjective voice
is apparent from that essay's opening sentence: "It has been a
long time now, and not many remember how it was in the old
days, not really" (*CE*, 237). Throughout "Golden Age, Time
Past," Ellison appoints himself a chronicler of hearsay. "So how
can they remember?" (*CE*, 239), Ellison asks at one point. "Or
some will tell you . . ." (*CE*, 240), he begins at another. The essay
concludes with the following warning: "Now the tall tales told as
history must feed on the results of their efforts" (*CE*, 249). For
Ellison, though, the line between official histories and unofficial
tall tales begins to blur. Ellison, who often said he had difficulty
with transitions, wrote a novel with a circular sense of time—
following *Finnegans Wake* and *In Search of Lost Time*—while expressing unease at the aesthetic forward march of jazz history.

But just as the New Critics used an ahistorical approach to
literary texts, the jazz revivalists of the 1940s venerated those
earlier Armstrong recordings by bracketing away their context,
and when Armstrong's recordings broke away from the seemingly "pure" realm of black jazz to venture into white American
pop, he ceased to be a practitioner of high art. It is inarguable
that Armstrong's recordings from 1926 to 1928 are indeed
among the most astonishing in the history of American music,

but they are not what generated material for Ellison, for those records, recorded for Columbia's Okeh label, were tunes by black composers and black musicians and recorded for a black audience; there is no recorded narrative of diversity for Ellison to appropriate for his own. When Armstrong branched out to record the work of a white composer, Hoagy Carmichael, in 1934, many of Armstrong's critics—including the biographer James Lincoln Collier—viewed it as a sign of artistic decline. In 1948, after Ellison was given his instruction to replace the Bolden reference to an Armstrong one, the Marxist critic Sidney Finkelstein used such a critique of Armstrong's performances of Tin Pan Alley tunes as an example of his broader thesis that an authentic art is impossible in a corrupt, capitalist culture: "Had a genuine, musical culture existed in America, one capable of cherishing its talents and giving them a chance to learn and grow, instead of destroying them, Armstrong might have been encouraged to produce a great American music. There was no such opportunity, however; instead, [only the] continual pressure to produce novelties, to plug new songs, or the same songs under new names."[10] Ellison would have dismissed such a comment as the kind of doctrinaire paternalism demonstrated by *Invisible Man's* Brother Jack, who ended up betraying the narrator to The Brotherhood. In fact, although Ellison was trained as a trumpet player and orchestrator, his praise of Armstrong was never on, say, Armstrong's use of glissandos, vibratos, and other technical features meticulously analyzed in musicological texts like Gunther Schuller's *Early Jazz* and *The Swing Era*. For Ellison, Finkelstein's Marxist reading of American culture was as predictable as the chord changes to "Sweethearts on Parade." " 'Are you alive, or not? Is there nothing in your head?' " Eliot asks in *The Waste Land* before concluding: "But / O O O O that Shakespeherian Rag,"[11] letting the musical performance answer for itself. Anyone wondering if there was more substance behind Armstrong's grinning need only listen to his dramatization of those popular songs into something richer and stranger. In 1933, Armstrong would record a magisterial version of "Sweethearts on Parade" and make a ferocious appearance in a Betty Boop cartoon singing "I'll Be Glad When You're Dead, You Rascal, You," and the contrast between setting and approach gives Armstrong a chance to transfigure, an effect that would have reminded Ellison of Eliot's use of the "Shakespearean Rag."

When Ellison replaced Bolden with Armstrong, the 1929 recording by Armstrong of Fats Waller and Andy Razaf's "(What Did I Do To Be So) Black and Blue" became what the narrator would take with him to the basement, and while it is a protest record by a black composer, it was also recorded when Armstrong had his first major exposure to a white audience as a trumpeter in the pit orchestra for the musical revue "Hot Chocolates." The tune, written for that revue, was sung by a dark-skinned woman who, in lyrics by Andy Razaf, laments, "Browns and yallers all have fellers / Gentlemen prefer them light." Armstrong, perceiving a broader message, eliminated the verse and created an early protest anthem. To be black, in his version, is to be black and blue, a remarkable statement for a 1929 pop record. The true meaning of the song is no longer found in Razaf's lyric, but in Armstrong's interpretation of it—a phrase like "Even a mouse ran from my house" might sound self-pitying or simplistic when sung by a less nuanced artist—and in the way he bends a "military instrument into a beam of lyrical sound."

The 1929 recording shows how lyricism emerges from repression in more than the obvious way; it's there in the conflict between the artist's freedom and the song's rhythmic and thematic straitjacket. The track opens with a sentimental, rhythmically literal riff on celesta, played by Gene Anderson, which is batted away by Armstrong's brassy, bluesy attack. Then he recapitulates Anderson's simple 5-1-2-3 / 6-1-2-3 minor phrase, a simple progression from an A minor to D minor, whose sentimental theme he subsequently dismantled with a blaring, dissenting high E atop a D-major chord. What follows is a series of mixed allusions, including additional blues variations, a trumpet onomatopoeia of a marching band snare-drum's "rat-a-tat-tat," and a parody of a bugle call, as if he were waking us up from a dirge. Armstrong's phrasing on trumpet and voice is supple, but what continues to astound is the contrast between his rhythmic variation and his rhythm section's relative stiffness. (The Armstrong of this period frequently engaged in jaw-dropping contrasts with his fellow musicians. On his version of Waller's "Ain't Misbehavin'," recorded three days before "Black and Blue," Homer Hobson's merely adequate trumpet is reduced to tonal rubble by the force of Armstrong's brassy detonations.) With Earl Hines out of the rhythm section, Armstrong lacked a peer. The metronymic quarter notes plonked out on Mancy Carr's banjo stand in dramatic contrast to Armstrong's graceful swing.

The Invisible Man also resists the constraining grips of his cultural moment, running from political orthodoxies and refusing to march lockstep with any political ideology. Instead, he "slip[s] into the breaks," finding the beat between the pulses and swinging hard. He is an antiliteralist, and even though he spends the entire novel searching in vain for a character named Mr. Emerson, he practices Emersonian self-reliance. Armstrong provides an alternative to the politicized factions of Harlem life:

Now I have one radio phonograph; I plan to have five. There is a certain acoustical deadness to my hole, and when I have music I want to *feel* its vibration, not only with my ear but with my whole body. I'd like to hear five recordings

of Louis Armstrong playing and singing "What Did I Do
To Be So Black and Blue"—all at the same time. Sometimes now I listen to Louis while I have my favorite dessert
of vanilla ice cream and sloe gin. I pour the red liquid over
the white mound, watching it glisten and the vapor rising
as Louis bends that military instrument into a beam of lyrical sound. Perhaps I like Louis Armstrong because he's
made poetry out of being invisible. I think it must be because he's unaware that he *is* invisible. And my own grasp
of invisibility aids me to understand his music.   (*TM*, 5–6)

Although Max Roach said that records were the textbooks for
jazz, the recording techniques of 1929 hardly convey the full
range of Armstrong's sound, and the three-minute 78 rpm record
was also a constraining form; Ellison recalled listening to a ten-
minute radio feed of the Armstrong of that era blowing chorus
after chorus of "Chinatown, My Chinatown," where the ideas
flowed much longer than the recording technology of the day
permitted. Why, then, does the narrator wish he could hear
recordings of Armstrong, when true jazz fans dream about hearing the real thing?

The answer has something to do with why Armstrong works
metaphorically for *Invisible Man*, for it was the conflict between
the mediated forms of representation and the liberating content
that interested Ellison. Ellison's Armstrong was a figure whose
art could transcend its context or occasion. So, for example,
when, according to Ellison's description, he "bends that military
instrument into a beam of lyrical sound," Ellison is probably
alluding to Armstrong's first cornet lessons as a boy imprisoned
at the Colored Waif's Home. (In a biographical essay on Armstrong, Martin Williams sidesteps the racial archaism of that
institution's name by simply referring to it as the "Waif's Home.")
According to Ellison, even though Armstrong learned the in-

strument in a military capacity, the blues, with their "bent" thirds and sevenths, gave Armstrong the freedom to find lyricism. While he is singing a song called "(What Did I Do To Be So) Black and Blue," his performance has no trace of self-pity, and a film of him singing the song to Kwame Nkrumah and a rapt Ghana audience in 1956 confirmed this fact. By the time the narrator turns to Armstrong to provide a soundtrack for his isolation, he has engaged in the silently subversive acts of stealing electricity from Con Edison and, anticipating the Liberty Paints episode—where he will cause an explosion by putting too much black into mixed paint—reddening the vanilla ice cream with sloe gin, dosing its sweetness with liquor.

But another concept that Ellison explodes is the distinction between artist and performer in the reception history of Armstrong. In *Ken Burns's Jazz*, the Ellisonian reading of Armstrong is at its most explicit when Burns shows an excerpt from the 1932 film "Rhapsody in Black and Blue." In that film, Armstrong, knee-deep in bubbles and wearing a leopard-skin suit, interprets the minstrel song "Shine"—a song describing "pearly" teeth and eyes shining out of black faces. But before the audience has a chance to react to the disturbing context of Armstrong's art, Burns carefully protects himself from charges of complicit exploitation with the redemptive reading of Armstrong first provided in *Invisible Man*. The black actor Keith David is heard telling PBS viewers that, however horrifying the minstrel-derived stereotypes seem, "Armstrong transcended it all." (The black actress Hattie Winston, in Gary Giddins's 1987 documentary *Satchmo*, is also heard saying that Armstrong "transcended it all," and the use of both actors could be seen as a use of what Barthes would call "inoculation," protecting Giddins and Burns from charges of exploitation.) Armstrong's mesmerizing performance is then intercut with Gary Giddins continuing in the redemptive Ellisonian vein:

What you are actually seeing is a very powerful, charismatic black man who is practically flexing his muscles at you because they are bared by the leopard skin, and singing the tune "Shine," which itself is a minstrel number, in such a way that it loses whatever minstrel or negative qualities it has, and playing this magnificent, unbelievable virtuoso trumpet. But the Armstrong effect was just too complicated for most people. They became embarrassed about it and they refused to see what was clearly on the screen, which was a brilliant, brilliant young man they're trying to imprison with these stereotypes and he's just breaking the chains right and left.[12]

Giddins's argument that Armstrong's performance transcends its problematic occasion is similar to Ellison's contention that Armstrong is "unaware that he's invisible," but there is also a crucial distinction: for Giddins, it is the "magnificent, unbelievable virtuoso trumpet" that renders his context absurd and demeaning for an artist of such a high stature (although he is portrayed as a form of parodic royalty in the film). Like the grandfather of *Invisible Man*, who advises the narrator to "overcome 'em with yesses, undermine 'em with grins," Armstrong has absorbed a cultural lesson the narrator only learns at the end.

For Ellison, the Armstrong effect is complicated, indeed. In a 1964 response to an essay on African American trickster figures by Stanley Edgar Hyman, Ellison goes so far as to compare Armstrong to an Elizabethan clown, arguing that his seemingly servile, minstrelsy-derived stage mannerisms were actually part of an elaborate power ploy:

Armstrong's clownish license and intoxicating powers are almost Elizabethan; he takes liberties with kings, queens, and presidents; he emphasizes the physicality of his music with sweat, spittle and facial contortions; he performs the magical feat of making romantic melody issue from a throat of gravel; and some years ago was recommending to all and sundry his personal physic, "Pluto Water," as a purging way to health, happiness, and international peace.   (*CE*, 106–7)

Armstrong, who did, in fact, recommend the laxative Swiss Kriss to the Duke and Duchess of Windsor, may not have been a deliberately subversive presence in the corridors of power, but he was certainly an irreverent one, getting away with behavior that would have been unthinkable coming from anyone else of any race. "Shakespeare invented Caliban. . . . Who the hell dreamed up Louie?" Ellison once asked Albert Murray in a letter. Postcolonial readings of *The Tempest* aside, Ellison posed that Armstrong—who, in the words of Duke Ellington was "born poor, died rich, and never hurt anyone along the way"—was a self-invented hero worthy of Horatio Alger. But in the world of criticism, autonomy is itself an invented concept, and there has been recent debate about who, exactly, *did* dream up Louis. At a panel at the Village Vanguard in May 2002, Krin Gabbard posed that it was, in fact, Ellison himself who dreamed up Louis, or at least our Louis: "Ellison created a Louis Armstrong that is now, I think, the Louis Armstrong that we have—it's as much because of Ken Burns as because of Ralph Ellison." Gary Giddins responds to the idea as "preposterous," adding that "the man who really created the Louis Armstrong all of us have been riffing off of—and who doesn't get the credit—is Dan Morgenstern." Morgenstern, the former editor of *Down Beat* and director of the Institute of Jazz Studies, has indeed made the kind of journalistic and archival dedication to Armstrong's rehabilitation that go beyond Ellison's literary tropes. But even though Morgenstern loved Armstrong and spent time with him, he never called him a trickster. Ellison may have marveled over Armstrong's apparent self-generation, but even the most autonomous of personae are still "created."[13] Louis Armstrong did indeed create Louis Armstrong, but he was misunderstood by many until figures like Ellison, Morgenstern, Giddins, Stanley Crouch, Ken Burns, and others reclaimed him to the point that it would be difficult to imagine an Armstrong backlash any time soon.

What *has* generated an enormous backlash, however, has been Ellison's legacy in the world of jazz repertory, particularly among critics who object to Jazz at Lincoln Center's policing of the boundaries of jazz's definitions. In a piece for the *New York Times* boldly entitled "What Jazz Is—And Isn't" (in what sounds like inverted allusion to the "Black is . . . black ain't" sermon from *Invisible Man*), Wynton Marsalis laid down what came to be called the neoclassical agenda: "Jazz commentary is too often shaped by a rebellion against what is considered to be the limitations of the middle class," he wrote.[14] "The commentators mistakenly believe that by willfully sliding down the intellectual, spiritual, economic, or social ladder, they will find freedom down where the jazz musicians (i.e., real people) lie. Jazz musicians, however, are searching for the freedom of ascendance." At the time of that editorial's 1987 composition, Marsalis determined that there were no musical developments in the past twenty years—especially rock, free jazz, or fusion—that could reach the "ascendance" privileged by Marsalis. The piece, like all other public statements penned by Marsalis, was heavily influenced by Albert Murray and Stanley Crouch. As Ted Panken observed in 1997, "Marsalis has worked tirelessly over the last decade to build a bully pulpit from which he speaks as advocate, spokesman, teacher and musical implementor of the aesthetic notions of continuity and inclusiveness intoned by Ralph Ellison and Albert Murray."[15]

When Crouch first discovered Marsalis as a brash, brilliant young trumpeter playing with Art Blakey's Jazz Messengers in 1980, the latter, like many young trumpeters, was playing in the mode of sixties-era Miles Davis (albeit with much cleaner technique), and showed little interest in Armstrong, Ellington, or other members of the Ellisonian pantheon. Crouch not only converted Marsalis to the joys of Armstrong, he had the eighteen-year-old trumpeter read Thomas Mann's *Joseph and his Brothers*—one of the key writers in Ellison's modernist pantheon. They would often pay visits to Ellison in his Riverside Drive apartment—where Marsalis, with his trademark southern charm, would attempt to disabuse Ellison of his notion that Thelonious Monk did not have technique.

In fact, in a personal correspondence, Crouch used Ellisonian criteria to argue that Monk not only had technique, he had elegance, a term Ellison thought too inelegant to apply to Armstrong. The most pervasive images of Monk are as an eccentric icon. Charlotte Zwerin's documentary *Straight, No Chaser*, for example, valorizes Monk's erratic behavior as integral to his jagged rhythms, peripatetic melodies, and percussive attack. Like Armstrong, Monk is now commonly regarded as merely a high modernist in signifying drag. Jazz at Lincoln Center, like Burns's documentary, is routinely criticized for their exclusion of trends from the past thirty years; such is the price of institutionalization. Jazz may be resistant to definition, but without specific parameters, it would be hard to imagine writing a grant proposal necessary for its institutional support. Ellison, who was fond of quoting Kenneth Burke's maxim, "When in Rome, do as the Greeks do," was more interested in examining a culture's origins than following its trends. Nevertheless, his impact on jazz's institutionalization is certainly ironic. "We do have institutions," Ellison told Robert O'Meally. "We have the Constitution and the Bill of Rights. And we have jazz." "At the time, I found this declaration bewildering," writes O'Meally.[16] Readers of *Invisible Man* might have reason to feel the same way. Wouldn't Ellison's novel, after all, appear to be an invective against institutions? When the novel's nameless narrator is first expelled from college for chauffeuring a white trustee on a detour that includes a confrontation with a sharecropper telling tales of incest, Dr. Bledsoe, the Machiavellian college president, offers the following denunciation: "College for Negroes! Boy, what do you know other than how to ruin an institution that took over half a hundred years to build?" (*IM*, 140)

In Ellison's bildungsroman, the narrator may not ruin institutions, but he certainly subverts many of them, including Liberty Paints (his failure to conceal the hidden black paint in "Optic White" results in an explosion), and organizations both Communist (The Brotherhood) and nationalist (the gang run by Ras the Destroyer). In the prologue and epilogue, the narrator— playfully calling himself Jack-the-Bear, after Duke Ellington's composition—retreats to a basement with only the music of Louis Armstrong to provide him solace, which the narrator calls "the invisible music of my isolation." The narrator also spends a fair amount of time in the early part of the book looking in vain for someone named Emerson (alluding to Ralph Waldo Ellison's namesake), but only finds true self-reliance when he escapes from the corruption and dishonesty around him to be alone with his record player. The Ellison of jazz writing may have inspired institutions, but the Invisible Man evaded them.

At his best, Ellison venerated his jazz heroes with a healthy layer of irony. In the final section of *Invisible Man*, the narrator, too protean for a stable definition, accepts the mistaken identity of the pimp, numbers runner, and con man Rinehart. Such has been the occupation of jazz musicians, recounted in explicit detail in memoirs by musicians including Miles Davis and Charles Mingus. What the Invisible Man calls "Rinehartism" is corrupt and duplicitous; it is an alternative form of institution building—even if that institution is a whorehouse. The name is derived from a "Harvard Blues," a blues song Ellison remembered Jimmy Rushing singing with Count Basie:

I wear Brooks clothes and white shoes all the time
Get three Cs and a D
Think checks from home sublime
I don't keep dogs or women in my room.
Rinehart, Rinehart, I'm a most indifferent guy
But I love my baby, that's no Harvard lie.[17]

Ellison, who would often work several jobs in order to be able to afford to cultivate what he called an "Ivy League" look as a Tuskegee student, embodied his own version of Henry James's notion that it was a "complex fate to be an American." For Ellison, such a complex fate was a collage that riffed on T. S. Eliot and Louis Armstrong with irreverence and abandon. If the result was a canonized novel and an exalted cultural position, Ellison would further exile himself with steadfastly contrarian opinions, and when those opinions became increasingly accepted, he simply went into exile altogether. After his retirement from his position as the Schweitzer Professor of Humanities at NYU in 1980—ostensibly to devote himself to his writing—he wrote and published virtually nothing of consequence before his death in 1994.

In those years of exile, though, implicit and explicit manifestations of his vision of African American—and American—culture were realized in what was a process of reclamation, whether it is at Henry Louis Gates's W.E.B. Du Bois Institute at Harvard or Jazz at Lincoln Center in New York. But Ellison's ironic role as an institution builder also splits his legacy in half. The Ralph Ellison of *Invisible Man* is transgressive. The Ralph Ellison of jazz criticism is traditional. The transgressive Ellison wrote a novel about a nameless narrator who defies black nationalists, Marxists, racists and well-meaning liberals and retreats into a basement with nothing left but stolen electricity generating a Louis Armstrong record. The traditional Ellison wrote essays and letters that brought Armstrong out of the basement and into serious literary consideration, but banished the jazz that was going on around him: he dismisses Charlie Parker for his "pitiful" tone, John Coltrane for his "badly executed velocity exercises," and "poor little lost Miles Davis" as "evil."[18] *Invisible Man*'s narrator is so resistant to fixed identity, he is never given a name. Nameless, he splices together an indeterminate identity in a satirical text that alludes heavily to Homer, Dante, Joyce, and Eliot, while also making references to Armstrong, Ellington, and Jimmy Rushing. There was something visionary about Ellison's idea that Louis Armstrong and T. S. Eliot were culturally inseparable, but there was something reactionary about his attitude toward the jazz innovations of his time. Ellison's narrator in *Invisible Man* is a daedalian, indeterminate hero, but his vision of jazz is more rigid than the rhythmic flexibility exhibited by the music itself.

In fact, while Ellison railed against rigid ideas on racial identity or political orthodoxy, his ideas on what jazz should and should not be were remarkably specific. It was Louis Armstrong's recording "(What Did I Do To Be So) Black and Blue" that not only provided a thematic and sonic analogue of *Invisible Man*'s "music of invisibility," but led to a parodic hallucination inspired by Faulkner and Dante as much as Armstrong's record. Shifting to an italicized dream narrative, the narrator sees a crowd listening to a preacher, proclaiming the parameters of the color line:

"I said black is . . ."
"Preach it, brother . . ."
". . . an' black ain't . . ."
"Red, Lawd, red: He said it's red!"
"Amen, brother . . ."
"Black will git you . . ."
"Yes, it will . . ."
". . . an' black won't . . ."
"Naw, it won't!"
"It do, Lawd . . ."
". . . an' it don't."
"Hallelujah . . ."
". . . It'll put you, glory, glory, Oh my Lawd, in the WHALE'S BELLY." (*IM*, 9)

The passage is a powerful display of Ellison's defiant wit. In his novel, blackness is too complex and indeterminate to be reduced to a single definition. In the mellifluous but deceptive cadences of the preacher, the dialectic of blackness will ultimately lead one to the whiteness that recalls Melville's "Whiteness of the Whale." Throughout the novel, it remains a fetish for whites and a protean trope for blacks. Does blackness mean following the course of the incestuous Jim Trueblood, the Machiavellian Dr. Bledsoe, or the rabble-rousing Ras the Destroyer? The quest for this blackness, ultimately, is a nightmare from which the narrator attempts to escape, and Louis Armstrong provides the only hope that an artist can overcome invisibility—the absurdity of these problematic personae—because "he's unaware that he's invisible."

But the parodic pulpit also leads to a contradiction between the idiosyncratic satirist in *Invisible Man* and the nostalgic music critic of the essays and the letters. Sometimes, Ellison sounds like his own satirical creation, promulgating, like the nightmarish preacher of the prologue, what "jazz is" and "jazz ain't," foreshadowing Marsalis's 1987 editorial, "What Jazz Is—and Isn't." While the novel's hero remained, as Ellington described Ella Fitzgerald, "beyond category," jazz constituted a specific cultural transformation for Ellison. Jazz *is* Louis Armstrong and Duke Ellington. Jazz *ain't* "the funeral posturing of the Modern Jazz Quartet," Charlie Parker, whose "vibratoless tone" produced "a sound of amateurish ineffectuality, as though he could not quite make it."

Ellison's canonical barometer was off on these artists, and not just because Parker actually *did* play with vibrato. The Modern Jazz Quartet, Charlie Parker, the pre-1968 Miles Davis, and John Coltrane are now the subjects of numerous reissues, scholarly studies, and repertory festivals. But many of the institutions that are canonizing these figures are indebted to Ellison nevertheless. Throughout the most vital years of jazz's development, its discourse was as underground as the *Invisible Man*. When Ken Burns's nineteen-hour *Jazz* documentary aired on PBS in January, 2001, it inspired the kind of critical acrimony engendered when a music of invisibility is brought into the cold light of public conversation. Ironically, it was Ellison who hovered over those debates, whether it was the documentary's conception of jazz as synonymous with liberal democracy (Ellison described it as America's "jazz-shaped" status), or the documentary's characterization of Louis Armstrong as the American Bach. Ellison was an intensely private man who was content to let his epigones do the public speaking. Jazz is a music that has resisted definition from its most canonized practitioners: Ellington asked that his music be called "Negro Folk Music" if it had to be called something.[19] Charlie Parker, when asked to define bebop, merely responded, "It's all music, man"; and Louis Armstrong, when asked for a definition of jazz, famously replied, "If you have to ask, you'll never know." It was Ellison's metaphors, images, and cultural understanding that will ultimately prove more important than the particular blind spots in his aesthetic vision, and it would be Ellison who would take those metaphors, even those of invisibility, out of the basement and onward to millions of television viewers.

In September 1965 Ralph Ellison appeared on a WNET program called "Bop: Jazz Goes Intellectual." Ellison had been on the committee that established the network, the first public broadcasting system in American history, and if jazz was going to go intellectual, he was going to have his say about it. The 1952 publication of *Invisible Man* had earned Ellison a National Book Award and a respectability never before enjoyed by an African American writer, and the new educational medium presented him with an opportunity to make an impassioned case for what he felt was a sorely neglected subject. "One of the most intriguing gaps in American cultural history sprang from the fact that jazz, one of the few American art forms, failed to attract the understanding of our outstanding intellectuals," said Ellison. "While, it is true, jazz in a limited sense has gone intellectual, the greater job of increasing our understanding is still to be done. A vacuum does exist in our understanding. It is a fact that for all their important contributions to American culture, no Edmund Wilson, no T. S. Eliot, no Cowley or Kazin have offered us insights into the relationship between this most vital art and the broader aspects of American social life."[20]

"With jazz, we are not yet in the age of history, but linger in that of folklore," Ellison had lamented in 1955 (*CE*, 242) . Half a century later, jazz is accused of lingering too much in its history; reissues crowd new releases in the cottage industry that is the jazz market, and the new releases are either criticized for being too derivative of pre-1968 styles, selling out to the commercialism of pop styles incongruous with what is thought to be "real jazz," or banished to the even smaller corner of an experimental market that loses its relevance with each passing trend. As jazz has more recently moved from folklore to history—from a scene of fans to an institution of historians and scholars—Ellison's influence is ubiquitous, from PBS to Columbia University to Lincoln Center. To be a jazz scholar at the beginning of the twenty-first century is to write in the shadow of Ralph Ellison, and he is the only canonical literary figure to have had such an impact on the music's current discourse.

This was not an influence Ellison achieved in any obvious way. *Invisible Man*, though framed with crucial references to Louis Armstrong, was not, like Dorothy Baker's hugely popular *Young Man With a Horn*, a novel primarily about music, even if it was the product of a conservatory dropout writing a buildungsroman with a jazz-shaped sensibility. Although his essays on Charlie Christian, Jimmy Rushing, and Duke Ellington are widely considered to be among the most significant essays on jazz ever written, he wrote to Albert Murray, "I wouldn't be a jazz critic for love or money."[21] Rather, Ellison has presided as a deus ex absentia over the current movements to keep jazz alive as a pedagogical and repertory subject. Recent texts, including Horace Porter's *Ralph Ellison's Jazz Country*, Robert O'Meally's anthology of Ellison's jazz writings, *Living With Music*, and Lawrence Jackson's *Ralph Ellison: Emergence of a Genius* have all provided evidence that jazz was a central subject for Ellison, informing his aesthetic sense as much as it served as an alternative to any political ideology. The consequences of those aesthetics, however, are only beginning to be apparent in jazz's repertory afterlife. In his lifetime, Ellison enraged, at one time or another, Communists, nationalists, conservatives, and liberals. After his time, Ellison's most prominent disciples have enraged jazz critics.

Jazz at Lincoln Center, the first jazz repertory ensemble enjoying equal partner status with a major symphony orchestra and opera company, was the brainchild of the trumpeter Wynton Marsalis and the writers Stanley Crouch and Albert Murray, all of whom were overtly influenced by Ellison. Jazz critic Gene Seymour has observed that Ellison's ideas ran through Murray, Crouch, and Marsalis "like an echo," that "Ellison was the wellspring for the ideals advanced by Murray, Crouch, and Marsalis."[22] Seymour, the only black jazz critic on the staff of a New York daily paper, wrote this in response to the 1996 publication of Ellison's *Collected Essays*. *Trading Twelves*, an epistolary exchange between Ellison and Murray from the 1950s published in 1999, reinforces Seymour's observations by revealing the two men engaging in a scathing critique of the jazz of younger musicians (most notably Charlie Parker, Miles Davis, John Coltrane, Thelonious Monk, and Charles Mingus), and a celebration of their heroes (a list that would include Louis Armstrong, Duke Ellington, Charlie Christian, Jimmy Rushing, and Count Basie). But Murray and Ellison had this dialogue not just as two middle-aged men of letters lamenting that the younger generation had gone horribly astray, but as writers who would influence the formation of the jazz canon.

In one of those letters, Ellison writes about attending a 1958 performance in Newport from "that poor, evil, lost little Miles Davis, who on this occasion sounded like he just couldn't get it together. Nor did Coltrane help with his badly executed velocity exercises. These cats have gotten lost, man."[23] Later in the letter, he describes a performance by Davis at the Plaza Hotel as "murder" and finds that in a performance by Duke Ellington, "Duke signified on Davis all through his numbers and his trumpeters and saxophonists went after him like a bunch of hustlers in a Georgia skin game fighting with razors."[24] Although Ellison never developed his objection to Davis in any critical fashion, it is too convenient to ignore the remark while venerating the prophetic power of *Invisible Man*. Ellison found high art in the incongruity between performance and the substance behind that performance. In his public appearances, Davis refused to provide a performance in Ellison's sense of the term. The Davis performances Ellison described are available on two different CDs, *Jazz at the Plaza* (Columbia/Legacy 85245) and *Miles Davis at Newport 1958* (Columbia/Legacy CK 85202), and listening to these cherished fetish objects heightens the irony of imagining a bemused Ralph Ellison in the background. When Davis plays Frank Loesser's "If I Were A Bell," for example, he wanders off the microphone, only dabbing a hint of the melody, with a delivery so emotionally muted—and muted with what came to be his trademark Harmon—it ironically comments on the "bell" of the song's title. Davis was emphatically not bell-like, and this was part of his appeal. Ellison's literary contemporaries James Baldwin and Norman Mailer would pay homage to him in their literary tropes just as Ellison had paid homage to Armstrong in his. Davis and Armstrong both shared an impeccable melodic economy and instinct for an emotive rhythmic attack, and this is particularly evident in comparing Armstrong's 1933 recording of Spencer Williams's "Basin Street Blues" with Davis's recording of the same tune thirty years later. Davis's muted, melancholic interpretation of the tune could be said to complement Armstrong's like the other side of a Janus mask, but Ellison merely observed that the blues without the particular kind of performance attached to it that he venerated was "fucking up the blues."

Ellison's narrator may have been in exile, but he preferred his jazz performers not to wear their alienation on their sleeves. "Invisibility, let me explain, gives one a slightly different sense of time," Ellison wrote in *Invisible Man*, "you're never quite on the beat" (*IM*, 5). Being "never quite on the beat" is a useful description of rhythms called, for lack of a better term, "swing." To swing, in a musical sense, is to be "never quite on the beat," to display rhythmic flexibility, free from the tyranny of the metronome, and, under the auspices of Jazz at Lincoln Center, it has become an institutional rubric. But swing is also an indeterminate rubric, and the subject of much debate and exclusion, often defined more for what it is not (as in "he can't swing") than for what it is. When Duke Ellington made his famous proclamation, in song, that "It Don't Mean a Thing if it Ain't Got That Swing," he probably did not realize that he was creating an institutional orthodoxy, and when Ellison wrote *Invisible Man*, he was writing more in a satire of institutions than in conscious effort to create new ones.

Although Jazz at Lincoln Center, *Ken Burns's Jazz*, and most jazz history curricula would, in fact, canonize the musicians that Ellison and Murray admonished in their letters, their method of admonishment served as a prototype for how jazz, a music built on principles of spontaneity and improvisation, could become an inscribed art form with remarkably strict parameters, not just harmonically and rhythmically, but culturally and historically. Jazz criticism was, up to that point, largely limited to journalism, where the subject of jazz is essentially a beat, and part of the critic's job is to search for the latest trends. Ellison's impulses were the opposite of the jazz critic's. He was wistfully looking back to something from the past, and bitterly repudiated the present. The ways of playing jazz might be developing less than a journalist would like to report, but the ways of institutionalizing jazz are changing, and Ellison's concerns about the cultural context for jazz and the relation between jazz and "American social life" are not the least of the reasons why.

"Teaching [jazz] formally might well have imposed too many thou-shalt-nots and imposed stability upon a developing form," Ellison has said. "Dance halls and jam sessions, along with recordings, are the true academy for jazz."[25] Ellison made that statement in a 1976 interview, years after dance halls stopped featuring the jazz Ellison loved. Although *Invisible Man* was a novel of the 1950s, the culture Ellison venerated was the music of the 1930s—the decade when Ellison was in his twenties and the music's appeal was at its broadest. By the time dance halls stopped featuring Jimmy Rushing and other musicians from his Oklahoma youth, jazz had to become something else, something that, like the Constitution and the Bill of Rights, he called an "institution." At the end of the twentieth century, journalists and scholars were writing about the "jazz wars," which, like the culture wars of the 1990s, were essentially a series of debates about who gets to be included in the canon and why.

When he appeared on "Jazz Goes Intellectual," Ellison was calling for a particular kind of intellectual and a particular kind of approach. Indeed, in calling for a new kind of jazz intellectual in 1965, Ellison implied that intellectuals had not written on jazz. In the 1930s, Otis Ferguson—edited by Cowley at the *New Republic*—was a critic who connected jazz to the "broader aspects of American social life" by promoting the interracial swing of Benny Goodman and Charlie Christian and making the first known case for the racial reclamations of Louis Armstrong's performance style. Ferguson's death in 1943 cut his career short, before he was able to make a contribution beyond journalism. Gunther Schuller had already established a reputation as a composer and collaborator with Mingus and Miles Davis, and was in the process of writing serious musicological studies of Armstrong and Ellington, but Schuller's studies stayed on discussions of major sevenths and landing tones, never on the "broader aspects of American social life." And Langston Hughes, a crucial early mentor to Ellison, certainly devoted much of his work to establishing a link between the sounds of Ellington and the lives of working African Americans in Harlem, but he did so as a lyrical poet and populist prose writer. Each of these approaches—journalistic, musicological, poetic—had its impact on Ellison, but he felt that none of them in isolation gave a complete account of an art that could hold up to close readings, inspire lyrical poetry, and provide an ongoing story for a general magazine audience.

In 1965 four people died in a racially charged riot in the Watts section of Los Angeles Bag. In that year Miles Davis released *E.S.P.*; Cecil Taylor *Conquistador*; Charles Mingus *My Favorite Quintet*; John Coltrane *A Love Supreme* and *Ascension*. This was to be the last period in jazz fully acknowledged to be both innovative and worthy of canonical status, and each of these recordings reveals a restless desire among the musicians to break away from conventional rhythm, harmony, and meter. The music and the riots both represented a breakdown of the African American communities Ellison loved. Black jazz musicians were less likely to turn to the blues, but to the European avant-garde for expression, and the resulting sounds were a violent assault on the music he cherished, nearly as much as the riots in Watts were a literal manifestation of the same. The events in Watts were the fulfillment of the breakdown of community and loss of individual will anticipated by Ellison in *Invisible Man* when the narrator participates in a race riot, caught between Ras the Destroyer and The Brotherhood. The jazz of that era, similarly represented a violent break within the black communities for which Ellison felt so much affection. The revolution that had begun in Minton's

Playhouse in 1941, where musicians were simply blowing choruses for each other and not for dancers—he would call bebop musicians "connoisseurs of chaos"—had turned even further inward. When he had to introduce Cecil Taylor on the 1965 program "Jazz: The Experimenters," Ellison could barely conceal his contempt for Taylor's New England Conservatory-derived clangor, describing it as an "interesting illustration" of the struggle between what he saw as the overtly European influences of the avant-garde and the Americana of traditional jazz. But the jazz of the era was speaking less and less for the African Americans of that community and more for a white, collegiate, increasingly marginalized elite. Ellison, too, was becoming marginalized from the black community and subject to charges of elitism. That year, Ellison received an award from *Book Week* for *Invisible Man*, declared by a panel of writers and editors to be the most distinguished novel of the postwar era, and also participated in a National Arts festival organized by president Lyndon Johnson. When the poet Robert Lowell protested the event, Ellison responded in an essay that "the President wasn't telling Lowell how to write his poetry, and I don't think he's in any position to tell Johnson how to run the government."[26]

If jazz, like the government, was indeed an institution, Ellison did think he was in a position to tell just about everyone how they should run it, and it was on public television—an institution that he did, after all, have a hand in developing—that he made a case for how that should happen, but it was a point that was as radical as it was antiquated. On the one hand, Ellison was proposing a radically new form of critical discourse that would factor race into the equation as never before. On the programs, Ellison gave backhanded introductions to Charles Mingus, as well as Cecil Taylor, both of whom were billed as "experimenters," but for Ellison, were committing musical acts of redundancy, experimenting on a form already experimental and slimly understood.

In this sense, Ellison's vision of jazz was anti-Hegelian. He did not believe that jazz was bound for a dialectical journey that would move ever upward to greater harmonic abstraction until it reached the equivalent of the end of history. Ellison's cohost on "Jazz Goes Intellectual" was one of the Hegelians, Martin Williams, the jazz critic for the *Saturday Review*, whose collections for Oxford University Press had become among the seminal works of jazz criticism in the 1960s. But while Williams was a champion of avant-garde artists like Taylor and Ornette Coleman, his method for analyzing them—and for inspiring general-interest audiences of the 1950s to take them seriously—derived from New Criticism. Williams received an M.A. from the University of Pennsylvania, and, like the New Critics, he performed close readings of jazz "texts" as a series of rhythmic changes that, in high modernist fashion, used complex techniques to reveal a cohesion.[27]

Before their appearance on the program, Williams had attempted to solicit an essay on Charlie Christian by Ellison for an Oxford University Press anthology, which Ellison declined to submit because of a book on jazz he claimed to be writing. After one of their joint television appearances, Williams fired off a note to Ellison telling him, "You don't know anything about jazz." In fact, "The Charlie Christian Story," the essay on the legendary Oklahoma guitarist that Williams had attempted to solicit, contained the kind of criticism Ellison felt was missing from the work of Williams and other jazz critics. "For while there is now a rather extensive history of discography and recording sessions," Ellison wrote in that essay, "there is but the bare beginnings of a historiography of jazz. We know much of jazz as entertainment, but a mere handful of clichés constitutes our knowledge of jazz as experience" (*CE*, 269). As LeRoi Jones had pointed out in his 1963 essay "Jazz and the White Critic": "Negro music, like the Negro himself, is strictly an American phenomenon, and we have got to set up standards of judgment and aesthetic excellence that depend on our native knowledge and understanding of the underlying philosophies and local cultural references that produced blues and jazz in order to produce valid critical writing or commentary about it."[28] There is little difference between Jones's statement in 1963 and Ellison's in 1965. The point that both were making was that musicology was too rooted in European conceptions of harmony and rhythm, while jazz journalism was too caught up in hipster auras and New Critical paradigms. What was missing, according to both Jones and Ellison, was an account of the cultural dynamic that produced this music, which, to both of them, was a phenomenon that was distinctly American and, to use the term Ellison preferred, distinctly "Negro." Despite their common ground, though, Ellison was even more hostile to Jones's approach than he was to Williams's, anticipating that the nationalist figure Jones, as Amiri Baraka would later become, would be a parody of Ras the Destroyer in *Invisible Man*. In a review of Jones's *Blues People*, Ellison wrote that his overtly sociological approach "would even give the blues the blues."

But when it was published in 1964, *Blues People*, as the title suggested, was the only existing work that attempted to integrate jazz with "American social life" by subjecting jazz "to a socio-anthropological as well as musical scrutiny." Ellison did not like Jones's conclusions, nor did he like the attitudes of many jazz musicians and political activists, even though many were influenced by his work. In 1965, it seemed, Ellison was trapped by his fame, his novelistic ambitions, his antiseparatism, and his increasing disdain for the new voices and sounds emerging around him. For Ellison, jazz historiography could only be a way of looking back. The figure that would link Williams's approach with Ellison's was, at least indirectly, T. S. Eliot. The New Criticism that Williams practiced for his M.A. as an English graduate student—and, indeed, his entire approach of formalism and close reading—would not have been possible without the prevailing influence of T. S. Eliot's principle of the "impersonality of the critic." But Eliot's poetry also diverted Ellison from his musical studies and into the literary realm where he was able to claim authority on jazz in the first place. The cultural synthesis would propel him away from music and toward novel writing, but also toward a reading of jazz that was as modernist as it was a story of ethnic crossing.

In a lecture called "Hidden Name and Complex Fate" given at the Library of Congress on January 6, 1964, Ellison spoke of the discovery of "The Waste Land" at Tuskegee. "I was intrigued by its power to move me while eluding my understanding," he said. "Somehow its rhythms were closer to jazz than were those of the Negro poets, and even though I could not understand them, its range of allusion was as mixed and varied as that of Louis Armstrong" (*CE*, 203). He would later say that making these connections prepared him to seek out Richard Wright, who in turn convinced Ellison to become a writer in the first place. Although their sensibilities would ultimately clash—Wright would tell an interviewer that he had little interest in jazz and that his interest in the blues was entirely based on his idea that it expressed the suffering of Negroes—the connection was one that Ellison repeatedly described as his "real transition to writing" (*CE*, 202), implying that, had he not found the connection between Louis Armstrong and T. S. Eliot, *Invisible Man* would have never been written.[29] But while Ellison would write and speak about this connection on several occasions, he never fully developed this particular cultural and aesthetic synaesthesia, leaving the work to scholars. Ellison did claim that his placing Armstrong next to

Eliot was "not a matter of giving the music fine airs—it doesn't need them—but of saying that whatever touches our highly conscious creators of culture is apt to be reflected here." Either Ellison was being ironic or self-contradictory.

Ellison was not the only writer to note the affinities between the allusive, fragmented aesthetic of modernism and the often elliptical, associative logic of a jazz solo.[30] A 1932 reviewer of Armstrong wrote that his "savage growling" was as "removed from the way we speak or sing—and as modern—as James Joyce," while an ad from that period comically headlined Armstrong as the "Master of Modernism."[31] Such a statement would be serious for Ellison, a connection that would later be explored in Alfred Appel's *Jazz Modernism* (2002). To establish that Armstrong was "highly conscious" and combat the hyperbole that he was a "savage," Ellison had to show how he transfigured the vernacular source material he performed in the spirit of Eliot's riffs on dance hall tunes. Indeed, Wyndham Lewis and Clive Bell both saw "The Waste Land" as a form of "jazz," although it is unclear exactly what they meant by the word. Such connections were made more specifically to Eliot's unlikely ethnic influences by the 1990s, when Ann Douglas's *Terrible Honesty* highlighted Eliot's childhood stint as a minstrel performer, and Michael North's *Dialect of Modernism* commented on Eliot's use of Negro dialect in his letters to Ezra Pound. Lawrence Jackson even claims that Eliot quoted an Armstrong recording of "China Moon" in "The Waste Land." And Ellison provided evidence that Eliot's poem—which he seemed to have read as a series of riffs—could itself be riffed upon. When, for example, Ellison discovered this line in the poem:

But
O O O O that Shakespeherean Rag—
It's so elegant
So intelligent

he was not only aware that "The Shakespearean Rag" was a rag-time hit by 1912, but was able to riff upon the riff in a mock-pastoral description of the college in *Invisible Man*, which concludes "And oh, oh, oh, oh, those multimillionaires!" (*IM*, 37) The allusion to Eliot is also a description of the college's benefactors, one of whom, Mr. Norton, is given the name of a publishing company. The narrator of *Invisible Man* is placed in opposition to this symbol of cultural production. Indeed, the narrator's journey with Mr. Norton is a commentary upon white and black cultural canons: after Norton is first introduced to Jim Trueblood, Trueblood, in the midst of telling a tale of waking up with his penis inside his daughter, says, "I sings me some blues that night that ain't never been sang before" (*IM*, 66). The narrator continues his self-destruction by taking Norton to The Golden Day, named for Lewis Mumford's book. The Invisible Man, himself lacking an identity, rocked his segregated institution's identity by giving it mixed signals: the bar is named for an influential study of architecture; Trueblood is linked to an influential musical style. Trueblood's outrageous, hallucinatory tale is rewarded with $100; the narrator, trying to do a job for the college, is expelled. It is a lesson that incestuous folk tales can be profitable, artful, even influential, but the link between incest and the blues is also Ellison's suggestion that if jazz is to be high art, it must be exogamous. Ellison, like Eliot, was shoring fragments against his ruins, and like Eliot, ended up creating a critical school in their wake.

Anyone writing jazz journalism since the 1990s has had to take a position on the Ellisonian school in what hyperbolically has been termed the "jazz wars," and how one felt about Jazz at Lincoln Center defined one's position on what jazz is and jazz ain't. These wars were meticulously and somewhat gratuitously detailed in a 1994 cover story for the *Village Voice* that told tales of empire building, rivalry, identity crises, and power plays: in short, the characteristics Ellison skewered with every institution he satirized in *Invisible Man*. That year, Ellison died at the age of eighty with an unfinished second novel and a career that seemed to his followers nothing short of tragic. Jazz would be a subject in some of his posthumous writings, including *Flying Home*, named for the Lionel Hampton composition, and sections from the unfinished manuscript published as *Juneteenth*, including a morally dubious jazz trombonist echoing the duplicitous Jim Trueblood as much as the bullshit artists Ellison enjoyed hearing at barbershops as a young man. But *Invisible Man* still remains the definitive guidebook to how the heroic image of Louis Armstrong can continue to be revered as a tradition while also acting as a transgressive muse. Ellison, whose narrator only wanted to imagine multiple recordings of Armstrong in his basement, inspired a movement that keeps his vision of Armstrong afloat with an endowed professorship in his name, scholarships, institutes, and more. Those institutions, like any other, were built to be challenged. One of the appeals of *Invisible Man* is that it grants a regenerative heroic status not to the person following the dictated rules of a cultural form, but to the one willing to cause trouble. Students of literature love these kinds of heroes, and students of jazz should continue valuing them, as well. From this perspective, the greatest tribute to Ellison could be to shake up the institutions set up upon his principles. Taking a cue from his novel, perhaps an underground figure can stir up the wrong paint, tap into the illegal electrical outlet, and give the offending speech. Who knows but that, on the lower frequencies, Ellison could still speak for jazz?

> Let us invent an idiom for the proper transposition
> of jazz into words! Something clean, sparkling, elusive!
>
> —HART CRANE

3

STOMPING THE MUSE

JAZZ, POETRY, AND THE PROBLEMATIC MUSE

"I try to hide in Proust, / Mallarme, & Camus, but the no-good blues come looking for me," writes Yusef Komunyakaa. When in 1935 young Ralph Ellison retreated to the library as a student at Tuskegee, making his first entry into Eliot's "The Waste Land," Louis Armstrong came looking for him, too. It made sense that Armstrong was a touchstone for Ellison, since Eliot pointed to so many references that Ellison wanted to master. But Ellison did not come unprepared. Years of hearing Jimmy Rushing and Charlie Christian in Oklahoma City, pouring over Wagner scores with William Dawson at Tuskegee, and, most significantly, internalizing the aesthetic of Armstrong gave him an ear for Eliot's allusive music. When Eliot jumped in the span of a single line from "I will show you fear in a handful of dust" (lifted from Tennyson's *Maud:* "And my heart is a handful of dust.") to *"Frisch weht der Wind / Der Heimat zu"* ("borrowed" from *Tristan and Isolde*), Ellison could have recognized that kind of fancy footwork from many an Armstrong allusion: on his 1929 trumpet solo on Fats Waller and Andy Razaf's "Ain't Misbehavin'," he nods to the Gershwin brothers with the opening motif from "Rhapsody in Blue"; on his 1930 recording of "Dinah," his solo flies through motifs from Verdi's *Rigoletto* to Oscar Strauss's

"My Hero," Gershwin's "Lady Be Good," Bagley's "National Emblem March," Romberg's "Lover Come Back to Me," a snake charmer's dance, and more—all in a mere two choruses.[1] In an oft-quoted maxim, Eliot said, "Immature poets borrow, mature poets steal." Armstrong was a mature artist.

Ellison was not the only one who saw a kinship between "high" modernism and jazz. Ellison discovered Eliot at the beginning of his creative life; Eliot came looking for Charles Mingus at the end of his. When he was ailing with ALS, Mingus wanted to set Eliot's *Four Quartets* to music, perhaps identifying with that poem's sonata form–driven conceit, "In the beginning is my end." He had been inspired by the Italian filmmaker Daniele Senatore's ardor for the poem, but perhaps he also saw in Eliot's method something akin to his own. Much recent Eliot scholarship has been fixated on his covert blackness, arguing that before he became an Anglican, anti-Semitic high priest of culture, lamenting the dross of urban rootlessness and ethnic diversity, he sang minstrel songs as a boy in St. Louis, and later bantered in African American dialect with Ezra Pound while revising "The Waste Land."[2] When he accepted an invitation from Marjorie Hutchinson in 1920, he even said, "I should bring a jazz banjorine, not a lute."[3]

Yet despite recent scholarship by such writers as Ann Douglas, Michael North, and David Chinitz that makes a convincing case for Eliot's covert minstrel and jazz predilections, he still seems a counterintuitve modernist muse for Ellison and Mingus. After all, both of them had their encounters with Langston Hughes, a poet who, on the surface, would seem to have more in common with both artists. A day after Ellison left Tuskegee behind and arrived at the Harlem YMCA, he tracked down Hughes, showed off his musical and literary prowess, and hounded the poet until he secured a job recommendation from him.

Hughes quickly became Ellison's mentor, giving him an introduction to Richard Wright, a dedication in his 1940 collection
Montage of a Dream Deferred, and even providing a jacket blurb
for *Invisible Man* in spite of never getting very far in reading
the book itself. But once Ellison was given the National Book
Award, he no longer had any need for Hughes and cast him
aside.

Mingus, always striving for literary respect, recorded and performed with Hughes in 1957, but those Harlem Renaissance
lyrics represented a vanquished era for Mingus. They had their
virtues, but did not measure up to the neurotic, bombastic, ambitious sound Mingus was hearing in his head, producing on the
bass, and scribbling on scores. In search of a poetic analogue, the
fledgling Ellison and the dying Mingus went for Eliot instead,
much as Eliot, in his early years, went for jazz.

Eliot was not alone. Jazz has fascinated poets since at least the
early 1920s—shortly after the first jazz recordings were committed to record—inspiring a disparate group of them to capture,
transpose, appropriate, and attempt to embody it. Among the
many poets who attempted to get their muses to swing were
William Carlos Williams, who paid tribute to Bunk Johnson;
John Berryman, who adopted the voice of Bessie Smith; Jack
Kerouac, who worshiped at the bench of George Shearing and
recorded with Zoot Sims; Elizabeth Bishop, who cast aside ses-
tinas for the blues when she wrote "Songs for a Colored Singer"
for Billie Holiday; Larry Neal, who bid farewell to Mingus's
porkpie hat; Jayne Cortez (the former Mrs. Ornette Coleman),
who followed the sinuous trail of Basie's nimble fingers; and Jay
Wright, who envisioned ethnic apocalypse to the strains of Albert
Ayler's atonal clangor.[4] The following accounts of Hart Crane,
Langston Hughes, Wallace Stevens, Frank O'Hara, Jack Kerouac, and Yusef Komunyakaa versifying their way into jazz are in

no way a complete account of the convoluted interaction between the media, but a crucial series of intersections where modernism and the Harlem Renaissance face off, and the Beats, a
New York School dandy, and a Last Poet trade choruses.

What is peculiar about the interest in jazz by such modernists
as Crane and Stevens is just how conterintuitive it is—and how
jazz musicians also saw an unlikely connection between the two
media. It is not so surprising that Crane and Stevens would not
have the same understandings of jazz as those who regularly took
in sets, listened to records, even talked and worked with musicians; what is surprising is that they tried to write jazz poetry at
all. When poets wrote in empathy with jazz musicians, they
spoke for the select few who understood the music, and it made
sense that, say, the Black Arts movement embraced jazz. The
jazz poems of Crane and Stevens reveal that the minstrel show
was not confined to the vaudeville stage: in order to write poems
of their climate, they had to engage in high modernist minstrelsy. Their poetic misreadings of jazz, in turn, reveal a great
deal about its role in American culture as a repository for repressed libidos and allegorical imaginations. When Charles
Mingus, Billie Holiday, and Miles Davis decided to put their
names on their own memoirs, they delighted and profited by engaging these very points of fetish. And yet Crane, Stevens, and
Eliot spent as much time aspiring to jazz as Ralph Ellison and
Charles Mingus spent yearning for high modernist credibility.
Like Al Jolson's Jack Robin, blacked up and looking into the image of himself in whiteface (or Jew face) chanting the Kol Nidre,
jazz and American poetry has often involved an *unheimlich* mas-
querade in which they each recognized the Other in themselves.

White modernists and black populists did not always run in
the same literary circles, but that did not stop Crane, Hughes,
and Stevens from writing their own versions of jazz poems. In

1922, Hart Crane announced his ambition to "forge an idiom of jazz into words! Something clean, sparkling, elusive!" Langston Hughes asked his publishers to call him "the original jazz poet" for staging poetry and music performances in 1926. And while there are no references to jazz in Wallace Stevens's *Collected Letters*, he did attempt in one poem, "The Sick Man," to resolve the music of black blues musicians of the South with a white choir in the North, calling for the kind of blues-based orchestral music that was already being scored by Duke Ellington, and ended up with an image that would anticipate Ellison's *Juneteenth*. A decade later, LeRoi Jones interrupted a Frank O'Hara poem to tell him about a racist police assault on Miles Davis, an occasion where a jazz musician could not only inspire a white poet but make him rethink his priorities—one alternative to the earlier fetishization of jazz by poets removed from the culture of the music and the actual people who made it. More recently, Yusef Komunyakaa offered his revision to Jack Kerouac's Beatification of Charlie Parker, showing the kind of verse that can result from poets as steeped in jazz as they are in poetry.

Despite the fascination of many modernist poets with jazz, the relationship between the two is less like a Charleston, in which we cannot "tell the dancer from the dance," than it is like a strange and paradoxical wrestling match. Jazz poems often reveal more about the poets and their limitations than about the music and its possibilities, and they are difficult to reconcile with the music itself; many of their images do not age particularly well. Crane made his pronouncements when jazz recording was in its infancy, even before Duke Ellington or Louis Armstrong made their first records. Stevens wrote his jazz-themed poem when the jazz canon was already being established, but he left no evidence that he took much interest in it. And Hughes's jazz poems were written in a separate realm from the white poets who wanted to appropriate it, but that did not stop Ellison and Mingus from gravitating toward Eliot.

Looking at Crane or Stevens through a jazz lens calls attention not to the mystery or ecstasy evoked by these poets, but rather shows where their aesthetic judgments date themselves. Today, both jazz and poetry are more ensconced in the ivory tower than ever, and it is remarkable to look back on the figures who were working alongside each other in a considerably more vital creative moment than our own, yet for whom an aesthetic dialogue would have been impossible. Such a dialogue would not necessarily include the "poetry-to-jazz" sessions that inspired Hughes to come up with a new avenue of self-promotion and collaborate with a less-than-enthralled Mingus, but does suggest the kinds of conversations that could have demystified Crane's poetic intentions or exposed Stevens to the kind of fusion between sonata form and the blues that he depicted as mere poetic conceit. Charlie Parker wished he could take a year off from performing and study with Stravinsky, but it is inconceivable to imagine Crane wanting to study the music he wanted to appropriate with Jelly Roll Morton or any other black musician. The canons of jazz and American poetry are often debated and challenged; there is also, however, a hybrid lineage of poetry that uses vocalizations, cries, instrumentation, and vocalese in a way that neither Crane nor Stevens could have imagined. Baraka, Madhubuti, and even Jon Hendricks are part of this line, as are the spoken-word and slam-poetry movements, the Last Poets, the Black Mountain Poets, and a host of other strains. These movements have obvious connections to jazz and benefit from the hindsight of history. Yet just because a poet knows about John Coltrane does not mean he will have the talent of a Hart Crane.

Hart Crane had abundant talent, but he lived in an age when the music was being invented, not historicized. In the 1920s, unless Crane was reading W.E.B. Du Bois's *Crisis*, or Louis Armstrong was thumbing through the T. S. Eliot's *Criterion*, there would have been fewer outlets to find out what one segregated group of artists were thinking about the other. "Man, your poems are weird," Billie Holiday allegedly said to Kenneth Koch after she heard him read from the New York White Pages accompanied by the alto warbling of Larry Rivers.[5] Holiday's remark to Koch was one of the few recorded instances of a jazz musician's response to a poet, and there was clearly much more that went unsaid. These poets were not necessarily writing with a comprehensive awareness of jazz history—a subject still in the process of revision—but the jazz history to which we currently have access allows us to examine some jazz poems in a larger historical and aesthetic context. Ellison emerged from the world of fiction to make his impact on how that history has been told. Although Hughes did not participate in shaping the cultural discourse of jazz so dramatically, he did show that being on the inside of jazz can be as much of a poetic inspiration as being on the outside, as Crane and Stevens certainly were. Hearing the jazz in poetry, or reading the poetry in jazz, requires going inside and outside the changes.

"CLEAN, SPARKLING, ELUSIVE"

Hart Crane might have been on the outside of jazz, but he desperately yearned for a way in. He makes his first direct reference to jazz in a letter to Allen Tate on May 16, 1922, in which he begins by talking about a dialectical realm of poetry that will somehow reach its synthesis in something he calls "jazz":

> The poetry of negation is beautiful—alas, too dangerously so for one of my mind. But I am trying to break away from it. Perhaps this is useless, perhaps it is silly—but one *does*

have joys. The vocabulary of damnations and prostrations has been developed at the expense of these other moods, however, so that it is hard to dance in proper measure. Let us invent an idiom for the proper transposition of jazz into words! Something clean, sparkling, elusive![6]

If Crane's letter had been written any later, his desire to "invent" a transposition of jazz into words would seem presumptuous at best and smack of paternalism at worst. The implication is that black people playing jazz might be capable of inspiring poetry, but not of writing it. Of course, Crane's manifesto reveals as much about poetic ambition as it says about appropriation. The most crucial point, though, is that Crane was writing two years before Hughes's first publications and a year before the first major jazz records were even cut. Although the music was in an embryonic stage in 1922, Crane instantly saw in it an alternative to the "damnations and prostrations" of Western literature. He found the vocabulary of modernism in jazz and used the gestation of one art form as a way to define his own emerging poetics, perhaps inspired by a similar impulse as Ellison when he initially reached back to Buddy Bolden to give voice to invisibility.

In 1922, the most widely available and successful jazz recordings were made by white musicians,[7] but Crane's interest in jazz appears inextricably tied to its blackness. In 1917, a year after the African American cornetist Freddie Keppard turned down the opportunity to make the first jazz record ("If I do, anybody can copy my phrases," he allegedly said), The Original Dixieland Jass Band would achieve fame, fortune, and infamy for making a hit out of "Tiger Rag," and Paul Whiteman's "Whispering" would sell two million copies in 1920. But there were only a few black musicians recording music that would now be considered jazz by 1922, a year before Louis Armstrong's first recording and two years before Ellington's. Crane's interest in the music was tied in with a racial allegory, and this was in a moment when black jazz performers were just beginning to be recorded. While white musicians were already appropriating the sounds and rhythms of jazz music, however, Crane did not do the same thing with his own rhythms. His poetry remains steeped in the conversational free verse of Whitman, the Shakespearian hubris of Melville, and, above all, the etherized sensibility of Eliot—and not the minstrel version of the poet dominating recent scholarship. He understood the complex web of allusion in Eliot—a style he would later emulate in *The Bridge*—but he did not draw an analogy to jazz's intricate nexus of musical references. Nonetheless, though, he could not have predicted how central Eliot would become to black artists like Ellison, Mingus, and M. B. Tolson, but he did see how central jazz was for his own vision.

Despite jazz's appealing immediacy for Crane, ironically he can only get to the music through layers upon layers of mediation and arcane reference. Crane, unlike Ellison, did not see the method behind jazz as akin to that of modernism; rather, he thought of jazz as a mood to be transposed into articulate speech. His approach was to scaffold the music in a mythological edifice akin to Eliot's use of Norse mythology in "The Waste Land" or Joyce's plundering of Homer and Shakespeare in *Ulysses*. Crane's interest in black culture stemmed from his own projections of its mystery, fascination, and, at least initially, his own guilt. "Black Tambourine" was written in 1920, after Crane learned that a job he landed in his father's hotel was made possible by the firing of a black handyman. Crane wrote this lyric for the fired black worker in response:

The interests of a black man in a cellar
Mark tardy judgment on the world's closed door.
Gnats toss in the shadow of a bottle,
And a roach spans a crevice in the floor.

Aesop, driven to pondering, found
Heaven with the tortoise and the hare;
Fox brush and sow ear top his grave
And mingling incantations on the air.[8]

Crane sees the Invisible Man "forlorn in the cellar," caught in a
dark limbo "Between his tambourine, stuck on the wall, / And,
in Africa, a carcass quick with flies." The poem seems to express
Crane's sympathy for the black man's threshold status "in some
mid-kingdom" between art and mortality. Yet he explained in a
letter that "Black Tambourine" is not meant as a political statement but as a placement of black people in an Aesopian tradition:

> The poem is a description and bundle of insinuations, sug-
> gestions bearing on the Negro's place somewhere between
> man and beast. That is why Aesop is brought in, etc.,—the
> popular conception of Negro romance, the tambourine on
> the wall. The value of the poem is only, to me, in what a
> painter would call its "tactile" quality,—an entirely aesthetic
> feature. A propagandist for either side of the Negro ques-
> tion could find anything he wanted to in it. My only decla-
> ration in it is that I find the Negro (in the popular mind)
> sentimentally or brutally "placed" in this midkingdom.[9]

Although he is writing on a politically charged subject, Crane
takes no particular position on race. While he never met the man
who lost his job, his invocation of Aesop rendered that black man
into a convenient poetic trope, whether or not he believed Aesop
to be black. But the Aesopian reference is also an interrogation of
widely held clichés: racists and antiracists both tend to mytholo-
gize the black man. According to Paul Mariani's *The Broken
Tower*, as a gesture of transgression Crane would fraternize with
the black workers in his father's hotel in 1921, picking up infor-

mation about black performers that would have been obscure to most whites. For a nonmusician to have access to recorded black jazz would have been a cutting-edge phenomenon even by 1922. But Crane had a knack for spotting monuments in the making: as a seventeen-year-old in 1917, Crane was already devouring *Ulysses* in serial form five years before the book's publication (and fourteen before its first legal U.S. printing) and writing verse in imitation of Wallace Stevens, whose first book would not be published for another six years. And so when Crane ventured to take that tambourine off the wall and explore its music, even if jazz was in its infancy, for Crane it was already primed for a high modernist journey into poetic allusion.

"For the Marriage of Faustus and Helen," written in 1922, is an urban poem the way that "The Love Song of J. Alfred Prufrock" is an urban poem or the "Loomings" section of *Moby Dick* is urban prose. Prufrock only finds rejection and despair in the city's landscape; Melville's Ishmael must escape the confines of the "Manhattoes" to satiate his wanderlust. The poet of "For the Marriage of Faustus and Helen" feels his mind divided by the "accepted multitudes" and seeks refuge from the banality of the "memoranda, baseball scores, / The stenographic smiles and stock quotations," escaping, if not exactly into jazz, then into a simulacrum of it. It is worth remembering that in his rhapsodic letter, Crane sought something mediated, not jazz itself but its "proper transposition into words." Making a proper transposition hardly sounds like poetic ecstasy and scarcely resembles the improvisations that struck his fancy. Crane would often write his first drafts semidrunk; perhaps listening to a Spanish Bolero, and even ranted on one occasion, "I am Rimbaud! I am Christ!"[10] In the cold light of day, his sober revisions would often contain not a single phrase from his initial outbursts, as evidenced in a comparison of the draft and final version of "Voyages." As fascinated as Crane apparently was by jazz, his own approach to craft was anything but improvised.

And it is not improvisation that Crane is necessarily after in the poem either. Instead, Crane takes the Faust legend and, rather than riffing on Marlowe's or Goethe's version, uses it as an occasion for his own overdetermined journey in which the speaker, after confronting aspects of city life ranging from the banal to the pornographic ("Smutty wings flash out equivocations"), finally dreams of losing his way on the subway and finding himself in a jazz garden party with a soundtrack provided by minstrel-like angelic figures invoking revelry and ecstasy:

> Brazen hypnotics glitter here;
> Glee shifts from foot to foot,
> Magnetic to their tremulo.
> This crashing opéra bouffe,
> Blest excursion! this ricochet
> From roof to roof—
> Know, Olympians, we are breathless
> While nigger cupids scour the stars!   (*WB*, 40)

As rhapsodic as these lines are, Crane never lets us forget the many layers of remove that exist between the poet and the subject. He addresses the Olympians who ascend to the poetic peak only to find themselves rendered out of breath (anticipating Frank O'Hara's "The Day Lady Died") when confronted with the inscrutable music performed by the (unfortunately termed) "nigger cupids." These black angels perform a music with "strange harmonic laws" that defy categorization or historical context, banishing all previous forms of music as "serene," rocked to somnolence in "patent armchairs." The music is still in embryonic form, waiting to be codified, and the "incunabula" Crane describes not only refers to books printed before 1501, the era of the historical Faust, but also the early stages of jazz's development in that embryonic moment of 1922.

The transposition of jazz into words really will not do justice to preserving this phenomenon, and Crane uses his rhapsodic language to hype the medium that would in many ways displace the textual centrality of the modernist poetry in which Crane thrived: the record industry ("The siren of the springs of guilty song— / Let us take her on the incandescent wax / Striated with nuances, nervosities / That we are heir to"). That "incandescent wax" "striated" with grooves would end up replacing text as the medium that would best capture the phenomenon Crane was recounting. By the end of the decade, when Armstrong's Hot Fives and Hot Sevens and Ellington's Washingtonians were sufficiently documented on records, finding their way to the "metallic paradise" of the Victrola, transposing jazz into words would be less important than transposing jazz into mechanically reproducible products. Although the black orchestra leader James Reese Europe recorded syncopated brass music up to his death in 1919, and was even billed as "The Jazz King," his music has no improvisation, no blues, no swing. The first black jazz recordings were probably by the backing band for Mamie Smith, the first African American singer on record, whose voice sounded more primed for the vaudeville stage than a speakeasy. But however unflattering the microphone was to her somewhat overbearing vibrato, and however debatable her connection to jazz even was, her backing musicians did record instrumentals in 1921—including the tinny clarinet of Garvin Bushell and the cornet of Johnny Dunn, who was allegedly blown off the stage by a young Louis Armstrong. The "New soothings, new amazements / That cornets introduce at every turn" have been interpreted in a canonical line of jazz history by Paul Mariani, who writes that Crane captured "not Debussy, but an American jazz

idiom, the equivalent of Louis Armstrong's brazen tonalities,"
even though it is certain that Armstrong's tonalities would have
never been available to Crane when he was writing the poem.[11]
There is no palpable difference between the recordings of Johnny
Dunn's less brazen tonalities and the Original Dixieland Jass
Band's hits from a few years earlier.

A black imitation of a white imitation of a black music sounds
convoluted, but it was a simulacrum Crane could follow. Crane,
languishing in Cleveland in 1922, pining away for the New York
he inhabited in adolescent spurts, imagined an "amazing open
air jazz garden." It is possible that Crane journeyed to Chicago's
Lincoln Gardens on the advice of the black hotel workers, but it
is more likely that Crane imagined a phenomenon that would be
played out just a few years later, when jazz records actually could
begin to capture the spontaneous excitement he yearned to transpose into words. Crane is writing about a public fantasy made
private—a possession of stardom only possible in an era when
records and films would compete with books. His conjured image of Helen is "stippled with pink and green advertisements"
and adored by a "million brittle, bloodshot eyes," and he longs
for her sound to be documented on wax and stuffed into a record
sleeve, ready for diva worship. None of Crane's biographers know
whether he actually trolled the Harlem underworld for rooftop
gardens, rent parties, and speakeasies. It is more likely that
Crane merely fantasized about such parties with his Chianti,
Victrola, and rapturous lines, captured and harnessed in Promethean fashion.

At first glance, "The Marriage of Faustus and Helen" seems to
have only a tangential relationship to the legend of Faust as conceived by Marlowe, Goethe, or Jonson.[12] But the charlatans of
Jonson's play do resemble the historical Faust, a nemesis of Martin Luther, who, like the figures Henry Louis Gates documents

as central to African American vernacular in *The Signifying Monkey*, is a trickster, using mirrors and tricks of light to conjure up simulacra of Helen and other historical figures. Faust's tricks were protocinematic performance pieces staging allusion and fantasy to seductive music for his audiences. Crane, too, describes the erotics of spectacle as he recounts fantasies of attending a "crashing opéra bouffe" whose star he has seen plastered all over billboards in Manhattan, and whose sound he desires, Prometheus-like, stolen from the musical gods and immortalized on wax. As Crane details this fan's imaginary journey on the subway to a seedy club of "smutty wings" and "[b]razen hypnotics," he attempts to achieve a "transposition of jazz into words." Crane's alchemical poetic jazz does not "raise . . . Helen's house against the Ismaelite," but shows how Helen's "siren . . . of guilty song" serenaded the kind of performance even the most intrepid of white bohemians rarely attended.

Crane's speaker is too "[d]ivided by accepted multitudes," "rebuffed by asphalt" and workaday Manhattan bustle. At every turn he is confronted by the simulacra of posters and advertisements across which "smutty wings" from Comic Opera placards "flash out equivocations." With his eyes "riveted to [the] plane" of his modern Helen's poster, he fantasizes about touching her and finding himself transported to the Harlem rooftop where she is performing a "crashing opéra bouffe," becoming one adoring eye in a captivated audience "rocked in patent armchairs." Yet however alluring this thought, he cannot cross the social divide to see such a "smutty" and "guilty" performance of Helen singing to the music of "nigger cupids," and so the poem ends with a wish to record this "siren of the springs of guilty song / . . . on the incandescent wax" of a record that he can listen to in the "cultivated storm" of his private quarters.

Even if the most successful jazz records were still by white musicians, Crane, perhaps through his jovial interactions with the black hotel workers, knew that the music really belonged to the "nigger cupids," whom he hoped could transport him into a sonic *Walpurgisnacht* in the comfort of his own living room. Despite his use of jazz as a vocabulary for his own modernist idiom, Crane does not go so far as to see jazz musicians as fellow craftsmen. What Crane imagined was not black jazz musicians as living human beings—like the hotel worker who could evoke guilt in "Black Tambourine"—but as mythological figures that could provide an imaginary escape from what R.W.B. Lewis called the "Wall Street Idiom" of the poem.[13] Within a year, there would suddenly be a burgeoning market for the figure Crane would prophetically invoke in section II of "For the Marriage of Faustus and Helen": the jazz-record collector. By then, that incandescent wax would document performances that would render Crane's immaterial fantasies into material history. Nineteen twenty-two was the last year that black jazz musicians operated outside of the recording industry, in a realm Crane characterized as "elusive." By the time he leapt to his death from the *Orizba* a decade later, in 1932, Louis Armstrong, Duke Ellington, James P. Johnson, Bessie Smith, and many other figures had already recorded a body of work more than worthy of Crane's "transposition." If he had lived longer, he might very well have revisited jazz after some of its central figures had documented their art, approaching the "striated nervosities" of Ellington's "Black and Tan Fantasy" or Armstrong's "West End Blues" with the same precision and lyricism that he applied to the Brooklyn Bridge or his grandmother's love letters. Crane's black man in a cellar in "Black Tambourine" was not the self-conscious record-collecting rhapsodist of "For the Marriage of Faustus and Helen." It would take Ellison, thirty years later, to synthesize these two conceits. That tambourine would eventually come off the wall.

HUGHES AND THE ABSTRACT TRUTH

Hughes not only took the tambourine off the wall, he brought the entire ensemble with him. If Crane came to jazz poetry from the outside, Hughes came to it from the inside. Even though Kenneth Rexroth claimed to have staged the first jazz and poetry performances in 1934, Hughes got there first in 1926. And while one of his celebrated contemporaries wanted to turn the Harlem Renaissance into the Renaissance—Countee Cullen turned away from the blues and toward Petrarch for poetic forms—no one could have ever accused Hughes of missing the music. He collaborated with Charles Mingus after giving him a rave review in the *Chicago Defender*, and made references to Armstrong, Parker, Holiday, and many other key figures throughout his work. When Hughes made his 1957 public-relations pitch as the "Original Jazz Poet," he was not trying to topple white modernists like Crane, whose remarks about his own jazz ambitions were made in private correspondence. And the Beats were not hard for Hughes to dismiss, either. "I don't know the beatniks," he told a reporter. "They all seem to be down in the Village and I practically never go down there. I stay up in Harlem."[14] When Hughes did go down to the Village to perform with Charles Mingus at the Village Vanguard in 1957, he encountered the figure that presented the greatest threat to his claim as Original Jazz Poet. Hughes had referred to Mingus as a "modernist with more of a beat to my ear" and had collaborated with him on a narrative piece called "Scenes from the City" in 1955.

When they recorded *The Weary Blues* together in 1957, however, it became clear that even though Mingus was making Hughes's kind of jazz, Hughes was not necessarily writing Mingus's kind of poetry, at least not the analogue to what he was creating as a composer. Mingus himself wrote lyrics to many of his compositions. In "Fables of Faubus," Mingus and Dannie Richmond engage in a call and response excoriating Arkansas's segregationist governor Orval Faubus with hard-hitting blues, jagged harmonies, and damning couplets scored right out of the dozens (rhyming "Faubus" with "ridiculous"). In contrast to the psychoanalytic pastiche of Mingus's autobiography *Beneath the Underdog* (1971), Mingus's lyrics are often remarkably straight-forward. In the lyrics to "Freedom," he plays the trickster: "This mule ain't from Moscow; this mule ain't from the South / This mule's had some hard learning; mostly mouth to mouth.[15] These lines tell the truth about getting behind the mule on southern plantations, but, unlike Emily Dickinson, they do not tell it slant. Mingus's vaster and more eccentric ambitions would be heard on the ambitious, atonal horn arrangements supporting these lines. Aldon Neilsen observed that "Mingus's own poetry tended to be premodernist in form," but, that said, even these seemingly simple lyrics to "Freedom" "could have been written by Hughes himself."[16] When it came to narrating racial struggles Mingus and Hughes were on the same page. But when it came to Mingus's own musical responses to Hughes's performance, they were not always on the same score. Mingus wrote "Chill of Death" in a gothic mode, *Beneath the Underdog* with a Jungian tinge, "The Clown" as an absurdist allegorist, and "Eat That Chicken" as a man loudly proclaiming his appetites. Hughes and Mingus came together in some ways, but on *The Weary Blues*, they can also be heard taking divergent aesthetic strategies as well. Mingus's own writing was not necessarily like Eliot's *Four Quartets*, but he must have found that it resonated with what he was doing musically. Mingus's language could find common ground with Hughes's, but it was not the only territory he wanted to cover.

Hughes's delivery sounds stranded in another era, self-consciously delivering lyrics without the music, audibly uncomfortable with the medium of recording, even though he is widely credited as an inventor of performance poetry. Although Hughes was the first poet to perform with jazz musicians, it is jarring to hear lines like "Good morning, daddy! Ain't you heard / The boogie-woogie rumble / Of a dream deferred?" ("Dream Boogie") delivered with his oddly affected Midwestern twang. The first side of the record was accompanied by polite revival versions of Dixieland and gospel by the critic Leonard Feather. From the opening notes of the second side, it is clear that Mingus is up to something less comfortably nostalgic. Before Hughes even utters a word, Mingus sets up a musical opposition to Hughes's style, bowing in contrasting fifths—from a G-major chord to a D dominant seventh—accompanying the tenor lines of Shafi Hadi. The chords then modulate in directions that add color and clangor without losing the melody while Hughes's "Consider Me" asks listeners to "consider" the peripatetic identity of a grown-up "colored boy":

Before me
Papa, mama,
Grandpa, grandma,
So on back
To original
Pa[17]

On the record, but not in the published poem, Hughes adds: "Spelled G-O-D," as if there was any question of the identity of "original / Pa," punctuated with a series of piano arpeggios and followed by a half-note thumping bass line. In the text of the poem, "original / Pa" remains mysterious while the speaker shares some of his woes of how hard he has to work for his "Sugar" (who has to work, too), and how he is "Black, / Caught in a crack / That splits the world in two / From China / By way of Arkansas / To Lenox Avenue."[18] Hughes's voice refers listeners to a journey all the way from China to Harlem (recalling Nick Kenny's lyrics to Ellington's "Drop Me off in Harlem": "If Harlem moved to China / I could think of nothing finer / Than to stow away on a plane someday and have them / Drop me off in Harlem"), charting a passage leading to a conflicted racial identity. Mingus's accompaniment to the poem's plaintive voice adds yet another cultural dimension, alternating between a bowing style resembling a contrapuntal melodic line from a Bartok string quartet to a more familiar sound: the pulsating quarter notes of a walking bass line. As a bass player, Mingus was dissatisfied with the role of mere time keeper, and his hypnotically thudding quarrels with the quarter note are a hallmark of his playing.

Like his accompaniment for "Consider Me," Mingus followed bowing with bass thumping, renouncing his dream of playing classical cello to pound walking bass lines as a jazz musician, a role he felt to be racially confining. As Mingus recounts in his *Beneath the Underdog*, his first instrument was cello, but he quit the Los Angeles Youth orchestra in protest after refusing to play the diluted version of Beethoven that the conductor put before him. After being informed by the orchestra director, "Most of you Negroes can't read," Mingus recalled in his autobiography how his friend, the saxophonist Buddy Collette, helped him make the transition from classical cello to jazz bass:

"Go get yourself a bass and we'll put you in our Union swing band,"
Buddy told my boy. "We can use you."
"Get a bass?"

"That's right. You're black. You'll never make it in classical music no matter how good you are. You want to play, you gotta play a *Negro* instrument. You can't slap a cello, so you gotta learn to *slap that bass*, Charlie!"[19]

Mingus did learn to slap that bass, enough to attain one of the most distinctive percussive attacks in the recorded history of the instrument.[20] Still, Mingus was never satisfied with his accolades. In a letter to Nat Hentoff from Bellevue, Mingus, listening to the Bartok string quartets, felt a pang of genre envy. "I am a good composer with great possibilities and I made an easy success through jazz but it wasn't really success—jazz has too many strangling possibilities for a composer," Mingus wrote. "If I want it right, Nat, guess I'll have to leave jazz—that word leaves room for too much fooling" (*BTU*, 340). Mingus was not necessarily fooling when he went back to that bow, but he was upsetting the assumptions of jazz and jazz poetry, the ones that made Buddy Collette tell him that he had to jettison the cello to slap that bass.

And so Mingus bows his way through some Bartokian lines—dark, brooding, atonally lyrical—to segue into folksy Hughes maxims like: "Curb your doggie / like you ought to do / But don't let that dog curb you" ("Warning: Augmented"). Equally incongruous is hearing Mingus play his own "Weird Nightmare"—as much inspired by his own insomnia and Scriabin as by Ellington and Fletcher Henderson—behind Hughes's "Motto":

I play it cool
And dig all jive
That's the reason I stay alive   (*CPLH*, 398)

Hughes was surely displaying a rich irony, with the speaker using playing it cool and digging all jive as a means of self-preservation. As someone who claimed not to know the Beats, Hughes

certainly knew how to signify on their appropriations. In the
year of "The White Negro" and Kerouac's *On the Road*, Hughes
took the language stolen by the white hipsters and stole it back
with a wink and a nudge while Verve records rolled the tapes. Yet
while Hughes used the argot of hip, his lack of a public sexual
persona made him the opposite of the stereotypical hypersexual
black man. That self-styled black sexual dynamo was pounding
the bass behind him, exuding the kind of power that tantalized
Mailer's hyperbolic imagination. And yet, Mingus had his own
muse to fulfill, one too expansive to fit into any hipster fantasy. If
Hughes was a poet who worked as an entertainer, Mingus was an
entertainer who aspired to poetry. As a poet whose verse adapted
the twelve-bar blues for a distinctive AAB six-line stanzaic structure as early as 1926, Hughes showed poets that the blues could
be a basis for poetry. Mingus, working under the shadow of Duke
Ellington, who had already proven the elastic capabilities of the
blues, wanted to demonstrate, as he argued in a letter to *Down
Beat* in 1951, that "all music is one."[21] Like Albert Murray, not
"interested in romanticizing what we'd grown up with," Mingus
adds European allusions to Hughes's mythology of cool bop dad-
dies, dreams deferred, and homages to Lenox Avenue.

Mingus cultivated an image of a genius trapped in the ghetto,
whose cultural aspirations outside the confines of Watts were as
confounding as they were impressive, and the standard for which
his legacy is measured is a European mode. In the documentary
Triumph of the Underdog, Gunther Schuller praises Mingus as a
"written-down composer," as if forms endemic to the African
American vernacular—the very forms Hughes celebrates in his
blues poems and his homages to Harlem—were insufficient in
truly measuring his greatness.[22] "Charlie Parker is in his own
way creating complete clearly thought-out compositions of
melodic line every time he plays a solo, as surely as one was ever

written down by Brahms or Chopin or Tchaikowksy [*sic*]," Mingus wrote in 1951, anticipating Jack Kerouac's manifesto a few years later contending that Parker's lines are as complex as Bach's.[23] Mingus had much to protest in the tumultuous fifties, but when he refers to his "best friend Nat Hentoff" in his memoir, he is not describing the patronage of a white liberal journalist but a friendship between equals, just as when he says "all music is one," he does not think himself beneath Beethoven—either as a teenage orchestra-member or as a composer. By 1957, Mingus's own life was rather different from the speaker of the Hughes poem who wonders "if white folks ever feel bad / Gettin' up lonesome and sad?" Hughes and Mingus both traveled in an interracial bohemia. Hughes would often play the role of native informant for guilty white liberals, brilliantly satirized in his poem "Dinner Guest: Me," in which it is up to him to report on the troubles of "Darktown, USA" amidst clinking cocktail glasses on Park Avenue.[24] Mingus responds to Hughes's lines with his bow, playing the kinds of melodies that captured his imagination as the brooding teenager who would write "Chill of Death." The plaintive accompaniment is neither bluesy nor swinging, evoking a café in Romania more than a Harlem speakeasy. Hughes, who documented his clashes with Charlotte Osgood Mason, his white upper-middle-class "Godmother" in *The Big Sea*, was a long way from the poem's speaker wondering if white folks ever felt bad. For the musician bowing those lines behind Hughes, "the ways of white folks" were even more demystified, since they were they ways of his white, upper-middle-class wives. Mingus may have had his own hostility to "white folks," but he also married them, inspired them, collaborated with them, confounded, infuriated, and challenged them.

What Mingus did culturally (and sexually), he also did musically, and this is not the least of the reasons why he felt more kinship with Eliot than he did with Hughes. It obviously had nothing to do with politics: Mingus's civil rights anthems and paranoia about Nazis could not be further away from a poet who once publicly declared that it is preferable to be less than welcome to "freethinking Jews." As an aesthetic credo, though, Mingus's never-adapted version of the *Four Quartets* was surely more than mere social climbing. It is more the acknowledgment of jarring, colliding influences—with the range of languages and the intersection between the classical and the vernacular—that drove Mingus to include Spanish maracas in *New Tijuana Moods*, indigenous South American folk music in *Cumbia and Jazz Fusion*, and leading "Taurus in the Arena of Life" with a Baroque piano part that then descends to a postbop harmonic swirl on *Let My Children Hear Music*. More importantly, though, the experience of playing Mingus is to embrace the willed merging of genres, sensibilities, and chords that were not made to be played together. Musicians call such chords "stacked" voicings and the uninitiated player might wonder why Mingus would, as he does in "Sue's Changes," stack an E Major over a B Flat—about the most dissonant combination imaginable—yet still achieve something shockingly melodic. The answers could come from the gospel church, the Ellington-Strayhorn tonal palette, the impressionists, Bartok. They could also be explained by Eliot's influential essay on metaphysical poetry, in which he invokes Samuel Johnson's idea that "the most heterogenous ideas are yoked by violence together."[25]

Mingus yoked many things together by violence. He was convicted of third-degree assault after punching trombonist Jimmy Knepper during a rehearsal, and the Village Vanguard honored his passion by never replacing a spotlight he smashed in a fit of rage one night. But his collisions were cultural, as well: he also showed how the yoking together of two seemingly disparate chords—or races, genres, or sensibilities—could make compelling music. Hughes, meanwhile, saw jazz not, as Ellison did, as an aesthetic outgrowth of Eliot's poetics, but as a retort to them. In "To A Negro Jazz Band in a Parisian Cabaret," for example, Eliot's famous clangor of three languages in "The Waste Land" (Bin gar keine Russin, stamm' aus Litauen, echt deutsch), is tweaked when Hughes directs the expatriate musicians to play their multilingual "thing":

> May I?
> Mais oui,
> Mein Gott!
> Parece una rumba.
> Que rumba!
> Play it, jazz band!
> You've got seven languages to speak in
> And then some.   (*CPLH*, 60)

By 1961, four years after his collaboration with Mingus, Hughes—who had witnessed the high modernist influence not only on his former protégé Ellison, but also on the black poet M. B. Tolson—again used jazz not as a form of high modernism but as a parody of it in "Ask Your Mama," in which Eliot's footnotes for "The Waste Land" become "Liner Notes for the Poetically Unhep." Hughes was demonstrating that "Ask Your Mama" could have an apparatus as exclusionary and deliberately misleading as "The Waste Land," and that the mythology of the Underground Railroad, the dozens, and bebop could be just as inscrutable and arcane as the Norse mythology so meticulously annotated in Eliot's notes. When Hughes described Mingus as "a modernist with more of a beat to my ear," it is unclear whether Hughes is placing Mingus in a musical tradition or a literary one, but Mingus's modernism was different from Hughes's.

Hughes's verse has a deceptive simplicity, and the pure lyricism of "The Weary Blues" may look pretty thin after the more obvious literary complexity of Eliot, Crane, and Stevens. But when Hughes took on, say, the blues as a subject, he didn't merely write about the blues, he wrote the blues itself. Establishing the blues as an American poetic form is no mean feat, and yet it is precisely this direct representation that invited such harsh criticism from James Baldwin, who criticized "The Weary Blues," "which copies, rather than exploits, the cadences of the blues."[26] Baldwin saw such forms as "hieroglyphics" for a coded Negro speech, putting the responsibility on the shoulders of the African American artist not only to reproduce those forms, but to dig beyond their attractive surfaces. "He has not forced them into the realm of art where their meaning would become more clear and overwhelming." If anyone questioned Hughes's claim to be the Original Jazz Poet, it was not because they thought he misunderstood the music, but because they wanted a poet to transform it into something else, much as jazz itself has been an art of transfiguration. Hughes's populism was not met with approval by high modernists like Albert Murray and Ralph Ellison. "I wanted to do something that was a bigger challenge than what Hughes was doing," recalled Murray, who, along with Ellison, preferred the hierarchical realm of Eliot. "We didn't have an urge to romanticize what we'd grown up with. It was the urge to see what we could do with it, achieve what others had achieved in other cultures."[27]

Mingus had aspirations similar to Murray's, was striving for a different kind of literary credibility, closer to the hierarchical modernism of Ellison. Hughes might have given Ellison his first literary break in 1937, but twenty years later, Ellison would be making high modernist claims for jazz at Hughes's expense, claiming that Eliot—of all people—could swing harder than

Hughes. According to Al Young and other poets who attended the Mingus/Hughes performances at the Vanguard, Mingus was looking for a different kind of poetry to work with, closer to the Beats—the same group targeted by Hughes as downtown interlopers. Gene Santoro wrote in *Myself When I am Real* that Mingus was "unhappy with some of Hughes's poetry: it was too lyric, too old fashioned."[28] Poets Al Young and Maureen Meloy recalled Mingus's complaints after one of their Vanguard performances in which Mingus said he wished he could work with Beat poets instead of Hughes.[29] The Beat poet who did work with Mingus was Kenneth Patchen, who acted as a Virgil for Mingus's journey to Bellevue in *Beneath the Underdog*. But Eliot, who initially called "The Waste Land" "He Do the Police In Different Voices," presented a more polyphonous chorus of colliding cultures as expansive and mentally unhinged as the composer of "Hellvue at Bellvue." The beginning really was in Mingus's end, and if he had combined his music with Eliot's *Four Quartets*, he could have tested Ellison's claims and finally put Eliot's "jazz banjorine" to use. In 1958, Langston Hughes told a reporter, "Jazz gives poetry a much wider following and poetry brings jazz the greater respectability that people seem to think it needs. I don't think jazz needs it, but most people seem to."[30] One of those people who thought jazz needed greater respectability was Charles Mingus. On their collaboration, you can hear him fighting for it.

"A TUNE BEYOND US, YET OURSELVES"

Hart Crane's jazz aesthetic may have been vague compared to Langston Hughes's, but he left a more substantial paper trail on the subject in 1922 than Wallace Stevens did prior to his death in 1955. A thorough study of Stevens's record collection at the

Huntington reveals no jazz—no black music at all, in fact, a dis-
appointing catalogue for a poet with such an aggressively American vision. He never went abroad, apparently out of fear that, like
Eliot and James, he would be overly influenced by European culture, and so defined himself with the mythology of his climate,
calling his first volume of poetry *Harmonium* (an instrument used
in American folk music) in 1923. A poem in that volume, "A
High-Toned Old Christian Woman," did contain a dandyish reference to moral laws "squiggling like saxophones,"[31] while its title
suggests a high pitched, "high yaller" character preaching high-
mindedness. "Mrs. Alfred Uruguay," from *Parts of A World*, begins
with a syncopated line, "So what said the others and the sun went
down,"[32] before describing the "brown blues of evening." Eleanor
Cook describes this line as "an Eliot ragtime rhythm,"[33] but since
Stevens did not offer us a context for this music, reading swing
into every instance of syncopation in his poems—and there are a
few—recalls the many critics who have pointed out the swing
rhythms in Beethoven's Sonata no. 32 in C Minor, op. 111. The
sounds may be there, but the cultural context is not. Despite the
possible racial connotations of "the brown blues of evening,"
Stevens did not explicitly refer to black music until "The Sick
Man" of 1950, and it is in this poem where Stevens gives us
more explicit clues about his views on jazz. It did not see publication until the Samuel French Morse edition of Stevens's *Opus
Posthumous* in 1957 and remains relatively obscure.

In his lecture "The Irrational Element in Poetry," Stevens
writes that poetry itself is the "true subject" of poetry. When
Stevens refers to a blackbird hovering over Haddam, Connecticut, a jar in sitting on a hill in Tennessee, or the Oklahoma landscape roamed by a firecat, he is embodying what he proclaimed
in a late lyric: a mythology reflects its own region. "The Sick
Man" evokes the music of the South, and to reflect that region

fully, Stevens has to confront African American music in search of what he called the "American Sublime." But what exactly did Stevens know about this music and when did he know it? "The Sick Man," written when the poet was seventy, is in the elegiac mode that characterizes much of his later work. Many of these later poems directly allude to the poet's earlier work in a questioning, even self-interrogating mode. "Have I lived a skeleton's life, / As a disbeliever in reality?" Stevens asks in "As You Leave the Room,"[34] after alluding to "Someone Puts a Pineapple Together," "The Well Dressed Man with a Beard," and "Credences of Summer." "The Sick Man" is similarly self-referential and self-doubting, while attempting synthesis between two kinds of music and two cultures. First, Stevens describes a band of black blues musicians in the South, then a celestial and presumably European choir in the North. A man lying in bed, apparently the sick man of the poem's title, yearns to bring these two concepts together, but his wish remains conceptual. In his fevered imagination, "Bands of black men seem to be drifting in the air" from the South, "Playing mouth-organs in the night or, now, guitars."[35] He also hears northern "voices of men" singing wordlessly and "[wa]its for the unison of the music of the drifting bands / And the dissolving chorals." In a solitude as anguished as that of Ellison's Invisible Man, Stevens's speaker seeks comfort through music, his imagined synthesis between the "tunk-a-tunk-tunk" blues rhythms evoked in "A High-Toned Old Christian Woman" and the kind of celestial choir he evokes in "Sunday Morning" from *Harmonium* and "Not Ideas About the Thing but the Thing Itself" from *The Rock* (1954):

And in a bed in one room, alone, a listener
Waits for the unison of the music of the drifting bands
And the dissolving chorals, waits for it and imagines

The words of winter in which these two will come together,
In the ceiling of the distant room, in which he lies,
The listener, listening to the shadows, seeing them,

Choosing out of himself, out of everything within him,
Speech for the quiet, good hail of himself, good hail, good
    hail,
The peaceful, blissful words, well-tuned, well sung, well-
    spoken.[36]

These words of winter directly allude to the "mind of winter,"
which, Stevens implored in "The Snow Man" from *Harmonium*,
one must have in order to attain his particular poetic perspective.
Although there is no evidence from Stevens's record collection
that he had firsthand knowledge of this kind of music, the images of black men playing guitars could have evoked strains of
Robert Johnson, Charley Patton, Skip James, and Son House
drifting through the air, or, given the multiplicity of strumming
guitarists, could even allude to James Reese Europe's bands of
the teens, in which dozens of banjo players would jangle in unison. Jean Toomer's *Cane* or the spiritual "Swing Low, Sweet
Chariot" could be yet another source for Stevens's band of black
men:

I looked over Jordan,
And WHAT did I see,
Comin' for to carry me home,
A band of angels comin' after me,
Comin' for to carry me home.

Whether Stevens is drawing from the spiritual, the secular, or
even the minstrel, the poet only left behind a textual trail for this
musical poem. The first published work of criticism on this
poem was a close reading by Helen Vendler published in the

New York Review of Books in 1997, and she identified the need for racial healing as the cause of the sick man's illness. "It is maddening for the sick man to hear these two musics, to know that there somehow must exist an American libretto that will unify these instruments and these voices, and to feel that he is called to compose that libretto if he is to survive," she writes. "Stevens did not live to invent such a text: but that he urgently wanted, at seventy, to conceive it and felt he would remain a sick man if he could not write it, says a great deal about the Americanness of his imagination, and about the moral responsibility—not sufficiently credited—underlying his work."[37] According to this reading, Stevens was a civil rights activist who, ailing, knew that there was some link between this black folkloric art and the European sonata form, and that he lamented the segregation of these forms. Vendler, a descendant of the New Critics, reads the poem without any outside context, making Stevens's racial views seem fit for a civics class.

Yet Stevens also called a poem "Like Decorations in a Nigger Cemetery" (*Ideas of Order*, 1936), a title that certainly means offense, even if it also has an odd form of identification with the ethnic group he maligns: in an apparently self-deprecating remark to the southern judge Arthur Powell, Stevens wrote, "My poems are like decorations in a nigger cemetery." Did he mean his poems were ornate, like the Rococo designs of those headstones he saw near his Key West retreat, or thrown together, like the makeshift memorials of the poor? While this title still remains a poetic ambiguity, another incident in Stevens's life does not. In 1952, two years after the writing of "The Sick Man," Stevens was about to preside over a National Book Award ceremony, where he already knew he would lose to Marianne Moore. Allegedly, after a two-martini lunch, he scanned the photographs of past judges on the wall and came across a picture of

Gwendolyn Brooks. "Who's the coon?" he asked. "I know you don't like to hear a lady being called a coon, but who is it?"[38]

Stevens apparently thought that black people could inspire poetry but not write it or judge it. Brooks did both, and also wrote such jazz-inspired poems as "Queen of the Blues" and "The Third Sermon on the Warpland." It is not surprising, therefore, that he was unaware that by the time he wrote "The Sick Man" in 1950, black musicians could be as complex in their creations as he was. A text that linked the blues with sonata form had already been written; it existed not in the world of high modernist poetry, however, but in the pantheon of jazz music. In 1943, seven years before the composition of "The Sick Man" (and nearly a decade before the Gwendolyn Brooks incident), Duke Ellington was challenging such categories when he premiered *Black, Brown, and Beige*, the most ambitious large-scale jazz work that had been written at that point. This work does precisely what Stevens's sick man wishes he could do: it takes a motif rooted in the blues and the gospel church—the section "Come Sunday"—and, like Beethoven's "Ode to Joy," develops it into many different themes, exploiting its harmonic, rhythmic, and emotional possibilities.

Not all of the critics were kind to *Black, Brown, and Beige* when it first premiered. John Hammond lamented that "it was unfortunate that Duke saw fit to tamper with the blues form in order to produce music of 'significance,' "[39] and it was not until Brian Priestly and Alan Cohen's musicological analysis of 1974 that Ellington's structural approach was given critical vindication. Within a year of the premiere of *Black, Brown, and Beige*, the *New Yorker* ran a profile on Ellington called "The Hot Bach," and Ellington himself was sounding off in print against classical music critics and other detractors unwilling to accept that his "story of the Negro in America" could hold up to technical scrutiny while also keeping up his credibility with jazz purists. Responding to Winthorp Sargeant in the *American Mercury*, who wrote, "Give him the chance to study, and the Negro will soon turn from Boogie Woogie to Beethoven," Ellington responded, "Maybe so, but what a shame! There is so much that is good in a musical expression in the popular field."[40]

Stevens's poetic consciousness (as opposed to his award-ceremony decorum) conveyed a deeper sense of diversity than Sargeant's absurd binarisms, particularly as they were directed against Ellington. Even though Stevens had an obsessive knowledge of classical music, his poems often suggest that new indigenous sounds were approaching. In "Not Ideas About the Thing But the Thing Itself," he juxtaposes a "scrawny cry" with "[a] chorister whose c preceded the choir."[41] The overall effect of these two modes—the choral and a "scrawny cry"—resulted not in mere clangor but a music that "was like / A new knowledge of reality." The musical solution to this clash was supplied by Ellington, and before he made it to Carnegie Hall with a blues-based sonata form, he made it to Hollywood with parody. In the 1934 film *Murder at the Vanities* featuring lyrics by Sam Coslow, vocalist Ivie Anderson tweaks highbrow convention as polite parody, easing the listener into radical rhythmic and harmonic innovation with entertainment, singing

> It's got those licks
> It's got those kicks
> That Mr. Liszt would never recognize . . .

The tune is called "Ebony Rhapsody" and captures the lascivious end of pre-Code Hollywood. In a scene called "Rape of a Rhapsody," Ellington and members of his orchestra interrupt an orchestral performance of Liszt's "Hungarian Rhapsody" with riffs and licks. The white symphony members are scandalized and leave the stage. A decade later, Ellington would be making more serious strides toward long-form composition with *Black, Brown, and Beige*, and by 1959—four year after Stevens's death—he would record a jazz rendition of Tchaikovsky's *Nutcracker Suite*.[42]

Yet even though Stevens publicly denigrated Gwendolyn Brooks in a drunken rant, his image of the Sick Man waiting to be healed by the fusion of North and South, white and black, and classical and the blues was not far off from the work of another African American writer: Ralph Ellison. When Stevens died in 1955, Ellison was already at work on the novel that he would spend the rest of his life failing to complete. What was eventually published as *Juneteenth* in 1999 centered on a dialogue between a racist northern senator ailing from an assassin's gunshot wound and a black jazz trombonist named Alonzo Hickman who had raised the senator when he was a mixed-race young man named Bliss. Like Stevens's Sick Man, Senator Sunraider must learn how to come to terms with racial mixing if he has any hope of healing. In an early passage from that book, which first appeared in Ellison's 1973 story "Cadillac Flambé," the senator, before his assassination, fulminates against black men in Cadillacs, using the same epithet Stevens directed toward Brooks:

> Indeed, I am led to suggest, and quite seriously, that legislation be drawn up to rename it the "Coon Cage Eight." And not at all because of its eight superefficient cylinders, nor because of the lean, springing strength and beauty of its general outlines. Not at all, but because it has now become such a common sight to see eight or more of our darker brethren crowded together enjoying its power, its beauty, its neo-pagan comfort, while weaving recklessly through the streets of our great cities and along our superhighways.[43]

Sunraider is shot down soon after suggesting this piece of legislation, and is only able to heal when he is able to answer the
salient question: Who's your daddy? The senator must listen to
his "dark daddy of the flesh" to accept that before he reinvented
himself as the race-baiting Adam Sunraider, he was the biracial
Bliss. And he must also come to see that the "Coon Cage Eight"
he disparaged at the beginning of the book could actually be seen
as something quite magnificent, definitively and weirdly American:

> *This was no Cadillac, no Lincoln, Oldsmobile or Buick—nor*
> *any other known make of machine; it was an arbitrary assem-*
> *blage of chassis, wheels, engine, hood, horns, none of which had*
> *ever been part of a single car! It was a junkyard sculpture mech-*
> *anized! An improvisation, a bastard creation of black bastards—*
> *and yet, it was no ordinary hot rod. It was an improvisation of*
> *vast arrogance and subversive and malicious defiance which*
> *they had designed to outrage and destroy everything in its path,*
> *a rolling time bomb launched in the streets.*   (*JT*, 347)

"An improvisation of vast arrogance": what a rich way to describe the music that would heal Stevens's Sick Man if he only
stopped to listen to it. When Stevens said "my poems are like
decorations in a nigger cemetery" or, in "The Man With the
Blue Guitar" (*The Man with the Blue Guitar*; 1937), remarked
"Tom-tom, c'est moi," he was somehow aware, like Crane with
his "nigger cupids" or Eliot with his "jazz banjorine," that he
needed to come to terms with the proposition Ellison made about
all Americans: that he, too, was "somehow black." Stevens's Sick
Man never had to confront his black daddy, nor did Stevens ever
make reparations to Gwendolyn Brooks. And yet Stevens's Sick
Man is, at least metaphorically, as trapped as Crane's black man
in a cellar, waiting for the kind of music that liberated Invisible

Man, yearning for the "peaceful, blissful words, well-tuned, well sung, / well-spoken." Although the Sick Man does not find blissful words the way Ellison's Sunraider discovered his inner Bliss, Stevens did acknowledge in his poetry that some lost chords were waiting to be discovered. Responding to a chorus in "The Man With the Blue Guitar," who interrogates his obscure poetics by complaining, "You do not play things as they are," Stevens gives a reply that could apply to a poetics of jazz as much as it could serve as a manifesto for his own eccentric Americana: "But play, you must, / A tune beyond us, yet ourselves."

WAITING FOR LEROI

The music evoked in "For the Marriage of Faustus and Helen," "The Weary Blues," and "The Sick Man" is not really the same music at all. Crane's Dionysian self-removal, Hughes's twelve-bar lyricism, and Stevens's racial metaphor of conceit were all coming from radically different places, and there was no stable criterion for the music they described. Crane, to his credit, did cross racial lines somewhat: he spent much time with Jean Toomer (the African American writer who cited "Black Tambourine" as an influence on *Cane*) and apparently attended jazz performances. By the time Hughes was staging his poetry-to-jazz readings with Charles Mingus in 1957, the divides that kept Crane, Hughes, and Stevens from experiencing the same music were slowly dissolving—at least on the fringes of urban bohemia. By the 1950s, Lawrence Ferlinghetti and Kenneth Rexroth were staging poetry readings incorporating jazz in San Francisco, Allen Ginsberg, waxing poetic about "angel headed hipsters contemplating jazz," became an international celebrity with the "Howl" obscenity trial. There were white Beat and New York School poets who shared Crane's fascination with jazz such as

Jack Kerouac, but unlike Crane, they had access to a fully developed music and, most crucially, were witnessing the same performances as black poets and artists. One of those poets was then known as LeRoi Jones, as accomplished and promising a jazz critic as he was a jazz poet. Jones and Frank O'Hara sat at the same table the Five Spot in the East Village and each wrote about Billie Holiday and Miles Davis. Even if O'Hara's Holiday was not exactly serving the same purpose as Jones's, their poetic impressions were achieved through dialogue with the music.

The arrival of Jones announced that jazz poetry would no longer be a divided world of weary blues, "nigger cupids," and sick men. When he was in the Beat phase of his career, his musical heroes were black, but his poetic influences were not. "For me, Lorca, Williams, Pound, and Charles Olson have had the greatest influence," he wrote in 1960.[44] A few years later, he made this pronouncement: "There has never been an equivalent to Duke Ellington or Louis Armstrong in Negro writing; even the best of contemporary literature written by Negroes cannot yet be compared to the fantastic beauty of Charlie Parker's music."[45] This claim might seem outrageous, but it is not far from the Ellison-Murray juxtaposition of Mann, Malraux, and Eliot with Ellington, Basie, and Armstrong. Jones's most enduring work was on that music, and in his most prophetic piece of writing, the 1963 "Jazz and the White Critic," he issued a challenge to traditional modes of analysis of the music on sociological and methodological grounds. To understand jazz, he wrote, one needed to address the "socio-cultural philosophy of the Negro in America," but also, most crucially, one needed to look beyond notation to understand the nuance and cadence of the music:

> Strict musicological analysis of jazz, which has come into favor recently, is also as limited as a means of jazz criticism

as a strict sociological approach. The notator of any jazz solo, or blues, has no chance of capturing what in effect are the most important elements of the music. (Most transcriptions of blues lyrics are just as frustrating.) A printed musical example of an Armstrong solo, or of a Thelonious Monk solo, tells us almost nothing except the futility of formal musicology when dealing with jazz. Not only are the various jazz effects almost impossible to notate, but each note *means something* quite in adjunct to musical notation.[46]

Jones's attack on European musicology was revolutionary for its time, bringing up how it was only in the age of recording—the "incandescent wax" of Crane's Promethean poem—that this art form defying notation could be preserved at all. What he does not provide is an alternative to these traditional modes of analysis, but he implies that the subjective realm of poetry could be the only way to describe those elusive effects of Armstrong or Monk.

Jones may have been the interrogator of jazz and the white critic, but he had not necessarily given up on jazz and the white poet, at least not on the poets in his social circle. Frank O'Hara was one of the poets Jones mentioned as among the "many young wizards around now doing great things that everybody calling himself a poet can learn from" and Jones himself was central to O'Hara's "Personism: A Manifesto."[47] "It was founded by me after lunch with LeRoi Jones on August 27, 1959, a day in which I was in love with someone (not Roi, by the way, a blond)."[48] O'Hara contended that his new movement in poetry would "undoubtedly have lots of adherents," "may be the death of literature as we know it," and is "too new, too vital, a movement to promise anything. But it, like Africa, is on the way."[49] With Jones as editor and Africa as its model for an emerging space for literary colonizing, O'Hara speculates on a poetry with the immediacy of a phone call and the flicker of a movie screen. It is in this moment that O'Hara's jazz poem is born.

There is a theory that the word "jazz" is derived from an African word meaning "faster," but for O'Hara, the subjects of Miles Davis and Billie Holiday had the opposite effect.[50] O'Hara's style, which he dubbed his "I do this I do that" approach, was usually characterized by its brevity. From the late fifties onward, O'Hara's poetry exuded the nonchalance of the gay sex symbol, the dandy, the hipster, and Museum of Modern Art curator whose poems were, as the title of his 1964 *Lunch Poems* would suggest, dashed off while taking a break from wielding considerable cultural power. The sonnet and the lyric are mixed effortlessly with the diary and gossip column. Despite his often flippant sensibility ("Mary Desti's Ass," "Lana Turner Has Collapsed"), O'Hara was no stranger to the elegiac mode, memorializing everyone and everything from his Aunt Mary and Jackson Pollock to Sergei Rachmaninoff to his own feelings. But Miles Davis and Billie Holiday broke up the everyday rhythm of O'Hara's verse, and Jones's influence was surely central in helping him discover exactly what that meant.

Jones literally breaks into O'Hara's "Personal Poem" of August 28, 1959, the day of the lunch that brought "Personism" into the world. Meeting Jones for the meal that inspired a new poetics of idiosyncratic introspection, O'Hara's charting of social climbing is interrupted with some other news around 52nd Street:

> . . . Moriarty's where I wait for
> LeRoi and hear who wants to be a mover and
> shaker the last five years my batting average
> is .016 that's that, and LeRoi comes in
> and tells me Miles Davis was clubbed 12
> times last night outside BIRDLAND by a cop

The incident Jones reports to O'Hara exemplifies the tragedy and irony of the jazz mainstream. A few weeks earlier, on August 2, Columbia records had released *Kind of Blue*, which would go on to become the top-selling album in the history of jazz. Although only recorded in two unrehearsed sessions, *Kind of Blue* has a deceptive simplicity that tests the limits of criticism. Davis's playing is as sparse as it is intense. "So What" is built on two chords and a walking bass line; "Freddie Freeloader" is a standard twelve-bar blues; "All Blues" is a 3/4 version of one. But on all of them, Davis packs an orchestra's worth of emotion into a single note, sometimes repeating it with a pained, lonely control. Davis said that the album was built around the pianist Bill Evans, the only white member of Davis's band (who, incidentally, had already given his notice), though he went uncredited in their collaborations.[51] "So What," with its insouciant shrug, was a way of playing it cool, but in contrast to Hughes's motto of digging and being dug in return, Davis plays it cool with a "fuck you" subtext, an elegant anger played with a romantic sheen. This would not be a bad description of much of O'Hara's work.

On August 27, when Davis was headlining at Birdland, he refused a policeman's request to "move along," received those blows to the head, and a cause celebre was born. The poem ends with O'Hara shaking hands with Jones, and the tone immediately turns glib: he refuses to give a nickel for a terrible disease "because we don't like terrible diseases," but the guilt of Davis's clubbing haunts him as he wonders if "one person out of the 8,000,000 is / thinking of me as I shake hands with LeRoi." O'Hara does not engage with Miles Davis as an aesthetic in this poem, only as late-breaking news. But that news makes O'Hara think about his own predilections and their consequences, that he is against Lionel Trilling and Henry James but for Donald Allen and Herman Melville. He and his friends identify themselves with a particular aesthetic perspective, but the social world can violate the artist with a clubbing by a nightstick.[52] Hughes's Simple said that the sound of bebop was like nightsticks on the heads of his people. There was more to the music, of course, but on August 27, 1959, it was the sounds of those nightsticks that resounded the loudest.

It was in the same summer that the death of Billie Holiday would inspire O'Hara to write his most celebrated poem. Like "For the Marriage of Faustus and Helen," "The Day Lady Died" begins with the banal and ends with the sublime, from catching a train and grabbing a hamburger to memory, mortality, and a beauty that defies notation. The worship of Holiday as a camp diva is surely a factor in O'Hara's gaze, but the influence of LeRoi Jones cannot be far behind either. With his Miles Davis reference, the usually apolitical O'Hara recognizes that the racial divide can come crashing down on his bohemian circle. Billie Holiday makes O'Hara rethink his priorities, too, but in a more immediate way. When the poem begins, O'Hara is bitchy, name-dropping, balance-checking, and couch-surfing:

> I walk up the muggy street beginning to sun
> And have a hamburger and a malted and buy
> an ugly NEW WORLD WRITING to see what the poets
> in Ghana are up to these days.[53]

Just as O'Hara dismissed the "terrible diseases" for which the panhandler asked for a nickel in "Personal Poem" right after getting the news about Davis, and just as O'Hara flippantly pronounces that Personism, like Africa, "is on its way," he blanches at the trendiness of poetry in Ghana, almost anticipating Saul Bellow's query about the "Zulu Tolstoy" in the thick of the culture wars decades later.

But if O'Hara is indeed living in a hierarchical aesthetic

universe—he was, after all a curator at MOMA—after thumbing through Verlaine with Bonnard illustrations, the Lattimore
Hesiod translation, and yet another postcolonial racial reference
with Genet's *Les Negres*, he sees a headline, has a memory, and
rethinks his construction of culture:

> and I am sweating a lot by now and thinking of
> leaning on the john of the 5 SPOT
> while she whispered a song along the keyboard
> to Mal Waldron and everyone and I stopped breathing.[54]

Hart Crane and his Olympians might have been "breathless"
when his "nigger cupids" scoured the stars, but Billie Holiday
was a mythological figure made flesh for O'Hara. Sweating and
remembering leaning against the john at the legendary Five
Spot bathroom (musicians remember its smells wafting on to
the stage), O'Hara remembers an artistic experience that leaves
him breathless but not speechless. Though O'Hara had entered
Harvard with the ambition of becoming a concert pianist, Holiday's genius defied any analysis he could have picked up in
music-theory class. Jones, who would not write "Jazz and the
White Critic" for another four years, may have been trying out
his invective against musicological analysis of jazz on O'Hara,
whose six odes for Rachmoninoff included comparative pronouncements ("sometimes the 2nd symphony sounds like Pur-
cell"), pedagogical reverence ("Good / fortune, you would have
been my teacher, and I your only pupil"), and a basis for autobiographical cross-media ("My difficulty is / readily played—like a
rhapsody"). Holiday demands a different kind of trope altogether, and that is only one of the reasons why Jones wrote of
her in 1962, "Sometimes you are afraid to listen to this lady."[55]

The performance O'Hara attended is legendary. Although
O'Hara's frame of reference for jazz was always associated with

clubs (Birdland in "Personal Poem" and in "Bosch," with a description of a figure who "put his mediaeval pianist's hands / on the thighs of a contemporary romance / listening to Brubeck at Birdland"), Holiday had been barred from playing in them ever since she lost her cabaret card after a drug arrest in 1947. The night at the Five Spot was an impromptu illegal performance at a venue where Thelonious Monk had been holding court Tuesdays through Sundays and the poets would read on Mondays. This was a Monday, and while there are many performances of Holiday during this period, the most raw and intimate is on a bonus track on the Columbia/Legacy reissue of *Lady in Satin*, where Holiday is caught unawares singing "The End of a Love Affair" without the orchestral accompaniment of Ray Ellis, and in the raw a capella track, each note sounds like a struggle against gargled phlegm and an eviscerated larynx. The entire album, recorded in 1958, is a masterpiece of singing and a triumph of pure pathos over a debilitated voice, but her wrecked vocal chords add to the drama of delivery and confirm LeRoi Jones's assertion that notation will tell you absolutely nothing of the pity and fear evoked from Holiday's ravaged throat.[56]

Although "inspiration" literally means "to breathe in," to be full of the spirit of the muse, this experience deflates him, a brief detente in the struggle between jazz and poetry. After Crane's desire for transposition, Hughes's claim for cultural ownership, and Stevens's cultural divide, there was a brief moment when the most memorable poem about the most elusive of all jazz singers could have only been composed in a crossing over from the rarefied world of MOMA to the angry bard of Newark. Half a decade later, that bard would change his name from LeRoi Jones to Amiri Baraka and cast off O'Hara along with all of his other white literary cohorts. The movements he would participate in were part of his own career moves, political convictions, and

turbulence of his moment, but they would also inaugurate a poetics of separatism where racial crossings were no longer permitted. Hughes's weary blues could not be understood by Crane or
Stevens—and even Mingus wanted to hear other sounds. O'Hara
would die soon after Jones became Baraka, and the America the
latter chose to sing did not take kindly to outsiders.

PROVED UPON THE PULSES

After World War II, the Beats tried to live up to jazz in a style
that embodied what Hart Crane yearned for in his letter. In contrast to Crane, with his meticulous revisions, the Beats idealized
the rapture of the first draft. While Allen Ginsberg stopped to
admire "angel headed hipsters contemplating jazz" in the midst
of an expansive Whitmanian litany in *Howl*, Jack Kerouac, in his
"Essentials of Spontaneous Prose," took Ginsberg's dictum "First
thought, best thought" and made a manifesto out of it. In "Essentials of Spontaneous Prose" and "Belief & Technique of Modern Prose," Kerouac lays down the laws for no laws, a guide to
the unrehearsed. "No pause to think of proper word but the in-
fantile pileup of scatalogical buildup of words till satisfaction is
gained, which will turn out to be a great appending rhythm to a
thought and be in accordance with Great Law of Timing,"[57]
Kerouac says, attempting Joycean wordplay by substituting "scatalogical" for "scatological," evoking an Ella Fitzgerald vocal improvisation more than excrement with his heap of images. And
so, in the spirit of his perception of improvisation, he insists on
"no revisions (except obvious rational mistakes, such as names or
calculated insertions in act of not writing but inserting)."[58] Kerouac makes no distinction between a mediocre talent or a Charlie Parker in his manifestos. In fact, in his "Belief & Technique
For Modern Prose," Kerouac proclaims, "You're a genius all the

time,"[59] an effective self-help tool, to be sure, but how does such an affirmation work in practice?

He seems to contradict this adage when he asserts in his "240th Chorus" that Parker is "Musically more important then Beethoven, / Yet never regarded as such."[60] In his 239th Chorus, Parker's 1955 death allowed him to play King to his Milton, giving him a chance to write verse adding to the graffiti proclaiming "Bird Lives":

Charlie Parker looked like Buddha
Charlie Parker, who recently died
Laughing at a juggler on the TV
After weeks of strain and sickness,
Was called the Perfect Musician.
And his expression on his face
Was as calm, beautiful, and profound
As the image of the Buddha
Represented in the East, the lidded eyes,
The expression that says "All Is Well"
—This was what Charlie Parker
Said when he played.[61]

Kerouac found in Parker's face the visage of the Buddha himself—but surely such a close friend of William Burroughs, "Old Bull Lee" in *On the Road*, would recognize those lidded eyes not as mere Chinoiserie but the nodding out of a junkie. And what is that opiated Buddha of Avenue B emanating? "All is well." Kerouac's meditation on Parker is akin to Ginsberg roaming the supermarket aisles with Whitman, but just as Whitman, as John Hollander observed, "looks easy and proves hard," Parker's apparent expression of "all is well" was really the result of hard living and an even harder art. For a musician playing breakneck hours to support a heroin habit, trying desperately to provide for

a family, underappreciated in the music industry (a fact be-
moaned by Kerouac, but also one that added to his Beat street
cred), so volatile and unreliable he is barred from Birdland, the
club bearing his nickname, all would probably not seem well to
the subject of the poem. (When Parker made a legendary, tortured recording of "Lover Man" in 1946, he followed the session
by setting himself and a Los Angeles hotel lobby on fire.) But
even if all was not exactly well for Parker, all is apparently well
for Kerouac, transported by some fetishistic Buddha, taking
calm from the riffs of a misunderstood genius and the unintentional martyr for scores of hipsters.

One poet disturbed by Kerouac's calm in the face of Parker's
torment was Yusef Komunyakaa. "To many the Beat Movement
was nothing more than the latest minstrel show in town with the
new Jim Crow and Zip Coons, another social club that admitted
hardly any women or blacks," said Komunyakaa in an interview.
"Yet they said that Charlie Parker was their Buddha."[62] Komunyakaa also meditated at the Parker Bodhisattva, including Parker
in his text for the performance piece *Testimony*. Like O'Hara,
Komunyakaa is breathless over jazz, but he does not get the
wind knocked out of him. At the end of "The Day Lady Died,"
O'Hara is jolted after Holiday's death interrupts what would
have been a prosaic summer day in the Hamptons. But for Komunyakaa, the art form exemplified by Holiday *is* his priority.
Komunyakaa faces jazz dead on, not just as a venerated tenth
muse, but also as an integral aspect of his daily life.

Komunyakaa's poetry has drawn on everything from his Viet-
nam tour to his childhood on the bayou—when he was still an-
swering to his given name of James Willie Brown, Jr. Yet beyond
his stated indebtedness to Tennyson, Whitman, and M. B. Tolson, jazz has been his most salient aesthetic ideal. In the essay
"Shape and Tonal Equilibrium," Komunyakaa credits jazz itself

with giving him poetic license: "I learned from jazz that I could write anything into a poem."[63] In contrast to Kerouac's manifesto, though, Komunyakaa also acknowledges that learning how to write *anything* takes something. For any musician, superlative improvisation is only possible after long practice. Commenting on his 1998 collaboration with free-jazz saxophonist and composer John Tchicai for *Love Notes from the Madhouse*, Komunyakaa defined their project in contrast to 1950s hipsters:

> If you think about the 1950s, we think about the typical Beat scene. You know, somebody pounding on the bongos and basses and maybe there's a horn in the background. Black berets, specs, and turtlenecks. What happened there is that there was a kind of mutual disrespect. So, I wanted something that was the opposite of that. Of course, we began by rehearsing.[64]

Komunyakaa takes the craft of jazz as seriously as he takes his own, and, for him, the art evokes the kind of self-consciousness the Beats self-consciously avoided. In "February in Sydney," he attempts to match Dexter Gordon's lyrical tenor with his lines, and the process is wrenching. In stark contrast to Vernon Duke's idyllic "April in Paris," it is the wrong time in the wrong place:

> I emerge from the dark theatre,
> passing a woman who grabs her red purse
> & hangs it to her like a heart attack.
> Tremelo. Dexter comes back to rest
> behind my eyelids. A loneliness
> lingers like a silver needle
> under my black skin,
> as I try to feel how it is
> to scream for help with a horn.[65]

Komunyakaa's speaker is screaming for help socially and aesthetically, wounded by the racism and sexual fears of the patron, seeking solace in the cadences of Gordon's tenor, a comforting figure so internalized by the poet that he is resting behind his eyelids. The needle of the record player—evoking a syringe—pierces him, and he tries to become one with the horn's cathartic scream. Komunyakaa, who was married to the Australian novelist Mandy Sayer, picked up a slight Australian affect in his distinctive hybrid diction, but the no-good blues comes looking for him every time, even when it is February in Sydney. Like Invisible Man, the speaker of "February in Sydney" flees his racialized surroundings to inhabit the music itself as a refuge.

Jazz is also the standard bearer in "Twilight Seduction," although the sexual threat comes not from the insult of a woman clutching her purse but from a competition with the music itself. Komunyakaa puts himself into a sexualized cutting contest with Jimmy Blanton, the bass player with the Duke Ellington orchestra who pushed the instrument into center stage with his thumping quarter notes. Blanton revolutionized and liberated his instrument before dying at the absurdly young age of twenty-one, an achievement that produces more than a little performance anxiety in the speaker:

> Simply
> because Jimmy Blanton
>   died at twenty-one
>   & his hands on the bass
>
> still make me ashamed
>   to hold you like an upright
>   & a cross worked into one
> embrace.[66]

With art trumping experience, Komunyakaa wonders if his love-making can match the sensuous swing of Blanton. And yet Komunyakaa is aware of his own powers, too: "I tell myself the drum / can never be a woman, / even if her name's whispered / across skin," he writes, alluding to Ellington's mawkish poem "A Drum is a Woman." Komunyakaa may not be able to thump out those quarter notes on an upright and—as of the writing of the poem—was long past immortalizing himself at twenty-one, but he joins in Jayne Cortez's feminist critique of Ellington's lyric:

> your drum is not invisible
> your drum is not inferior to you
> your drum is a woman
> so don't reject your drum
> don't try to dominate your drum.[67]

Tweaking his musical deity, Komunyakaa dispenses with Ellington's metaphor altogether, implying that his own descriptions of musically driven sexuality can convey rhythm without violent objectification.

By the poem's end, the "Twilight Seduction" has given way to the night, and Komunyakaa expresses preference for the indeterminate crevices of the unseen. Like Stevens, who intoned in "Restatement of Romance" (*Ideas of Order*), "The night knows nothing of the chants of night. / It is what it is as I am what I am," Komunyakaa revels in darkness. He reclaims the color scorned by the woman in the club described in "Februrary in Sydney" and embraces its indeterminate mystery:

> because so much flesh
> is left in each song,
> because women touch themselves to know

where music comes from,
my fingers trace your lips to open up
the sky & let in
the night.[68]

Komunyakaa's music adapts the metaphors of Ellington's tones
and rhythms—while offering a critique of the imagery of "A
Drum Is a Woman"—and in so doing illuminates the mysteries
of the night, with all their musical and poetic inspirations and
erotic implications. Ellington, who called his memoir *Music Is
My Mistress*, also identified his art with sexual conquest, but it is
Komunyakaa's evocation of improvised seduction that conjures
up the closest words to Ellington's pitch. The image of the mistress would also appear in "Copacetic Mingus," in which Mingus's act of playing is described as "Running big hands down /
the upright's wide hips, / rocking his moon-eyed mistress / with
gold in her teeth."[69]

There was a craft to this seduction, of course, one that Mingus liked to boast about, a metaphor for the music that would
have wide appeal, not just for the poets, but the musicians themselves. For many poets, jazz has not only been an inspiration, but
a dare. Crane demonstrated more trepidation over "transpos[ing]
jazz into words" than toppling Eliot or Whitman, and eventually
dismissed his attempt as an "impotent" wish, as if the music itself were an aural form of Viagra. With a similarly fretful admiration, O'Hara uses Billie Holiday's performance at the Five
Spot not only as an elegy for the singer's death, but also as a
metaphor for his own waning fecundity, in which Holiday's
mere presence knocked the wind out of him. Langston Hughes
nerved himself up enough to pit his poetry against the volatile
genius of Charles Mingus. The poets did not always win the
cutting contest. Mingus's distaste for Langston Hughes's poetry

resulted in a jarring collaboration, with Mingus's avant-garde bowing undercutting Hughes's plain-spoken lines; Hart Crane's evocation of "open air jazz gardens" reveals much about jazz and the white imagination before it became codified in the age of mechanical reproduction; Wallace Stevens's poem about an imaginary union of white and black music exemplified his quest for the American Sublime while revealing his ignorance about interracial musical collaboration.

Perhaps some of the difficulty in transposing jazz into words has been that, as the musicologist Scott DeVeaux has observed, "There is no single working definition of jazz, no single list of musical characteristics."[70] Batting away terms like *swing* or *the blues* as perhaps knowable but not really definable, DeVeaux offers a counterattack to the repertory regimen inspired by Ellison. The most successful jazz poetry results when the music has been, in the words of Keats, "proved upon the pulses," when it has become so internalized, the poet no longer needs to transpose it at all. When the music of Ellington was proved upon Komunyakaa's pulses, he and Jayne Cortez versified dissents to "A Drum Is A Woman." But while Komunyakaa resisted calling music a mistress, Ellington spoke for many other musicians when he associated his art with illicit sex. Ellington's memoir was an allusion to his dictum: "Music is my mistress. She plays second fiddle to no one." Music as a mistress would prove an apt metaphor that would engage some of the musicians themselves when they put their names to their memoirs. For jazz memoirists, music would not only be a mistress, but the musicians would be pimps and prostitutes. That image would play second fiddle to no one.

I was fascinated by . . . the enticing walks of prostitutes and by the limping walks
affected by Negro hustlers, especially those who wore Stetson hats, expensive
shoes with well-starched overalls, usually with a diamond stickpin (when not in
hock) in their tireless collars as their gambling uniforms.
—RALPH ELLISON

4

LOVE FOR SALE

HUSTLING THE JAZZ MEMOIR

"All writers are selling somebody out," wrote Joan Didion. When
it comes to jazz autobiography, Didion's maxim is not just a
metaphor. Jazz may not have actually been born in the red-light
district of Storyville, but it certainly flourished there. The music's myths and legends have not strayed far from the oldest
profession—and when jazz musicians tell their own stories, selling somebody out is inevitable. The legendary New Orleans
trumpeter Buddy Bolden was never recorded, but he was remembered for playing "blues and all that stink music" in a sweaty,
crowded dive called Funky Butt Hall, back when prostitution in
Storyville was still the law of the land. By 1917, the vice squad
had shut down all of the red light districts around the time that
the Original Dixieland Jass Band was cutting "Tiger Rag"; jazz
recording began when Storyville went straight. For the record
industry, it was the beginning of a new era, but for Funky Butt
Hall, it was the end of one. The mythological figure of Bolden,
who probably contracted syphilis from one of those working
girls in Storyville, was, like Nietzsche, rendered catatonic from
the illness, spending his final years in a sanitarium.[1] "I thought I
heard Buddy Bolden shout, open up the window and let the foul
air out," Jelly Roll Morton sang in his "Funky Butt Blues."[2]

It is a long way from Funky Butt Hall to Jazz at Lincoln Center, and yet the canonizing of jazz cannot fully fumigate the bad air of the music's origins. "It was the good music that came from the bell of Old Bad Air's horn that counted. Old Bad Air is still around with his music and his dancing and his diversity, and I'll be up and around with mine" (*IM*, 581), wrote Ralph Ellison on the final page of *Invisible Man*. Ellison also wrote of his childhood fascination with pimps and prostitutes, and when *Invisible Man*'s narrator is mistaken for the hustler Rinehart, it is not entirely a bad thing. Ellison may have influenced what many critics consider to be a conservative jazz canon, but he also introduced a method for separating the dancer from the dance, taking the prostitute and the pimp out of their milieu to admire their style, just as the young Ralph Waldo did on the streets of Oklahoma City. Identifying the sharp-dressed man ordering the tricks as just another trickster, Ellison's Rinehart justified the pimp as an aesthetic phenomenon. A hundred years after Bolden's lines were first heard down Perdido Street, a 2001 *New York Times* article by the historian Robin D. G. Kelley praised Miles Davis's "pimp aesthetic" while offering the qualification, "I'm not suggesting that he needed to be a real pimp to embrace the aesthetic."[3]

The truth is, though, that Davis *had* been a real pimp, a trade that was also a temporary gig for Louis Armstrong (whose mother and first wife were prostitutes), Jelly Roll Morton, and Charles Mingus, whose pimp stories dominate his autobiography. *Miles: the Autobiography*, published after 1970s blaxploitation and 1980s gangsta rap, showed the pimp's swagger, revealing that by the 1990s pimping could only give you bragging rights in the publishing industry.[4] Like most jazz autobiographies, Davis's book is ghostwritten, a largely suspect litany of myths, half-truths, and unsubstantiated claims. "I had a whole stable of bitches working the street for me," Davis recalls in his autobiography, even if his most reliable biographer, John Szwed, was not so sure how active Davis actually was in the procurement business. Charles Mingus had similarly dubious accounts of his own role as a pimp, and his extravagant sexual exploits—including turning out adoring girlfriends on the streets and squiring twenty-three Mexican whores in a single night—are doubted by those who knew him best. Billie Holiday, meanwhile, had a similar mixture of shame and fascination with the life, remembering her degradation but still admiring the clothes. "All the big time whores wore big red velvet hats then with bird-of-paradise feathers on them," she recalled before setting up some particularly grisly anecdotes about her underage sexual exploitation.[5] In *Lady Sings the Blues*, Holiday recalls first hearing the music of Louis Armstrong at Alice Dean's whorehouse. "A lot of white people first heard jazz in places like Alice Dean's, and they helped label jazz 'whorehouse music,'" Holiday writes (*LSB*, 10).

When Davis, Mingus, and Holiday put their names on these books, they were practicing literary versions of the hustle. Davis and Holiday each claimed they never read their own autobiographies, and Mingus, who lamented that his heavily edited autobiography was whitewashed, also said that he filled his book with implausible sexual exploits and other tall tales to "make a pile of money." Jazz autobiography is a genre of streetwalking on many levels, paying the bills while the musicians practice their more "authentic" art. When Billie Holiday sang "Fine and Mellow," no one doubted that she put her entire being into every tortured phrase. When she put her name on *Lady Sings the Blues*, knowing readers were aware that the book was ghostwritten by William Dufty, and the *New York Post* editor filed copy chock full of tabloid fodder and lurid tell-all.

From the perspective of textual scholarship, jazz autobiography is the red-light district of African American narrative. Many contemporary critical perspectives, however, embrace such seed-iness. Among them is that of the "pimpologist," who, following the spirit of Ellison and his creation of Bliss Proteus Rinehart, explores an underworld profession that has become a cultural fetish. "If a pimp is what you wanna be, / You're gonna have to learn pimpology," says the rapper Too $hort. There are many places to start. Since 1999, three documentaries, *American Pimp*, *Pimps Up/Ho's Down*, and *Pimpology* have appeared to glowing reviews, with cult followings that are equal parts lurid fascina-tion and ironic admiration. It is a long way from the 1931 publi-cation of *The Second Oldest Profession*, when its case studies of the "Negro Pimp" were recounted with shame by white street-walkers.[6] When Hamlet tells Polonius, "Sir, you are a fishmon-ger," or Middleton's Courtesan complains that "[o]ur pimp's grown proud," the pimp was a Renaissance put-down. Today, Iceberg Slim's 1969 *Pimp* remains a cult classic and terms like "mack daddy" and "big pimp" have become tongue-in-cheek honorifics.

The jazz memoirists, on the cusp between shame and cultural fascination, play both sides of the game. Ellison showed that the zoot-suited numbers runner could be a figure of ironic pride, but hip hop culture has changed exactly how the black procurer is li-onized, demonized, and fetishized. Hearing how jazz musicians told their own stories of the game—or told those stories to ghostwriters, transcribers, and heavy-handed editors—not only provides a glimpse of the transformation from fishmonger to mack daddy over the course of the twentieth century, but also of the precarious and liminal place jazz continues to hold in Amer-ican culture. *Lady Sings the Blues* has more pages about the house of ill repute where Billie Holiday first heard Louis Armstrong and Bessie Smith than it does on how she took their musical examples and transformed them into a distinctive vocal style. And Mingus's memoir says much more about his sexual prowess—as both the handler and the rapacious lover—than it does about the mixed-race teenage prodigy in Watts stealing away from the streets to study twelve-tone harmony. What Billie Holiday was aware of in 1956—not as an author, but as a businesswoman— holds even more true in the twenty-first century: turning tricks tells a more compelling story than practicing scales. There are more accounts of black pimping in early twenty-first-century America than there are of black virtuosity. Ellison's Rinehart taught us that the pimp persona can itself be a finely honed art, but the distinction between the musical dedication of Billie Holiday, Charles Mingus, and Miles Davis and the swagger and strut of the streets is one that is understood less and less every day. We read jazz memoirs in search of the artist beneath the ghostwritten hype—to hear the music beneath the hustle.

"ONLY SLIGHTLY SOILED"

I guess I'm not the only one who heard their first good jazz in a whorehouse.
—BILLIE HOLIDAY

Lady Sings the Blues is the bane of Billie Holiday scholars, but a source of endless fascination for the fan, the fetishist, and most of all, the intrepid pimpologist. Ghostwriter William Dufty circulated many half-truths, unsubstantiated claims, and outright fabrications in the book, and many of the tapes and transcriptions that supposedly provided the basis for it have never materialized. Holiday was apparently unwilling or unable to write it, and Dufty's book should be read more as an engrossing account of the manufacturing of Holiday's image than as a reliable source of information.[7] Nevertheless, none of Holiday's official biogra-

phers dispute that Lady Day was a working girl. Indeed, Stuart
Nicholson's research reveals that she was an even younger working girl than the already lurid accounts offered in Dufty's book.[8]
Dufty narrates Holiday's teenage prostitution as though in a
pulp novel, and the effect is as exploitive and calumnious as it is
compulsively readable. Although Holiday is credited with composing a few of the standards in her repertoire—"Fine and Mellow," "Billie's Blues," and the lyrics to "God Bless the Child,"
"Don't Explain," and "Lady Sings the Blues"—her art can usually be found less in composition than in interpretation. When it
comes to her reading of the great American songbook, it is she
who is imposing her experience on material written by others.
When it comes to recounting her experiences, however, she de-
fers agency to her ghostwriter. Holiday-Dufty made much of
her claim that she first heard the music of Bessie Smith and
Louis Armstrong at Miss Dean's whorehouse. However clichéd
the sentiment or ghostwritten the prose, the statement ought
not be denied.

There is no better evidence of the musical impact of Holiday's
whorehouse experiences—first as a Victrola listener, then as a
working girl—than her 1952 recording of Cole Porter's "Love
for Sale."[9] Porter originally wrote the prostitute's melancholy
sales pitch for the 1930 revue *The New Yorkers*, in which the
sight of the tepid white vocalist Kathryn Crawford hawking "ap-
petizing young love for sale" inspired *World* drama critic Charles
Darnton to attack the number as "filthy" and "in the worst possible taste."[10] Within a year, Porter replaced her with the biracial
Elisabeth Welch and reset the scene from Reuben's to the Cot-
ton Club. Welch, who would go on to a decades-long cabaret career, described Porter's song as "a street cry," recalling, "I always
had a sympathy for prostitutes. I knew some in Paris. They make
me cry."[11] Welch's own affinity for the material and Porter's racial

crossing helped make the song palatable for an audience more comfortable with prostitution as a black thing.

Holiday's own experiences, or at least the stories that are told about them, evoke the same pathos that inspired Welch, but Holiday goes beyond Welch's sympathy into empathy. With Holiday, the artist and subject are one, infusing the song's deft bravado with a haunting vulnerability. Holiday, singing over Oscar Peterson's rubato chords with no other instruments to cushion the wear and tear of her voice, sneers Porter's couplet, "Love that's sweet and unspoiled / Love that's only slightly soiled," and the crack in her voice on "slightly" reveals a fissure that the performance reopens. The words and music may belong to Porter, but the experience is Holiday's alone. As Holiday's cabaret confessional progresses, Peterson's accompaniment moves to a more rhythmically steady stride, but her voice is no less vulnerable. The sexual syncopation of swing is brought to elegiac slow motion as the experience of putting her life on display deepens the ennui. "If you want the thrill of love / I've been through the mill of love," Holiday snarls, with the cleverness of the line all but swallowed up by bitterness. This recording does not feature Holiday's voice at its most ravaged—it was seven years before her death, and six before the string-drenched last will and testament of *Lady in Satin*—but it is weathered enough, already at the point where the question is no longer, "Will she hit every note?" but, "What note will she choose?" or, finally, "Why should she bother?" A conversational sigh meant more than pitch for the late-period Lady Day. At this point in her career, Holiday was aware that her self-destruction was part of her theater.

On that 1952 recording, Holiday's own experience defines the performance more than Porter's words and music, and it is difficult not to conflate it with her case history of teen (or, if Nicholson is to be believed, preteen) prostitution in *Lady Sings the*

Blues. These stories can only be read through the filter of Dufty, but as Holiday's account of selling her wares is given in the pugnacious voice of her memoir, she is somewhere behind the scenes silently giving her stamp of approval to the product. In a few pages, Holiday, at thirteen, first sees prostitution as a chance to escape life as a domestic. "I had my chance to become a strictly twenty-dollar call girl—and I took it" (*LSB*, 23), she first observes, only to realize quickly, "I didn't have what it took to be a call girl. In the first place, and for damn good reason, I was scared to death of sex" (*LSB*, 24). Holiday's reasons are "damn good," indeed. In *Lady Sings the Blues*, she says she had already survived molestation from a relative and rape from a neighbor. This money was anything but easy. Indeed, it was such excruciatingly painful work, she was almost relieved when she was eventually hauled off to jail.

These stories, like the accounts of physical abuse, drug addiction, dashed love affairs, and future prison sentences that follow in the book, can only be deciphered through decoding the layers of ventriloquism involved in the storytelling itself, leaving her readers to wonder who is doing the selling out. When Holiday sings Porter's words and makes them hers, her experience trumps his lyrics. When her story is filtered through a ghostwriter, however, her own agency in the exploitation of her image comes into question. On November 10, 1956, Verve recorded selections from *Lady Sings the Blues* during a concert at Carnegie Hall. The excerpts included accounts of how Holiday arrived at her vocal style, but are ultimately slanted toward descriptions of the whorehouse where she picked it up. Yet for reasons that remain unclear, the selections are read not by Holiday, but by Gilbert Millstein, a book reviewer and editor who was best known for helping to make Jack Kerouac famous with a rave review of *On the Road* in the *New York Times Book Review*. "This is Billie

Holiday's story," Millstein says, sounding like the "Voice of Doom" from the film noir classic *Naked City*. It is jarring to hear Millstein speak for Holiday with his noir affectations and dead-pan delivery:

> Mom and Pop were just a couple of kids when they got married. He was eighteen, she was sixteen. I was three. I was a woman when I was six [*sic*], big for my age with big breasts, big bones, a big fat healthy broad . . . Alice Dean used to keep a whorehouse on the corner nearest our place, and I used to run errands for her and the girls. When it came time to pay me, I used to tell her she could keep the money if she'd let me come up in her front parlor and listen to Louis Armstrong and Bessie Smith on her victrola. I guess I'm not the only one who heard their first good jazz in a whorehouse.   (Verve 314 517658-2)

A 1950s white man reciting irony-free lines about having "big breasts" and being a "big healthy broad" on stage at Carnegie Hall (this was not played for laughs like Milton Berle in drag) was making quite a leap. But what is most astonishing about this recording is the way it changes crucial details and misleadingly strings together sections from Dufty's book to emphasize even further Holiday's connection to the whorehouse. In the book, Holiday/Dufty include many childhood anecdotes after the opening describing her parents' marriage when she was three, and her admission, "I was a woman when I was sixteen" (*LSB*, 9), comes four pages later. In Millstein's performance for the benefit of a Carnegie Hall audience and future record listeners, he discusses her burgeoning sexuality in the sentence that follows "I was three," skipping the latency period altogether. He also changes her age from "sixteen" to "six," announcing, "I was a woman when I was six." Beating Stuart Nicholson's muckraking of Holiday's role in the child sex trade by a few decades, Millstein's version of the line makes her "big breasts" sound anatomically implausible and transforms "Billie Holiday's Story" into a pedophile's fantasy.

Holiday hovered somewhere in the background, hearing "Billie Holiday's story" narrated through the filter of two white journalists. While warming up to sing her first song, did she notice that the rate of her sexual development was accelerated by a decade? If she had, would she have even cared? "The singer herself was concerned with only two things," Nicholson claimed— "money and publicity."[12] The 1956 Carnegie Hall performance by Holiday and Millstein did not get in the way of either, leaving unanswered questions of agency and autonomy. Who is the prostitute and who is the pimp? Is Billie behind the scenes pimping her horrors while she relaxes between numbers, or is she prostituting her story with these two men? All we know is that Holiday's life is up for sale, with Dufty's prose and Millstein's voice doing the bidding.[13]

Holiday's art is above all of this, but her genius can only be found as she makes an intensely personal statement through, most of the time, the writing of others. In this respect, defining what makes Holiday significant exhausts the supply of similes and metaphors writers generally dole out in place of any empirical system. Whitney Balliett, for example, wrote that Holiday's voice in the 1950s "gave the impression of being pushed painfully in front of her, like a medicine ball."[14] Francis Davis called her simply "our lady of sorrows."[15] With a thin tone and limited vocal range—which became more limited as her emotional range deepened—Holiday's art would have gone unrecognized without recording. Listeners who would never dare to self-destruct so spectacularly, or, if they did, could never express the experience with such eloquence, marvel at how she takes Tin Pan Alley and adapts it to her own sense of time, whether she's nodding off, sounding off, or licking her wounds. Elizabeth Hardwick associated her with insomnia, Frank O'Hara with poetic asphyxiation. Even Amiri Baraka, a man not easily intimidated, remarked, "Sometimes you are afraid to listen to this lady."

Holiday did not navigate her way through the multiple octaves of the great Sarah Vaughan, the scat dialectics of Ella Fitzgerald, or the associative audacity of Betty Carter. She did not need to; hers was an art that needed no technical dexterity to justify its liberties. If there was an Icarus-like price to be paid for this gift, it was not only the ravages of drug addiction and romantic warfare, but the amount of exploitation she underwent to put herself out there, body and soul. *Lady Sings the Blues*, whoever is responsible for narrating it, conflates and confuses the boundary between exploitation and performance. A dozen pages after Holiday recalled how her first sexual encounter was "rugged enough to finish me off men for a while," the ever prescient John Hammond puts Holiday in front of a microphone. Eighteen and terrified, Holiday's resistance to mechanical reproduction assumes phallic proportions:

When we got there and I saw this big old microphone, it scared me half to death. I'd never sung in one and I was afraid of it. Nobody was wise to how scared I was except Buck, of the famous team of Buck and Bubbles, who was around for that session. Buck dug what was the matter with me and tried to snap me out of it.

"Don't let these white folks see you get scared," he begged me. "They'll be laughing at you." He finally got me to stand near it, told me I didn't have to look at it or even sing into it, just stand near it. He was getting nowhere until

he started to shame me, telling me I didn't have the nerve
to go through with it.   (*LSB*, 37)

"Buck" is Buck Washington, the vaudeville performer, pianist
and nominal leader on the date, who, just three days earlier, had
also accompanied Bessie Smith fearlessly growling "Do Your
Duty" into the same microphone. Nervously warbling "Your
Mother's Son in Law," Holiday had not learned yet to give fear
in return. As she sang a song about eagerly ensnaring a man and
grasping too tightly, she sounded as though (as Ethel Waters put
it) "her shoes were too tight."[16] The recording studio reversed
the racial dynamics of Florence Williams's whorehouse, where
Billie felt more at ease with the white clients:

> With my regular white customers, it was a cinch. They had
> wives and kids to go home to. When they came to see me it
> was wham, bang, they gave me the money and they were
> gone. I made all the loot I needed. But Negroes would keep
> you up all the damn night, handing you that stuff about "Is
> it good, baby?" and "Don't you want to be my old lady?"
>
> (*LSB*, 25)

This is either a genuine memory of Holiday's or a white Negro
fantasy of Dufty's. Either way, the memoir shows that no matter
how fast young Elenora Fagan grew up, by the time she was a legal eighteen, she had renamed herself Billie Holiday but was still
scared of the microphone. Unlike her call-girl days, when she
claimed her preference for white customers—and even ended up
in prison for refusing to service a black man who happened to
have police connections—she found racial solidarity in her new
profession, initiated by a fellow black performer into one of the
first integrated ensembles in the history of American recording.

Holiday said she was happy to get $35 for the gig. It was a new kind of hustle, and by the time the anecdote made it into *Lady Sings the Blues*, she was more shrewd at how to profit from it. By 1956, a white man was working for her byline, and that microphone was no longer so scary.

But the jazz-conservatory training Billie received at Alice Dean's—where she had her first listen to Bessie and Louis and worked her way through the mill of love—never fully left her. She was on the arm of violent pimps and hustlers in her later years, including the thuggish John Levy, brutal enough to fit the masochistic lyrics of "My Man" ("He isn't true / He beats me, too / Oh, my man, I love him so") and meet the standard she once explained she needed for a relationship: "To suit me a man has got to be dominating at all times."[17] With chapter titles named for Holiday songs, *Lady Sings the Blues* blurred the lines between Holiday's songbook and a litany of tumultuous love affairs, run-ins with the law, life on and off heroin, and the perpetual stabs at artistic longevity for the failed call girl. Beyond the ghostwriting and the great American songbook, there is still Holiday herself. Between childhood exploitation and middle-aged martyrdom, she reclaimed her sexuality and spread the word. On "Swing, Brother, Swing," recorded for an air-check with the Count Basie Orchestra in 1937, the twenty-two-year-old Holiday sounds all but invincible, accenting each syllable with a percussive relentlessness. "There ain't nothing gonna hold me down," insists the young, lusty Holiday, spurred on by a Basie band pulsing out quarter notes in hypnotic, lascivious syncopation. After rhapsodizing about the "hot rhythm," she hollers to Basie's drummer, "Come on, kill me, Jo"—a death wish as intoxicating as it was prophetic.[18] Three years before that prophecy was fulfilled under police guard in Metropolitan Hospital, the ghostwritten Holiday reminded us that, as much as she was making a commodity out of her blues, she still "didn't have what it took to be a real call girl." Nonetheless, Holiday's stock was low when she died three years after her memoir's publication—with only $854 to her name—but the posthumous Billie Holiday quickly became a hot property. After she became a martyr, sales of her book, along with her entire recorded output, sky-rocketed. They have never been out of print. "If you want to buy my wares / Climb with me onto the stairs," sang Holiday on "Love for Sale." It is a trick that keeps on turning.

BASS INSTINCTS

> When a young up and coming man reaches out to prove himself, boss pimp, it's making it. That's what it meant where I come, from—proving you're a man."
> "And when you proved it what did you want?"
> "Just to play music, that's all."
>   —CHARLES MINGUS, *Beneath the Underdog*

At the end of *Beneath the Underdog*, Charles Mingus imagines a conversation with the late trumpeter Fats Navarro. When the subject turns to Mingus's pimping days, Navarro's interest is at its most acute. "Mingus, you start telling about me your book and you gonna write then you modulate and go into something completely else. . . . But you got me so interested in your bitches and whores where you coulda made a million, I want you to go on and tell me that."[19] Navarro should not have worried. Even after *Beneath the Underdog* was trimmed from an unwieldy 875 pages to a more manageable 366, Mingus's tales of his life as "boss pimp" were sharpened, expanded, and chiseled into a com-mercially viable prose. The real Navarro, who died at the age of twenty-six in 1950, did not live to see Mingus achieve recogni-tion as perhaps the most significant jazz composer after Duke Ellington, and he certainly could not have imagined that it could be possible to make a million selling the pimp's image. Before anyone could see Mingus's manuscript, it had assumed a legendary status. When its title was changed from *Memoirs of a Half Yellow Schitt Covered Nigger* to *Beneath the Underdog*, most critics of the finished product assumed that in the editing process its content was likewise "whitened up beyond repair," distilled into "weak tea,"[20] and that Mingus's mack-daddy strut must have surely been slowed down. But while much of his memoir ended up on the cutting-room floor, the pimp stories survived, making them assume an even greater proportion of the memoir than Mingus had intended. He had been toiling over his manuscript for more than a decade, and by the time he relented to Nel King's edits for a 1971 book, he had become so financially desperate that he conceded to her suggestions. Besides, pimp stories had suddenly become good for business. Iceberg Slim's lurid *Pimp*, marketed as "autobiographical fiction" by the independent publisher Holloway House in 1969, could not stay on the shelves, eventually selling over two million copies worldwide. Mingus had claimed he resorted to pimping in lean times, but by 1971 nasty stories of the sex trade could provide material for a potboiler.

When it comes to sexual exploits, *Beneath the Underdog* is dismissed by many of Mingus's friends and intimates as dubious. The book's subtitle, "His World as Composed by Mingus," should direct readers against taking him too literally when he describes his superhuman sexual stamina (and tendency to make his lovers pass out from sheer exhaustion) or his reputation as a bad-ass pimp. But while the book may be "composed by" Mingus, it does not exaggerate his musical achievements—if anything it glosses over them to make room for a portrait of the artist as a young pimp. Mingus was not confined by periods or movements in jazz. He was the only major figure to emerge from the bebop era to look back and develop the orchestral revolutions brought about by Ellington and Strayhorn, the New Orleans polyphony of Jelly Roll Morton, even the cadences and shouts of the gospel church, and weave them into something idiosyncratic, strange, and vital. When most bebop musicians were trying to emulate Charlie Parker's breakneck flights on a single melodic line, Mingus was thumping behind him while also thinking in multiple voices (much as he later composed his memoir with multiple selves). The blues holler of "Eat that Chicken," the civil rights invective of "Fables of Faubus," the neurotic orchestral sweep of *The Black Saint and Sinner Lady* (the only jazz album with liner notes from the artist's psychiatrist, also a major player in the memoir), and the enduring elegy of his ode to Lester Young, "Goodbye Porkpie Hat," should provide sufficient bragging rights for a legendary story. It is compelling enough to contemplate how a mixed-race kid from Watts was able to develop a powerful, percussive, and rigorous bass technique without having to resort to apocryphal pimp stories. While composing his own life, however, Mingus did not spend much time describing his distinctive and harmonically challenging compositions.

The music Mingus produced was enough for a legendary life story, but unlike Duke Ellington, whose ghostwritten *Music is My Mistress* is a charming series of triumphs with its nasty words carefully hidden beneath a regal veneer, Mingus foregrounds the violence, including an on-stage knife fight with Ellington trombonist Juan Tizol that earned him the distinction of being the first musician fired from Ellington's band. From stays in Bellevue to failed large-scale compositions, Mingus spent much of his time railing against the white man, lamenting jazz's marginal status, and trying with varying degrees of success to take matters into his own hands. In the spirit of Ellison, who had claimed that jazz was already an "institution," Mingus used his expulsion from venerable institutions (especially the ensemble of his idol, Ellington) and his experience in less illustrious ones (Belleveue's psychiatric ward, inspiring "Hellvue at Bellvue") to use whatever means he could to push jazz in his own image. He started his own record labels, wrote a letter of protest to President Eisenhower insisting that jazz musicians be eligible for unemployment insurance (to sweeten the deal, Mingus offered to play a gig at the White House pro bono), and tried to start a school, a project that ended with an eviction that was preserved for all time for television cameras and Tom Reichman's 1968 documentary.[21] Mingus felt certain he was above it all, writing to the critic Nat Hentoff from Bellevue that he'd had enough of the degrading business of jazz. Winning *Down Beat*'s Best Bass Player poll year after year was meaningless to him. He wanted to be Bartok, wanted to have some dignity—wanted, in short, to be canonical.

It would have been difficult for Mingus to inflate his musical significance in *Beneath the Underdog*, and he does not even bother. Like Billie Holiday in 1956, the Mingus of 1971 knew that musical genius was not enough to sell books, and after a late-sixties hiatus from music—including the hospital stay and a stint as a photographer—he was ready to sell an edited version of his life story. His widow and executor, Sue Mingus, says there are more than fifteen hours of tape of Mingus talking about his music—surely enough material for an alternative musical autobiography. *Underdog* does have fleeting stream-of-consciousness descriptions of a Charlie Parker jam session here, a conversation with the pianist Art Tatum there. But for the most part, the music provides the backdrop to a sexual cutting contest with the always menacing white man. Norman Mailer thinks jazz is orgasm? This book provides pages of orgasms, along with enough phallic presence to confirm any White Negro's assumptions of black-male sexual superiority and violent rage. But Mingus provides these excursions within a psychoanalytic framework. The Mingus of *Beneath the Underdog* is not only a boss pimp, he is a neurotic, self-reflective boss pimp. Lying on his analyst's couch recounting his sexual transactions with enough guilt and stream-of-consciousness reveries to fill several sessions for Alexander Portnoy, *Beneath the Underdog*'s Mingus is the lover, the mad-man, and the poet rolled into one. The book's carnal foreground-ing was an idea after Mingus's heart. "He wanted to be a pimp, he wanted to be a gangster, he wanted to be a musician, he wanted to be a great lover. And, you know, he considered himself all of these people," said the drummer Dannie Richmond. Note the order of significance. Richmond was Mingus's favorite drum-mer, the most malleable with respect to the twists and turns of Mingus's idiosyncratic rhythms. If he was as insightful into Min-gus's identity preferences as he was to his use of quarter notes, then *Underdog*'s pimp-heavy structure makes sense.

Most of the pre-edited typescript is in the form of rambling dialogue, a mode that came naturally to Mingus. (In his memoir, Miles Davis recalled becoming so exasperated with Mingus's in-cessant rambling on a road trip he threatened to break a bottle over his head.) Many of the prose passages do not appear until Nel King's second edit, and one of the passages certainly added at the eleventh hour is the description of Mingus's pimp cousin, who eventually comes to be called Billy Bones. In Mingus's an-notated typescript, he meets his pimp cousin without much fan-fare, showing up with his girlfriend Ina, whose love for Mingus is so profound she lets him turn her out on the streets for his first pimp job. Their dialogue is more or less preserved in the fi-nal version, although the girlfriend becomes Donnalee, named for Charlie Parker's tune. Billy Bones is given added descriptions that tell of his extravagant fashion, bank account, and charisma. In the post–Iceberg Slim era, Random House and Nel King needed to flesh out the pimp and hustle him:

> On the street, he wore expensive, proper clothes, appropriate for the San Francisco climate, and walked around in hundred-dollar Stetson shoes. He lived a kingly life, like a man on a continuous vacation with interruptions to see his florists or talk to his chef or instruct his brokers. He was perfectly at home with people of any financial or social position or any color and his attitude was, "We're all at the top of the Mark together. I can afford it and I assume you can too." He could afford anything because he was the Black Prince of Pimps and called my boy cousin and he was waiting at the airport in San Francisco.   (*BU*, 235)

For the Mingus of the early 1950s, such extravagance would have still been somewhat exotic. Even though he had already played behind Lionel Hampton, Duke Ellington, and Louis Armstrong, the work was not always steady in those journeyman years. He turned down a job at the post office to tour with Charlie Parker (who subsequently stiffed him for drug money), and was still taking on demeaning day jobs just to keep the wolves at the door. Just as the Billie Holiday of *Lady Sings the Blues* coveted the prostitute's feathered hat and swore off cleaning homes forever, Mingus looked on that "black prince of pimps" with his Stetson shoes with awe. This admiring description occurs only shortly after Mingus is tormented over turning his girlfriend out for tricks. "To be a pimp, one would have to lose all feelings, all sensitivity, all love. One would have to die! Kill himself! Kill all feeling for others in order to live with himself. Not to think. To keep going because you're already going. Mingus couldn't be this . . . a pimp" (*BU*, 212). It did not take long for Mingus to conclude otherwise—even to find that the pimp persona only added luster to his own. It is unclear whether this last-minute additional description of Billy Bones was in Mingus's own voice or the insertion of Nel King, approximating the streetwalker worship of Iceberg Slim, with Random House trailing behind Holloway House in search of another bestseller. The artist and the moralist are horrified. The pimpologist is intrigued. The publisher rubs its hands with glee. For a book that makes a principled turn away from the life, it also spends a fair amount of time gazing at it longingly, reveling in its minutiae for nearly a third of the completed text.

The Mingus of *Beneath the Underdog* thinks Billy Bones is a genius, but Billy Bones is really an invention of Mingus himself. Until Ellison's book came along in 1952, a figure like Rinehart the Runner had never been rendered into such a protean novelistic trope. Until Iceberg Slim's book came along in 1969—and when Iceberg Slim was still going by Robert Beck, he overlapped with Ellison at Tuskegee—no literary blockbuster had been entirely pimp-driven. Mingus put himself more in the Ellison camp, drawing clear distinctions between the struggle of the artist and the easy money of the hustler. When Mingus is under the sway of Billy Bones, he renders him into a Stetson-hatted sage: "You think your bass player is a genius? My Billy is the genius. He once got high and read three entire law books in two weeks—he only slept a few hours a day. When he finished he told me 'Reading is just like conversation. Once you realize that, you can remember it all'" (*BU*, 244). When Mingus describes his own musical affinity and ability to keep up with Ellington, Tatum, and Parker shortly after learning how to "slap that bass" and study his share of Bartok, Schoenberg, and Stravinsky, there is recorded evidence to back up this claim. These tales of Billy

Bones may be the kinds of folk legends Mingus heard about the most well-heeled hustlers, but these are claims that are harder to substantiate. What makes it difficult to sort out the history and mythmaking in *Beneath the Underdog* is Mingus's tendency to leave the recorded realm of music to get to the belt-buckle notches of his own sexual conquests. One of the book's few descriptions of musical craft as detailed as its descriptions of sexual technique occurs early on, when Mingus is first given that lesson from Buddy Collette. "Play it with the cover on," advises Joe Comfort, the bassist referred by Collette, assuring him that if he practices his instrument in the case, by the time he takes it out, his slaps will resound even more powerfully. "When you take it out, there's nothing to it" (*BU*, 70). It is an astonishing metaphor. The young Mingus is trying to find his way into experience, with the barriers only making him stronger. Once the bass is out of the case, he is unstoppable.

This passage is followed by some graphic sexual advice from Collette's father, who instructs him on the fine art of foreplay. After assuring Mingus about the "sweets" a girl wants and how a man must hold back and tease her until she begs for it, Pop Collette likens the act to a commercial transaction, and implies that if Mingus follows his advice, he will have a bright future as a fancy man: "Now, Charles, you try that on the next little girl you get. Watch the difference to her response. See if she don't tell you these very words: 'Charles, I never had it done to me like that in my life!' And see if you don't want to pay me fifty to one hundred dollars for the results you get" (*BU*, 74). This father-son parallel is amusing—and was even said to be the basis of a 1980s sex manual—but the latter lesson almost cheapens the earlier one. Sure, Mingus is embracing the flesh, a libidinous romantic with a hustler's ambition. But it does not take long for Mingus, learning to be a genius musician and, according to his street-corner bragging, a genius lover, to be given cynical advice from an older figure, not unlike the grandfather of *Invisible Man*, who advises the young narrator to "undermine 'em with grins." In world of sex and money, Mingus's gifts must be subordinated to the market, and if he follows the advice of the Collettes, learning about love and music has already become an act of prostitution. This conflation comes at the expense of why Mingus was compelling in the first place—his music. Plenty of men have internalized the kind of advice Pop Collette gave to Mingus. But Mingus alone was able to free that instrument from its case and do what he did with it. If this sounds sexual, it is, but the sexual metaphor is also an attempt to make Mingus's creative process comprehensible to a titillated audience. The sexual advice is generic; the music lesson is idiosyncratic.

Toward the end of the book, Mingus makes a dramatic renunciation of the pimping game, but the lesson of Billy Bones is never lost on him. In the decades following Mingus's death in 1979, jazz has found the kinds of institutional venues he dreamed of when he was writing to Nat Hentoff from Bellevue of the degradations of the jazz life, yet those institutions have yet to give him his due. Nineteen hours of *Ken Burns's Jazz* only afforded him two and a half minutes, and even when his eightieth birthday was celebrated in 2002, Jazz at Lincoln Center only devoted a single program to the occasion—in contrast to the entire year of programming set aside for the Ellington and Armstrong centenaries. A posthumous orchestral composition revived by the musicologist and Mingus friend Gunther Schuller in 1989, *Epitaph* still perpetuated the idea that there was somehow more meaning in a broad orchestral score than there were in the vital interactions and improvisations with his smaller ensembles on *Mingus Ah Um* (1959), *Mingus Dynasty* (1959), the group of live performances from 1964, *Mingus at Monterey* (1964), *The Black Saint and the Sinner Lady* (1963), and beyond. When Mingus goes on extended musical dialogues with Eric Dolphy on live recordings of "So Long Eric" and the full scale conversation of "What Love" from 1964, their musical symbiosis is something no score can touch—nor would it ever need to. As Mingus's music continues to be performed by the rowdy repertory ensemble the Mingus Big Band, and his legacy is still touted from reissues to clubs to the concert hall, it will take a certain amount of hustling to affix Mingus's epitaph just how he wanted it. If Dannie Richmond was correct and "pimp" was Mingus's first persona of choice, then that identity led the vast and complex array of creations he left behind for future audiences to analyze, unravel, and enjoy. While Mingus still pushes his way into the pantheon, it is the least we could do for him.

ON THE CORNER

> I had a whole stable of bitches out on the street working for me.
> —Miles Davis

Early on in Miles: *The Autobiography*, Miles Davis tells a story about a primal scene that took place in a cab with Charlie Parker. The year is 1945, and Davis is nineteen, still matriculated at Juilliard, and still receiving checks from his dentist father. After a day of classes, the young trumpeter would prowl 52nd Street in search of Parker, making a reputation for himself in jam sessions, and becoming as noted for his playing as he was for his obsessive pursuit. Finally, he achieved his dream and connected with Parker, becoming a crucial sideman in the burgeoning history of bebop, only to find himself caught in traffic and witnessing the leader of a musical revolution helping himself to fried chicken, heroin, whiskey, and, courtesy of a willing female companion, a blow job. Davis, who had barely learned to hold his liquor and still "wanted to quit every night" trying to follow up Parker's harmonic flights with a limited range and a Harmon mute, indicated his discomfort to his leader. "So you know what that motherfucker said?" Davis asked of Parker, using a favorite epithet. "He told me that if it was bothering me, then I should turn my head and not pay attention."[22] Parker, he went on to say, was like a "father figure" to him, and even if he was in for a bumpy ride, it was a lesson he never forgot. This was around the time that Davis said that "people used to say I had eyes like a girl" (*MA*, 97). When Davis decided to become a man, he would follow Parker's instructions and avert those eyes, transforming the act of looking away into a carefully constructed persona, a stage manner that was interpreted as rudeness, shyness, or even a political statement. In the next decade, he would go on and off heroin, mourn the death of Parker, hone his chops on monumental Blue Note and Prestige recording dates, talk his way into a Columbia recording contract, and find himself on the path to international celebrity. Somewhere in the middle, he was also a pimp. Davis was instructed by his father figure to feign a cool indifference to sex and power, and whether women were doing the hustle for him, or whether he was hustling his own legend, Parker's lesson was never forgotten.

Miles: The Autobiography is hustling a product: the belligerent, testy, protean legend of Miles Davis. If the book is to be trusted, it would be easy to assume that Miles's pimping days were as important to his image as his embouchure or contrapuntal lines with saxophonists Sonny Rollins, John Coltrane, and Wayne Shorter. The book's ghostwriter—really, its author—is the poet Quincy Troupe, whose own self-promotion was chastened when he was forced to withdraw from appointment as poet laureate of California after a routine background check revealed a forged college degree. Troupe is clearly in awe of Davis's mystique, as evidenced by *Miles and Me*, Troupe's own memoir about the making of Davis's autobiography. Every utterance, gesture, and outfit is worshipfully recounted in excruciating detail, and Troupe lets his readers know that as much of a "bad motherfucka" (to use both writers' preferred term) Davis was, he was not afraid to stand up to him to win some respect in their masculine cutting contests and their more thoughtful reflections on horses, art, and African heritage. The truth is, though, that as much as he liked to show off how he could spar with the trumpeter known as the "Prince of Darkness," he buys Davis's act unconditionally and uncritically. No one could tell Miles Davis what to do, and when it came to writing his autobiography, Davis could only have a willing disciple be his Boswell. The biography was cobbled together from a series of tape-recorded interviews in which Davis would tell anecdotes, usually ending in a quiet, tough-guy triumph for the trumpeter, unafraid to curse and insult white people in power, unremorseful in his (selective) tales of spousal abuse, and unrelenting in his insistence that he "changed music five or six times," despite the fact that the fifth or sixth time included synthesizer-drenched versions of 1980s hits like Michael Jackson's "Human Nature" and Cyndi Lauper's "Time After Time." He may have abused women and recorded commercial trifles for the last decade of his life, but Miles Davis, so the legend of Troupe's book would have it, never made a false move in his life. Those moves were made with the strut and swagger of the mack-daddy pimp, and it was Troupe who was, like the young Davis scrunched in that cab with Parker, sitting in awe at the excesses of a genius, doing what he was told and made to feel grateful just to be along for the ride.

The story Davis tells in Troupe's book is mostly one of success. "I knew some great musical shit was about to go down; I could feel it in my bones. And it happened. It went all the way down" (*MA*, 218), Davis says about a musical turning point in 1957. "My second great quintet," he says when introducing a photo spread of his 1964–1968 quintet. Anyone already attuned to the genuine importance of these bands would find no cause for argument there, but as a rhetorical device—especially for readers who are not already committed Davis fanatics—a little of this goes a long way. When Davis was at the pinnacle of his fame, a sharp-dressed man who would turn heads in the middle of a Cassius Clay fight, he basked in his glory. When he is done wrong—by those short-sighted critics who were championing his rivals like free-jazz artists Ornette Coleman and Cecil Taylor in the 1960s or questioning his move to fusion in the 1970s, or pushing a return to the styles Davis abandoned in the 1980s— Davis constantly emerges as the contrarian hero, coming up as the champion of artistic integrity and unrestrained profanity.

His segue into pimping is an exception. It is a low point in his life. In 1951 and 1952, following Parker's narcotic descent, Davis would sell people out any way he could just to get his next fix. Here is Davis's version of those dark days:

> I started to get money from whores to feed and support my habit. I started to pimp them, even before I realized that this was what I was doing. I was what I used to call a "professional junkie." That's all I lived for. I even chose my jobs according to whether it would be easy for me to cop drugs. I turned into one of the best hustlers because I had to get heroin every day, no matter what I had to do.   (*MA*, 136)

In the period when Davis claimed to be working as an actual pimp, even his pimp style suffered as a result. "Where I used to be a fashion plate dresser, now I wasn't dressing so well" (*MA*, 143), Davis confessed. What Robin D. G. Kelley identified as

Davis's "pimp aesthetic" in a 2001 *New York Times* article was less apparent when Davis was actually living the life as it was when he got clean, where his Brooks Brothers clothes would have surely impressed Ellison and Rushing's Rinehart. "Pimps in African-American culture and folklore are more than violent exploiters of women," wrote Kelley. "They are masters of style, from the language and the stroll to the clothes and the wheels."[23] When Davis's habit could not even afford him a $5 conk, those girls were allegedly strolling for him, but not bringing in enough green to allow him to dress the part.

In short, Davis did not present pimping as something to be proud of. Why, then, does John Szwed, Davis's most reliable biographer, feel that he inflated his "fancy man" image, when his own research indicated that Miles was not quite the mack daddy presented in Troupe's book? Like the intimates of Mingus who insisted that his pimping stories were largely exaggerated or even fabricated to enhance the commercial viability of his memoir, Davis's pimping stories, as grim as they were, also reinforced Troupe's perception of him as a "bad motherfucka." But why did Davis, who in his refusal to grin for white audiences supposedly did wonders for the African American image, tarnish his own just to sell a few more books? The pimp life had its pitfalls, but the pimp aesthetic has a perennial appeal, and Davis exercised it most powerfully not as a leader of the "whole stable of bitches" he claimed were working for him, but of the musicians and reputation in jazz history that he kept in his grip. If Billie Holiday's appeal reached to the scores of young women reclaiming her as a battered victim and feminist icon, Miles Davis's appeal reached to the scores of young men who chart jazz history through his charismatic leadership and, in his canonical moments of the 1950s, tailored Italian suits.

This is the standard line on Miles Davis's current reputation in jazz: in the 1940s, he sat at the feet of Charlie Parker and refined his craft, using the middle register for maximum emotive impact with striking melodic economy and a use of space and silence as ingenious as John Cage's. By 1949, when he was fronting his own ensemble for sessions that would be repackaged as "The Birth of the Cool," he took the breakneck eighth- and sixteenth-note runs of bebop and put them in slow motion—in effect a style that reflected the nodding off that Charlie Parker and other beboppers were doing in their heroin fogs—making the lines more discernable to outsiders and more useful as carnal soundtracks. (As a testimony to this enduring appeal of Davis's music, Fantasy and Columbia both released *Miles Davis for Lovers* CDs.) By 1955, Davis had kicked heroin and formed one of the greatest small groups in jazz history, including the little-known tenor saxophonist John Coltrane. The revolutions went on: the orchestral records with Gil Evans, the second great quintet with Herbie Hancock's impressionist splashes, Tony Williams's volcanic controlled freedom, and Wayne Shorter's modulating mind games. Then came acid, fusion, the Fillmore, rock-star status, a silent period, and those embarrassing 1980s covers.[24] By then, the sexagenarian Davis still needed to prove that he was a "bad muthafucka" as he sported a jeri-curl weave and expressed his enthusiasm for Phil Collins, and if he needed to sell some pimp stories to Simon and Schuster, that is exactly what he would do.

Could Davis have been anticipating his pimp appeal when he recorded "Love for Sale" six years after Billie Holiday? If he did, he certainly had a more eloquent way of expressing it during the Eisenhower era than he did during the Reagan years. It would have been unthinkable for the *New York Times* to publish an article lauding Davis's "pimp aesthetic" in 1958, as it did in 2001, but Davis, using Cole Porter's tune, was able to take on the voice not of a wounded streetwalker who has been "through the mill of love," but of the procurer profiting from her wares. In 1958, Davis recorded the song twice, first with the same quintet that, with the exception of drummer "Philly" Joe Jones, would appear on *Kind of Blue* the following year—including Bill Evans on piano, Paul Chambers on bass, John Coltrane on tenor saxophone, Julian "Cannonball" Adderley on alto saxophone—and also as a sideman for Adderley's "Something Else." The version with Davis's ensemble features the trumpet resting the melody on a delicate, intricate piano vamp from Evans, but the Adderley version is even more revealing of Davis's cool detachment from the hustler pose. The ensemble plays it both raw and cooked, beginning with Hank Jones's elegant, impromptu arpeggios, with an even more exaggerated weltschmerz than Oscar Peterson's intro to his duet version of the song with Holiday. But that lyricism is cut by the pulsating Latin rhythms from Art Blakey's drums, initiating something far less mannered than Evans's understated piano vamp from the Davis recording that same year. Following the ironic lyricism of Jones's cascading intro and Blakey's thudding yet controlled Latin rhythms, the tune then slips into the half-note swing that drove Davis's other version from 1958.

When Davis comes in to state the melody, he does what by then had become his trademark through his versions of "My Funny Valentine," "Bye-Bye Blackbird," "It Could Happen to You," and many other standards by white composers: he plays the notes he feels like playing and discards the rest with a graceful nonchalance. On the first A section, the melody is discernable, although he ends the last "sale" in a moody, extended ninth tone. By the time he begins the "Let the poets pipe of love" bridge, he is taking more liberties. While Blakey's rumblings are emanating underneath, Davis has deviated from the melody, navigating upwards to evade the issue playfully. With his icy mute, Davis's rendition does not convey the prostitute's sorrow, but the pimp's sly swagger, selling his product without feeling any pain. It is a masterpiece of elegance and impeccable melodic choices, telling a story of degradation while harmonically floating above it. There is more pure elegance in the 1958 "Love for Sale," more of a balance of lascivious sales pitch (driven by Blakey's orgiastic fills and Latin excursions) and refined harmonic explorations than there is in the brutal narrative of Troupe's book. The 1958 "Love for Sale," like the many explorations from the great American songbook made by Davis between 1949 and 1967, was a masterpiece of interpretation as transfiguration. The oldest profession was the subject of Porter's song, and like Holiday, who knew the subject from the inside, Davis struts around the song's periphery, showing a sly indifference and subtle retelling of Porter's story. The bullying braggadocio of Troupe's memoir is not heard in this tale, a story of the streets far more nuanced than Davis—or at least Troupe's Davis—put into words.

Indeed, there is more substance in either version of Davis's "Love for Sale" than in all the pages of *Miles: The Autobiography*, a more impressive statement on streetwalking than his autobiography's proclamation that he "had a whole stable of bitches working for me." Davis, after all, was conscious of his own self-promotion: he had love for sale—and eros, rage, and melancholy for the taking—and charged as much as he could while exhibiting contempt for the club promoters, journalists, and fans who bought the product. Some say he was shy, that he wanted to escape the performer's role, that he had, in effect, to pledge a *non servium* in response to the racist trappings of black performance in the 1950s. As we have all become Ellisonians and Armstrongians now, these gestures seem more multifaceted than they did in the 1950s, but there has been a bigger change in the racial dynamics of popular performance. Between that 1958 recording and the 1989 publication of Troupe's book, though, the pimp aesthetic identified by Kelley had been outed, foregrounded, and marketed, from 1970s blaxploitation to 1980s hip hop. Ellison's Rinehart was no longer a stop along the way of a complex and tortuous path of identity and self-realization. What the Invisible Man calls cynical "Rinehartism" was itself a destination, a fetish, a transposition from an underworld pose of power to the mainstream.

Davis was not about to let the opportunity pass for his pimping power to make the transition from the shamed moments of addiction and failure in the early 1950s to part of his concocted legend in the late 1980s. Just as Davis avoided Coleman Hawkins and other worthy potential leaders in 1944 on his way to latching on to the cult of Charlie Parker, he had his eyes on what would become a legend most, even if it meant hustling his lowest moments to sell it. It was a long way from Ma Rainey's "Hustlin' Blues" or Lucille Bogan's "Tricks Ain't Walkin' No More," where the life of the hustler was one to be renounced. Though the tales of pimping and addiction hardly seem appealing in Troupe's book, a pimpologist looking back on the 1950s could view Davis's 1958 "Love for Sale" as straddling the ground between a life to be renounced and a style to be fetishized. But the Davis of 1958 who played "Love for Sale" was coming from a cultural moment not far removed from the Ellison of 1952 who crafted Bliss Proteus Rinehart. Before Miles Davis lived the life, he became a masterful trumpet player, with far more technical dexterity than he is normally given credit for. It took hard work, discipline, and aspiration to sit through those Juilliard classes by day, keep up with Charlie Parker at night, and develop a distinctive trumpet style in the presence of such masters of the instrument (with far flashier technique) as Dizzy Gillespie and

Fats Navarro. Davis may have disparaged the Juilliard experience as just some "white shit," but he never stopped poring over scores of Ravel, Bartok, and Stravinsky, and often liked to lord his conservatory training over his less-schooled peers. Despite what some Beat poets might have said, becoming a jazz virtuoso is, in many ways, precisely the opposite of the easy money and the hedonistic thrills of the sex trade. Sharp-dressed hustlers were a dime a dozen; there was only one Miles Davis.

It is unfortunate that such an obvious point must be belabored, but in our moment of pimp worship, the players and the playas must be carefully distinguished. Robin D. G. Kelley's *New York Times* article reclaimed Davis as a proto-playa, marveling at his mack-daddy images on record covers and identifying the degrees to which his "pimp aesthetic" informed each phase of his musical development. This reading of Miles as a trickster-pimp figure is partly true, but Davis himself was ambivalent about how far to push the persona. As harsh as *Miles: The Autobiography* was in its horrific treatment of women and unabashed hubris in the persona of the "bad motherfucka," there were other signs that Troupe wanted to push the book's pimp narrative more than Miles. In an interview with *People* conducted before Troupe did his interviews for the book in the late 1980s, Davis claimed that he was less of a pimp than a playa, accepting money and gifts from women, but not necessarily directly working the trade. Whether he practiced directly in the sex trade or not, the construction of a Miles Davis that had "a whole stable of bitches" says more about the gangsta figure promulgated by Troupe and authorized by the ailing and cynical Davis of 1989 than it did about the Miles Davis that matters the most: the musical innovator and interpreter, whose "five or six" changes of music may not necessarily all have been equally valid, but who cannot be denied the first three or four. Davis's first wife, Irene, the drummer Stan Levey, and the saxophonist Allen Eager deny that Davis could have been practicing the trade, and until the actual tapes of Troupe's interviews with Davis become available (for now, there are only transcripts), it is impossible to know where Davis ends and where Troupe begins. In *Miles and Me*, Troupe, in characteristically self-serving fashion, claims that Davis devoured the galleys of the book and loved every word. A transcript of their appearance together at the Studio Museum of Harlem shows the trumpeter unfamiliar with its contents, with Davis stopping Troupe at one point to ask, "Did I say that?" In his incendiary review of the book, Stanley Crouch identifies where the book follows Jack Chambers's biography *Milestones* too closely to be coincidence.[25] *Miles: The Autobiography* is essential reading for anyone who wants to know how the trumpeter allowed himself to be mass-marketed, but it should certainly not be trusted for its textual integrity.

There is no doubt that Davis, whatever role he played in the sex trade, did pick up on masculine codes of power copped on the street. When he could still be clubbed by a policeman at the height of his fame in 1959, such a pose was a black man's access to power when the official venues were so hostile. But Davis's lowest moments should not be confused with his highest achievements. He consistently confounded audiences—especially white audiences—with the ugliness of his behavior and the beauty of his music. That he was a genius and a hustler is unquestionable, but in a moment when the line between hustling and entertainment becomes increasingly blurred—when the rapper Nelly can market an energy beverage called Pimp Juice—that genius should not get lost in street-corner transactions. "Pimp" has more street cred than "genius" or "artist," yet it is this style that can lead new listeners to the substance of Miles Davis. But whatever initially attracts listeners to him, they nonetheless will also encounter how he directed a session of minimal chords and slow tempos and turned it into a quiet musical revolution on *Kind of Blue*, emulate the sob of a Spanish widow on *Sketches of Spain*'s "Saeta," foster a collective improvisation and harmonic audacity in that Herbie Hancock-Wayne Shorter-Ron Carter-Tony Williams quintet the trumpeter was quite justified in calling "great" in Troupe's book. Those days of ordering tricks may or may not have occurred as described in those grim days of 1951 and 1952, but Miles's life as mack—and even his persona as a mack—is but an aspect of a complex musical life, one that, in his finest moments, was anything but a cheap transaction. Reading Troupe's memoir is a necessary part of the Miles Davis experience, even described by one critic as "more fun" than Szwed's more accurate and responsible biography. But there was nothing Miles Davis the man could have done to overshadow Miles Davis the musician. Reading Troupe's book, you can take the journey from Charlie Parker's fellatio all the way to Davis's final moments of coked-up, moribund electronic noodling. But no matter how much *Miles: The Autobiography* wears its pimping proudly, the hustler's sales pitch cannot drown out the music.

CODA: MUSIC SPEAKS LOUDER

Thought I heard Buddy Bolden shout
Open up that window, let that bear there out
I said: open up that window, let that foul air out
'Cause I thought I heard buddy Bolden say
    —JELLY ROLL MORTON, "Funky Butt Blues"

After Allen Ginsberg's reveries, Frank O'Hara's Billie-Holiday-inspired gasp, James Baldwin's Jamesian yearning into the mysterium of the bebopper, and Norman Mailer's assertion that "jazz is orgasm," one would think that when jazz musicians had a chance to tell their own stories, they would clear the air of their usual literary representations. "Open up that window, let that foul air out," Jelly Roll Morton sang in "Funky Butt Blues," and at the end of *Invisible Man*, Ellison is ambivalent about the pain and pleasure invoked by jazz's red-light-district origins. "Old Bad Air is still around with his dancing and diversity and I'll be up and around with mine," he writes. This allusion celebrates the music without endorsing the legacy of exploitation that has haunted jazz since legal prostitution ran amok down Perdido Street. It is a delicate balance to achieve. Anyone looking to the jazz memoir in search of a corrective to the misuses and abuses of the music in American writing will be disappointed. ("Persons attempting to find a moral will be banished," the famous disclaimer to *Huckleberry Finn*, belongs in front of jazz autobiographies as well.) "You done took my blues and gone," wrote Langston Hughes, but in the autobiographies of Holiday, Mingus, and Davis, when they take their blues to mass-market publications bearing their bylines, they linger in the whorehouses where the music's legends began. Holiday and Davis let their ghostwriters do their hustling for them. Mingus, after seeing the manuscript pass through so many editors and typists, did take literary matters in to his own hands more than Holiday and Davis, but loaded his autobiography with more tales of pimping—most of them disputed—than musical mastery. The typescripts available for public viewing show an editor's strong arm in the final revisions pushing the pimp angle with an eye on the bottom line.

"Can the subaltern speak?" asked Giyatri Chakravorty Spivak in an influential essay on Bengali literature.[26] In jazz autobiography, when the subaltern does speak, that speech often reinforces the hustle behind the music without revealing the complexity. Pimping may be dangerous work, but it offers the illusion of easy money. Fats Waller's sister told a story of seeing her father dressed to the nines around 1910, and in imitation of something she overheard at a grocery store, said, "Hello, pimp." Waller *père* let it be known that unlike the sharp-dressed hustlers on the street, he actually worked for a living.[27] Billie Holiday, Charles Mingus, and Miles Davis certainly worked for a living, too, and when their stories collided with the life, their narratives only became more complicated, learning a lesson from the hustle, but learning it the hard way. To believe that "jazz is orgasm" is not to see the music as hard work but as primitive ecstasy incarnate. As "jazz is orgasm" seems increasingly dated, "Hello, pimp" is not going away. "Pimp" has more currency in popular culture than ever before (while the currency of "ho" still has a long way to go). The African American minstrel performer Ernest Hogan changed the lyrics of his 1896 song "All Coons Look Alike to Me" to "All Pimps Look Alike to Me," just barely softening the sting of a hit he would eventually regret ever writing. The latter word has since been reclaimed, but the painful repercussions of the former word still resound. The subaltern may speak in jazz autobiography, but it is not a speech that brings the music very far from its red-light origins.

In this respect, the jazz memoirists are consistent with a larger literary landscape of novelists and poets who were fascinated by the music, but often added to its myths. There has been more literary material about the life surrounding the music—or its aura—than about the music itself. Whether it is Hart Crane's "nigger cupids," James Baldwin's junkie bebopper, or Frank O'Hara's breathless invocation of a tabloid headline and Bowery evening, the mechanics of the music are less important than the feelings they invoke, the lifestyle they accompany, the muse they feed. Louis Armstrong comforted Invisible Man in his basement, Bessie Smith saved Holden Caulfield from phonies, Billie

Holiday inspired Frank O'Hara to rethink his priorities, Charlie
Parker was considered a potential murderer by LeRoi Jones. The
mythological can be as fascinating as the metaphorically apt and
historically accurate. But rare is the creation of Richard Powers's
Strom brothers, captured with meticulous precision with their
scales, modes, and heightened awareness. Rarer still is Ellison's
Invisible Man, donning and discarding the threads or Rinehart
the Runner while keeping that Louis Armstrong record on his
turntable and in his prose. After the angelic invocations, the ethnic interplay, and the pimping and whoring, there is finally the
music, stripped away, still vital in the most profound isolation.
Writers, speaking from the isolation involved in producing the
printed word, envy the group activities responsible for jazz's most
enduring moments.

Musicians did not need writers to justify their art, but there
were those remarkable instances when literary writing and jazz
were astonishingly matched. When Thomas Pynchon culled Ornette Coleman's music, biography, and the middle name of Thelonious "Sphere" Monk for his alto-player character McLintic
Sphere in his debut novel *V.* (1963), he had already studied with
Nabokov at Cornell, played along with Parker records on alto in
the navy, and came a little too late and too influenced by the
modernist *Evergreen Review* to be a Beat, no matter how much
pot he smoked. Pynchon, a former physics and engineering major whose first professional writing job was as a technical scribe
for Boeing, was under the sway of Jack Kerouac—as late as
1984, he still considered *On the Road* to be "one of the great
American novels"—but he was also too steeped in the production of the music and the equations and linguistic translations of
science to underestimate its complexity. In a book divided between the often misguided quests of Benny Profane and Herbert

Stencil, Sphere is the smartest character in the book, the one whose motto articulates a balance between hipster insouciance and the intellect's self-consciousness: "Keep cool, but care."[28] Unlike many Pynchon characters, Sphere is no paranoid, but he is not a figment of the Beat imagination, either.

Sphere's dense grooves are only comprehended by, in Pynchon's estimate, "a dreamy 10 percent" of the crowd taking him in, but to that knowing 10 percent, what seemed like chaos was actually deliberated. This jazz was not merely a Mailerian "orgasm," but a new way of conceiving musical ecstasy. Like Coleman, Sphere played on a white plastic alto, and what he did with it divided listeners. He is caught by Pynchon playing at the V Note, a club based on the actual Five Spot, an allusion to the Half Note, where Coleman also played, the roman numeral for five, and, of course, the book's title:

He blew a hand-carved ivory alto saxophone with a $4\frac{1}{2}$ reed and the sound was like nothing any of them had heard before. The usual divisions prevailed: collegians did not dig, and left after an average of $1\frac{1}{2}$ sets. Personnel from other groups, either with a night off or taking a long break from somewhere crosstown or uptown, listened hard, trying to dig. "I am still thinking," they would say if you asked.[29]

Ornette Coleman, like McLintic Sphere, also divided listeners. Roy Eldridge thought he was "jiving," Miles Davis thought he was obviously "screwed up inside," even Thelonious Monk, who wrote a composition called "Nutty," said "Man, that guy is nuts!"[30] Mingus did cautiously "dig," calling Coleman's seeming disdain for regular meter and chord changes "playing wrong right." In retrospect, Coleman's music seems less like an assault and more like an extension. "Lonely Woman" sounds unsettled but is firmly grounded in the language of blues and bebop, as jangled and atemporal as a Robert Johnson recording, but, as a denizen at the V Note remarks, filling in the notes Charlie Parker missed. "Free Jazz" was a Coleman album title and the label of a movement associated with him, but where some scandalized listeners heard anarchy, Pynchon, who found balance in Sphere in an imbalanced world, actually made Coleman's aesthetic the guiding principle of his book. As W. T. Lahmon argues, "Keep cool, but care is the difficult program the novel follows."[31] Coleman leads listeners on a difficult program, too, not necessarily abandoning structure, but forcing listeners to rethink their conceptions of it. When Coleman was embraced by John Lewis, Gunther Schuller, and Martin Williams around the time of the Five Spot revolution, they saw links to theory, assaults on harmony and rhythm that really had their own logic. It took a while for Coleman to take to this: when Schuller tried to teach him how to read music, he became physically ill and stopped the lessons.

Eventually, though, Coleman came up with a theory: "harmolodics"—a concept that put harmony and rhythm, as he put it, "in unison." (Like a sexual act, he liked to explain—being in unison without being in unison.) One theorist of language, not music, who found a kinship with Coleman was Jacques Derrida, who interviewed Coleman for a Parisian journal and joined him on stage for a concert. The audience was largely not interested in what he had to say. But even the postsructuralist found that structure itself was inescapable, that the idea of improvisation, ironically, could be deconstructed. In an unpublished interview, Derrida demonstrated that, while he claimed to be musically illiterate, he could see that there was something profoundly self-conscious about this "freedom":

Even when one improvises in front of a camera or a microphone, one ventriloquizes, or leaves another to speak in one's place the schemas, the languages that are already there. There are already a great number of prescriptions that are prescribed in our memory and in our culture. All the names are already preprogrammed. It's already the names that inhibit our ability to ever really improvise. One can't say whatever one wants. One is obliged more or less to reproduce the stereotypical discourse. And so I believe in improvisation and I fight for improvisation, but always with the belief that it's impossible.[32]

Pynchon does not necessarily believe that improvisation is impossible, but he does not think it is arbitrary, either. Rather, he found in Coleman what Stevens would have called a "blessed rage to order," providing a wry antidote to a world of conspiracy. Coleman (or Sphere) may have filled in the notes that Parker missed, but Pynchon did not miss a beat when he placed Parker in one of the most comic and apocalyptic moments in late twentieth-century fiction, once again placing jazz accurately in an ambitious historical and aesthetic sweep.

Even more than the Beat apostles who scrawled "Bird Lives" through Lower Manhattan and beyond, Pynchon immortalized Parker in prose as associative, surreal, and visceral as a Parker solo. In his mammoth 1973 novel *Gravity's Rainbow*, Pynchon's hero, Tyrone Slothrop, on a government-sponsored acid trip—when LSD was used by the military to simulate schizophrenia during World War II—hallucinates that he is flushed down a cosmic toilet flanked by a pre–Nation of Islam Malcom X to the strains of a Parker performance of Ray Noble's "Cherokee." Pynchon, who claimed to play Parker alto solos in the navy, was surely aware that Parker famously spoke of playing the tune in a jam session when a new harmonic vocabulary crystallized for him:

> I'd been getting bored with the stereotyped changes that were being used all the time at the time, and I kept thinking there's bound to be something else. I could hear it sometimes, but I couldn't play it. Well, that night I was working over "Cherokee" and, as I did, I found that by using the higher intervals of a chord as a melody line and backing them with appropriately related changes, I could play the thing I'd been hearing. I came alive.[33]

Pynchon uses Parker's awakening for Slothrop's own disturbance of his dogmatic slumber, but it is a world where he goes literally underground in more corporeal realms than Ellison's basement dweller:

> The song playing is one more lie about white crimes. But more musicians have floundered in the channel to "Cherokee" than we have got through from end to end. All those long, long notes . . . what're they up to, all that time to do something inside of? is it an Indian spirit plot? Down in New York, drive fast maybe get there for the last set—on 7th Ave., between 139th and 140th tonight, "Yardbird" Parker is finding out how he can use the notes at the higher ends of these very chords to break up the melody into *have* mercy what is it a fucking machine gun or something, man he must be out of his *mind*.[34]

Pynchon has identified a moment of racial upheaval, harmonic discovery, and scientific turmoil, and he sets it in a toilet. By the end of the scene, Parker is heading through the septic tank with the future leader of the Nation of Islam and a misguided soldier of the greatest generation. Joyce wrote about the "nightmare of history," but Pynchon was writing about the hallucinations of time past and time future. A student of Nabokov and follower of Kerouac, Pynchon knew the hipster lingo, but could also do the math and play the riffs. As a tiny part of a gargantuan post-modern tome, Pynchon's use of bop and its cultural unconscious is peerless.

Parker rarely surfaced from the cultural underground, and the one time he is seen speaking on camera he issues a fierce retort to a discourse uncongenial to his sense of time. In 1952, the year *Invisible Man* was published, Parker made his only television appearance, and his host showed palpable signs of a crisis in etiquette. The program was *Stage Entrance*, and the host, *New York Post* columnist Earl Wilson, was so perplexed about how to address Parker and Dizzy Gillespie and present them with their *Down Beat* awards for 1951, he had to ask jazz critic Leonard Feather for advice on screen. "What am I supposed to say to them? Am I supposed to say, 'Hey, man?'" "Just talk to them," Feather replied, but Wilson did not bother to hide his disdain for Parker, who had already ruefully called himself "the world's most famous junkie." Parker, whose only other filmed performance was a duet with Coleman Hawkins where the audio was lost, was given this one opportunity to appear in the main-stream, countering Wilson's slights with the most artful signify-ing. His eyes flashing furious glances barely betrayed by a smirk, Parker counters insult after insult before deciding that his virtu-osity would provide the most eloquent way of saying, "fuck you."

EARL WILSON: And this is the *Down Beat* award for Best Alto Sax Man of 1951. Nice to see ya.

CHARLIE PARKER: Thank you.

EARL WILSON: And, uh, Diz, this is to you from *Down Beat* for being one of the top trumpet men of all time.

Congratulations, Diz, uh, I mean Dizzy. I got a little in-
formal there. You boys got anything more to say?

CHARLIE PARKER: Well, Earl, they say music speaks louder
than words, so we'd rather voice our opinion that way, if
you don't mind.[35]

"Music speaks louder": for Parker, his harmonic rewriting of
American vernacular culture was the only way he could "come
alive" and offer a withering dissent to the Earl Wilsons and any
other scribes who had the authority to write columns and offer
awards on television while professing an unashamed ignorance
of their art. The tune that Parker played with Gillespie and a
rhythm section was Tadd Dameron's "Hot House," an uncom-
promising bebop riff on Cole Porter's "What Is This Thing
Called Love?" where Porter's dandyish lyrics and melody are
stripped of decorum and replaced with angry eighth-note lines
that Parker issued with a furious dexterity, yet without a trace of
effort or awareness of his audience. As long as that horn was in
his mouth, Parker could remake culture any way he wanted, and
at thirty-two, two years away from death, could be called a "boy"
by Earl Wilson, throwing the introduction back at him by offering a withering musical response with baffling harmonics. These
"boys" had something to say for themselves, indeed, and writers
on the caliber of Pynchon rarely wrote about what they were
saying.

Parker also surfaces in Rafi Zabor's 1997 novel *The Bear Comes
Home*, which begins as a Kafkaesque joke and ends as a spiritual
and intellectual quest, all through the language and culture of
jazz. Just as Kafka's Gregor Samsa has to face life trapped in an
insect's body with a human consciousness, Zabor's Bear is an actual brown bear, who just also happens to quote Shakespeare and
Blake, engage in allusive puns, have tormented love affairs with

women, and play alto saxophone in a style influenced by Parker, Jackie McLean, and Ornette Coleman. Parker had to prove to Wilson that he was not just a "boy" winning an alto poll but a man of substance, and the Bear appears to be a freak show when he is actually a complex, tortured artist, doing circus tricks for a gig when what he wants to do is create. Zabor's training ground for the novel was the life of a jazz critic in which musical performances had to be vividly captured on deadline, while also keeping track of trends, anecdotes, reputations, volatile personalities, wounded egos, and an eccentric industry that prides itself on its underground status while still hustling for the next gig. Zabor's Bear goes through a familiar struggle endured by human protagonists of many a bildungsroman: he falls in and out of love, gets arrested, finds and loses inspiration, achieves then forfeits creative and professional success. Even though he looks like he belongs in a circus or a zoo, he really wants to be able to play like Sonny Rollins on "Doxy."

The struggle between art and commerce is a familiar story, but Zabor's novel is not merely a rewrite of *Lost Illusions*. Most writers find music to be, as Hart Crane put it, the most "elusive" of subjects, but Zabor, a jazz drummer, can talk harmonics and rhythms as well as he can revel in image and sustain an otherworldly metaphor. Charlie Haden, Billy Hart, Arthur Blythe, and Lester Bowie and are among the real jazz musicians who interact with this talking, wailing bear, but their interaction feels like eavesdropping in the stairwell at the Village Vanguard, with all the inside jokes, puns, and working musician's argot—as opposed to mere hipster cant—familiar to the jazz world.

The conceit of self-aware banter and the performing trained attraction is immediately apparent in the novel's opening. The novel begins with the Bear dancing in the street to a disco cassette while his keeper, Jones, takes donations. It is not until they walk up the stairs of their shared tenement apartment that they begin bantering about indulging their Epicurean yearnings for fresh salmon on meager budgets, alluding to *King Lear*, and, finally, sharing choruses of King Pleasure's vocalese of Charlie Parker's "Parker's Mood." The Bear lets us know how hard it is to live in what Crane called the Aesopean "midkingdom," except that he is the one making the allusions, jokes, and critical judgments:

> The Bear put the saxophone to his mouth and arpeggiated his way through a typically murderous late-fifties Coltrane turnaround—C major 7, E-flat 7, A-flat major to B 7, E major to G 7, and finished on a resonant C, which he flatted slightly for emphasis, "You try that with paws, mutha. You develop an embouchure for a snout. Yeah, you know me. Sure. Could *you* do that?"[36]

This music, the Bear tells us, is difficult to play. Living in a squalid flat and eating chopped meat, the Bear sees the humor of his own conceit—that coming up with inspiration while keeping up with the circle of fifths is hard enough. Maintaining animal instinct with an overactive brain is even harder, especially if one *is* an animal. Just as the jazz memoirists had to prostitute themselves in the name of the music's own regenerative creative rewards, the Bear's routine is beneath him, so much so that Wynton Marsalis is mentioned as condemning him for "degrading the image of the jazz musician." This is a joke, of course, but at the novel's end, it is clear that the thing about the Bear that would seem to be the most degrading—literally, the most dehumanizing—is what frees Zabor to speculate about what is actually going on in a highly self-conscious performing artist's inner life:

He felt his body find its ease, his lungs expanding on the inbreath tone enriching itself on the out. He doubletimed the next few bars, did a little accent-switching turnaround, thank you Bird, into the release, and felt cell after cell in the large dark shape of himself begin to come alight. Oxygen. Inspiration. I like it. He took the saxophone from his snout for a two-bar lag and laughed aloud as his heart began to open—lots of room in there, and something more knowing than emotion. Yes, he thought, as he had sometimes on the tour but never at the beginning of the first set, this is what the music's for.[37]

"Music is nothing," the composer and saxophonist Wayne Shorter likes to say. "What music is for is something."[38] Shorter's resistance to verbalizing the music's importance is not unusual for musicians—particularly spiritually inclined musicians, and Shorter is a Buddhist—who are shy of unpacking their own mystical experiences. But it is a writer's job to verbalize, and it is a difficult task to integrate exactly what music is for while also navigating characters, style, images, and narrative. But the Bear's entire outrageous conceit and strange journey is all about what music is for. Jazz is often in the service of another literary project, and this is where the mystification and misreading often comes in. Zabor's absurd metaphor actually elucidates much reality of the jazz life. There is something so unreal about the conditions of a working jazz musician, something so ridiculous that an artist of Parker's stature would have to endure the indignities of an Earl Wilson's condescension, that fantasy becomes the last refuge of the ingenious.

And Ellison, who had the ingenious metaphor of invisibility in response to the absurdity of the American racial imagination, applied those imaginative powers to Parker as well. Even though his words were hardly sympathetic, they were at least written on a level worthy of his subject. Ellison, dissenting from the "Bird Lives" crowd that had become a vocal majority among jazz fans by the time he wrote about him in 1964, issued these blistering lines:

> Parker operated in the underworld of American culture, on that turbulent level where human instincts conflict with social institutions; where contemporary civilized values and hypocrisies are challenged by the Dionysian urges of a between-wars youth born to prosperity, conditioned by the threat of world destruction, and inspired—when not seeking total anarchy—by a need to bring social reality and our social pretensions into a more meaningful balance.
>
> (*CE*, 261–62)

Ellison surely knew better than to confuse Parker's music with the "Dionysian urges" of his addictions, but by the time he wrote this essay, Ellison himself was already a figure functioning well above ground, writing speculatively about the jazz "institutions" that would eventually be built according to his principles. Many of the writers in this study limited their understanding to such urges: they were the sexy part of the equation, the most convenient metaphorical fodder. The musicians were often happy to play along, in the tradition of Funky Butt Hall, autobiographical pimping, and beyond, often embracing the stereotypes to signify and survive. Jazz has appeared in a number of guises in American writing: as orgasm, as preadolescent fetish, as protest, as "a beam of lyrical sound," as primitivism, as ethnic crossover, as modernism, as something "clean, sparkling, elusive," as conjecture, as an "angel headed hipster," as breathlessness, as the Buddha, as pimping, as signifyin'—but seldom as itself.

Derrida said that improvisation, though he fought for it, is impossible, but Ellison saw that it could be a metaphor and a private language of signifying that he could transpose into words and spread to anyone who would listen. Ellison's claim that Parker operated in the "underworld of American culture" is quite literally true, and one look at his exchange with Wilson would have made a good case for staying there. Many a misreading has produced memorable writing, and many accurate readings have not. "The White Negro," for example, misses the music but succeeds as polemic; "The Sick Man" drew upon Stevens's rich trove of elegiac tropes even if it was composed in apparent ignorance of Ellington. But once in a while, the lights in the cave can offer an illuminating flicker—made especially vibrant by stolen electricity. Ellison's own narrator, the most sublime of all jazz listeners in American letters, was himself a creature of the underworld, left in solitude with Armstrong's growl and wishing he could duplicate the experience five-fold. But when Ellison's hero retreats to his basement, he also reminds us that literature can transform the way we understand an artist and understand ourselves in the process. "They say music speaks louder than words," sneered Parker, but once in a while, the words come that are worthy to stand with the music. Ellison's Armstrong still speaks for us, and still speaks for the possibility that jazz can inspire and transfigure the American writer.

NOTES

NOTES TO INTRODUCTION

1. Donald Barthelme, "The King of Jazz," in *Hot & Cool: Jazz Short Stories*, ed. Marcela Breton (London: Bloosmbury, 1990), 237–38.

2. In Ken Burns's *Jazz*, when asked for a definition, Marsalis, who has placed himself in the role of jazz definer more than any other major figure, replied: "I think it means copulation."

3. For more on Coltrane's practicing methods, see Bill Cole, *John Coltrane* (New York: Schirmer, 1976), 120–21, and J. C. Thomas, *Chasin' the Trane* (New York: Doubleday, 1975), 102–3.

4. On musicians' resistance to the word "jazz" and its various attempted definitions, see John F. Szwed, *Jazz 101* (New York: Hyperion, 2000), 18–34.

5. Ralph Ellison, *Invisible Man* (New York: Random House, 1952), 6. Hereafter cited as *IM*.

6. Hart Crane, *The Letters of Hart Crane, 1916–1932*, ed. Brom Weber, (London: Oxford University Press, 1968), 89.

7. Wallace Stevens, *Opus Posthumous* (New York: Alfred A. Knopf, 1989), 118.

8. Albert Murray and Stanley Crouch have argued, though, that *The Great Gatsby* has narrative similarities to W. C. Handy's *The Beale Street Blues*: "For Daisy was young and her artificial world was redolent of orchids and pleasant, cheerful snobbery and orchestras which set the rhythm of the year, summing up the sadness and suggestiveness of life in new tunes. All night the saxophones wailed the hopeless comment of the BEALE STREET BLUES." This "hopeless comment"

performed by the white musicians suggests that black musicians could have done it better. See Albert Murray, *The Omni American* (New York: Dutton, 1970).

9. For an extended discussion that connects Morrison's novel to the music alluded to in its title, see Kristin K. Henson, *Beyond the Sound Barrier* (New York: Routledge, 2003).

NOTES TO CHAPTER ONE

1. For the Howe-Ellison debate, see Irving Howe, "Black Boys and Native Sons," in *A World More Attractive: A View of Modern Literature and Politics* (New York: Horizon Press, 1963), 98–122, and Ralph Ellison, "The World and the Jug," in *Shadow and Act* (New York: Random House, 1964). For Saul Bellow's oft-quoted remark on the "Zulu Tolstoy," see "Mr. Bellow's Planet," *New Yorker*, May 23, 1994, 35.

2. Amiri Baraka, "Somebody Blew Up America," *Counterpunch*, October 3, 2002.

3. Amiri Baraka (as LeRoi Jones), *Black Music* (New York: Morrow, 1967), 186.

4. See Eileen Southern, *The Music of Black Americans* (New York: Norton, 1997), 63–147.

5. For more on ethnic crossover and modernism, see "De Modern Do Mr. Bones," in Susan Gubar, *Race Changes: White Skin Black Face in American Culture* (New York: Oxford University Press, 1997), 134–68.

6. Powers's novel richly engages with the irony that blacks and Jews found musical convergence amidst political turmoil, and his book will be explored in detail at the end of this chapter.

7. For more about Adorno's attacks on jazz, see "Perennial Fashion—Jazz," in *Prisms*, trans. Samuel Weber and Shierry Weber (Cambridge, Mass: MIT Press, 1981), 129, as well as "On Jazz" and "Farewell to Jazz," in Theodor W. Adorno, *Essays on Music*, trans. Richard Leppert (Berkeley: University of California Press, 2002). Although Adorno mentions Louis Armstrong (comparing him to a castrato) and Duke Ellington (noted for his appropriation of Debussy and Ravel, but attacked for adapting them into "hot" music), his descriptions of the music reflect a knowledge of whiter, more sanitized versions of the mu-

sic. There has been recent debate about how much jazz Adorno actually experienced, but it is clear from reading his essays that, regardless of his knowledge or lack thereof, his mind was made up. Recent essays on Adorno and jazz include Theodor A. Gracyk, "Adorno, Jazz, and the Aesthetics of Popular Music," *Musical Quarterly* 76, no. 4 (Winter 1992); Richard Quinn, "Playing With Adorno: Improvisation and the Jazz Ensemble," *Yearbook of Comparative and General Literature* 44 (1996), 57–67; and Urlich Schoenherr, "Adorno and Jazz: Reflections on a Failed Encounter," *Telos* 87 (Spring 1991).

8. For a notable exception, see John F. Szwed's excellent "Really the (Typed-Out) Blues: Jazz Fiction in Search of Dr. Faustus," *Village Voice*, July 2, 1979, 72.

9. J. D. Salinger, *The Catcher in the Rye* (New York: Little Brown, 1951), 114–15. Hereafter cited as *CR*.

10. J. D. Salinger, "Blue Melody," *Cosmopolitan*, September 1948, 50. Hereafter cited as *BM*.

11. Saidiya Hartman, *Scenes of Subjection: Terror, Slavery, and Self-Making in Ninteenth Century America* (New York: Oxford University Press, 1997), 4.

12. Chris Albertson, *Bessie* (New York: Stein & Day, 1972), 216.

13. LeRoi Jones, *Dutchman* (New York: Morrow Quill Paperbacks, 1964), 35.

14. Mezz Mezzrow, *Really the Blues* (New York: Citadel, 1946), 112.

15. Anatole Broyard, "Keep Cool Man," *Commentary* 11 (April 1951): 361–62.

16. For more on Broyard's passing, see Henry Louis Gates's "The Passing of Anatole Broyard," in his *Thirteen Ways of Looking at a Black Man* (New York: Vintage, 1997), 180–214.

17. Ellison wrote that Mailer "thinks all hipsters are cocksmen possessed of great euphoric orgasms and are out to fuck the world into peace, prosperity and creativity. The same old primitivism crap in a new package." Ralph Ellison and Albert Murray, *Trading Twelves* (New York: Modern Library, 2000), 197–98.

18. See Mary V. Dearborn, *Mailer: A Biography* (New York: Houghton Mifflin, 1999), 116.

19. In the liner notes to *A Love Supreme*, Coltrane wrote, "During the year 1957, I experienced, by the grace of God, a spiritual awakening which was to lead me to a richer, fuller, more productive life." (GRP B000003N7G, originally released on Impulse! in 1964.)

20. The idea that race is more of an aesthetic choice than biology is a guiding principle behind the jazz writings of Albert Murray and Ralph Ellison, but it has been made most explicit by Stanley Crouch, who, although he is accused of barring white musicians from the jazz canon, is really a champion of what he calls the "Negro Aesthetic," of which he claims white musicians including Benny Goodman, Stan Getz, Joe Lovano, and Bill Charlap are exemplars. For more of Crouch on the distinction between "sounding white and being white," see Kerry Howley, "Cold Fusion," *Reason*, June 27, 2003, http://www.reason.com/hod/kh062703.shtml.

21. Norman Mailer, *Advertisements for Myself* (Cambridge, Mass.: Harvard University Press, 1992), 341.

22. Dearborn, *Mailer*, 120.

23. See W. J. Weatherby, *Squaring Off: Mailer Vs. Baldwin* (New York: Mason/Charter 1977).

24. Dearborn, *Mailer*, 133.

25. Fred. L. Standley, ed., *Conversations with James Baldwin* (Jackson: University Press of Mississippi, 1989), 237.

26. James Baldwin, "The Black Boy Looks at the White Boy," in *Collected Essays*, ed. Toni Morrison (New York: Library of America, 1998), 270.

27. Baldwin, *Collected Essays*, 272.

28. George J. Searles, ed., *Conversations with Philip Roth* (Jackson: University Press of Mississippi, 1992), 20–21.

29. *Ken Burns' Jazz, Episode 9: The Adventure, 1956–1961*, directed by Ken Burns, 999 min., PBS Home Video, 2001, DVD.

30. *Ken Burns' Jazz.*

31. Anatole Broyard, *Kafka Was the Rage* (New York: Vintage, 1997), 117.

32. Philip Roth, *The Human Stain* (New York: Vintage Books, 2001), 115. Hereafter *HS*.

33. When I asked Powers if Mann's novel was on his mind when he was writing the book, he replied, "On every page, in every paragraph, and not just in the interrogation of music and cultural ownership, but the question of high art's complicity through the violence of defining culture out on the streets. Zeitblom says 'The bombs are raining down on our cathedrals and our art museums and concert houses. It was our own belief in the purity of this supreme culture that has brought this on.'" January 15, 2003. Taped telephone interview.

34. Richard Powers, *The Time of Our Singing* (New York: Farrar, Straus and Giroux, 2003), 431. Hereafter *TS*.

35. Miles Davis, with Quincy Troupe, *Miles: The Autobiography* (New York: Simon and Schuster, 1989), 243–44.

36. John Hamans, Review of Richard Powers' *The Time of Our Singing*, *New York*, January 20, 2003, 85.

37. Sven Birkerts, Review of Richard Powers' *The Time of Our Singing*, *New Yorker*, January 13, 2003, 86.

38. For more on African Amrerican music prodigies, an essential text is James Weldon Johnson's *Autobiography of an Ex-Colored Man* (1912), in which musical mastery gives Johnson's narrator entree into a world of privilege. But even though the narrator, a classically trained pianist, finds success as a Ragtime musician, it is not as seductive as the appeal of spurious whiteness. Also see Stanley Crouch, *Don't The Moon Look Lonesome* (New York: Pantheon, 2000). Crouch, writing in the spirit of Ellison and Murray, uses his jazz expertise to give a detailed account for the actual process by which jazz is produced with his interracial star-crossed lovers, Carla, a white jazz singer, and Maxwell, a black tenor player. For a review of Crouch's novel, see David Yaffe, "The Jazz Singer," *The Village Voice*, June 7, 2000.

39. The title is the only one among Dylan's forty-three albums in quotation marks.

1. Rushing's version departs from Lovie and Austin's lyrics, which read, "Until you meet some of my demands" rather than, "Until you come under my command." The latter, presumably, was deemed more authoritative for the imposing singer, who, three hundred pounds, called himself "Mister Five-by-Five."

2. *Ralph Ellison: An American Journey.* Directed by Avon Kirkland, 2002.

3. In Kirkland's documentary, Henry Wingate recalls that Ellison "became unglued and began to cry, repeating, 'I'm not an Uncle Tom, I'm not an Uncle Tom.'" In his memoir *New York Days*, Willie Morris allowed Ellison to retort, "What do you know about my life? It's easy for you. You're just a straw in the wind. Get on your motorcycle and go back to Chicago and throw some Molotov cocktails. That's all you'll ever know about." Kirkland's version, corroborated by Morris's son, paints Ellison as the kind of helpless victim his own work avoided depicting. Since Morris's memoir is not exactly a monument to honesty, though, I would sooner believe the judge.

4. "The unfortunate fact remains that to define one's individuality is to stumble upon social barriers which stand in the way, all too much in the way, of 'infinite possibilities.' Freedom can be fought for, but it cannot always be willed or asserted into existence. And it seems hardly an accident that even as Ellison's hero asserts the 'infinite possibilities' he makes no attempt to specify them," wrote Howe. For the full essay, see Irving Howe, *A World More Attractive* (New York: Horizon Press, 1963).

5. Jerry Watts, *Heroism and the Black Intellectual: Ralph Ellison, Politics, and Afro American Intellectual Life* (Chapel Hill, NC: University of North Carolina Press, 1994), 55.

6. "'American Culture is of a Whole': From the Letters of Ralph Ellison," *New Republic* March 1, 1999.

7. Ralph Ellison, *Collected Essays* (New York: Modern Library, 1996), 247. Hereafter *CE*.

8. Dizzy Gillespie with Al Fraser, *To Be or Not to Bop* (Garden City, N.Y.: Doubleday, 1979), 295–96.

9. Miles Davis, with Quincy Troupe, *Miles: The Autobiography* (New York: Simon and Schuster, 1989), photo insert.

10. Sidney Finkelstein, *Jazz: A People's Music* (New York: International Publishers, 1948), 106.

11. T. S. Eliot, *The Waste Land and Other Poems* (New York: Signet Classic, 1998), 38.

12. *Ken Burns's Jazz, Episode Four: The True Welcome*, directed by Ken Burns, 999 mins., PBS Home Video, 2001, DVD.

13. I must take some credit—or blame—for this exchange, for on a panel with Gabbard and Robert O'Meally at the MLA convention in December 2000, I gave a paper entitled "Signifyin' Something: Ralph Ellison's Louis Armstrong," which claimed that Ellison's Armstrong influenced Burns, and thus our inescapable view of him as a heroic and redemptive figure whose apparent minstrelsy is really transformed into high art. For more of the fallout from that panel, see Robert O'Meally, "Ralph Ellison Inspired Jazz in the Concert Hall," (*New York Times*, May 27, 2001), in which O'Meally claims that "Gary Giddins is also an Ellisonian."

14. Robert Walser, *Keeping Time: Readings in Jazz History* (New York: Oxford, 1999), 338.

15. Ted Panken, "Wynton Marsalis: Interview," at http://www.jazz house.org/library/index.php3?read=panken1

16. Ralph Ellison, *Living With Music* (New York: Modern Library, 2001), xi.

17. A superlative Rushing performance of "Harvard Blues" can be heard on *Rushing Lullabies* (Columbia/Legacy CK 65118).

18. Ralph Ellison, *Trading Twelves* (New York: Modern Library, 2000), 193–94.

19. Mark Tucker, *The Duke Ellington Reader* (New York: Oxford University Press, 1993), 218, 452.

20. The only known tape that exists of this program is at the Library of Congress. It was part of a series that ran on WNET in the fall of

1965. The programs included "Bop: Jazz Goes Intellectual," with the Dizzy Gillespie quartet, and "Jazz: The Experimenters," with Charles Mingus and Cecil Taylor.

21. Ellison, *Trading Twelves*, 193.

22. See Henry Louis Gates Jr., *Thirteen Ways of Looking at a Black Man* (New York: Vintage, 1997), 39.

23. Ellison, *Trading Twelves*, 193.

24. Ibid., 194.

25. Ellison, *Living With Music*, 262.

26. Kirkland, *Ralph Ellison: An American Journey*.

27. See Krin Gabbard, *Jazz Among the Discourses* (Chicago: University of Chicago Press, 1996), 12–13.

28. LeRoi Jones, "Jazz and the White Critic," in *Black Music* (New York: Morrow, 1967), 20.

29. On Wright's connection to Eliot, see Craig Hansen Werner, *Playing the Changes* (Urbana: University of Illinois Press, 1994). Hansen finds that *Native Son* contains nearly as many allusions to Eliot as does *Invisible Man*.

30. In *Thinking in Jazz* (Chicago: University of Chicago Press, 1996), musicologist Paul Berliner writes extensively on musical quotations. See 98–99, 102–3, 257–58.

31. For more on this review from the *Daily Express*, see Laurence Bergreen's *Louis Armstrong: An Extravagant Life* (New York: Broadway, 1997), 243.

NOTES TO CHAPTER THREE

1. For these insights on allusion, I have alluded to Krin Gabbard, "Miles Davis and the Soundtrack of Modernity," in *Cinema and Modernity*, ed. Murray Pomerance (New Brunswick: Rutgers University Press, forthcoming).

2. Recent books that have made the case for this "other" T. S. Eliot have become so pervasive, it now seems like conventional wisdom that the vicar of high modernism who set his racism and anti-Semitism to

verse was also fascinated with jazz as a young man. These studies, mentioned in the previous chapter, include Ann Douglas's *Terrible Honesty: Mongrel Manhattan in the 1920s* (New York: Noonday Press, 1995), Michael North's *The Dialect of Modernism* (New York: Oxford, 1994), and David Chinitz's *T. S. Eliot and the Cultural Divide* (Chicago: University of Chicago Press, 2003).

3. Chinitz, *T. S. Eliot and the Cultural Divide*, 19–52.

4. For comprehensive anthologies of jazz and jazz-inspired poetry, see Sascha Feinstein and Yusef Komunyakaa, eds., *Jazz Poetry Anthology* (Bloomington: Indiana University Press, 1991) and item, *The Second Set* (Bloomington: Indiana University Press, 1996).

5. David Lehman, *The Last Avant-Garde* (New York: Doubleday, 1998), 109.

6. Hart Crane, *The Letters of Hart Crane, 1916–1932*, ed. Brom Weber (New York: Hermitage House, 1952), 89.

7. See Leonard Feather, *Encyclopedia of Jazz*: "The Original Dixieland Jass Band . . . recorded for Victor in 1917. These were the first jazz discs ever made; no Negro jazz orchestra was recorded on a major label until King Oliver's first session six years later" (24).

8. Hart Crane, *White Buildings* (New York: Boni and Liveright, 1926), 5. Hereafter *WB*.

9. Crane, *Letters*, 58.

10 See Malcolm Cowley, *A Second Flowering* (New York: Penguin, 1988), 191–215.

11. Paul Mariani, *The Broken Tower: A life of Hart Crane* (New York: W.W. Norton, 1999), 92.

12. The poem begins with a quotation from Act IV.iii of Ben Jonson's *Alchemist*, in which Dol Common, in a "fit of raving," rhapsodizes about "rais[ing] the building up / Of Helen's house against the Ismaelite, / King of Thogarma, and his habergeons / Brimstony, blue and fiery."

13. Cited in Harold Bloom, ed., *Modern Critical Views: Hart Crane* (New Haven: Chelsea House, 1985), 120.

14. Arnold Rampersad, *The Life of Langston Hughes Volume II, 1941–1967: I Dream a World* (New York: Oxford University Press, 1989), 280.

15. Charles Mingus, *Mingus Mingus Mingus Mingus Mingus* GRP/B000003N7Y, 1995 (Originally released on Impulse!, January 1963).

16. Alson Lynn Nielson, *Black Chant: Languages of African-American Postmodernism* (New York: Cambridge University Press, 1997), 187–88.

17. Langston Hughes, *The Collected Poems of Langston Hughes*, ed. Arnold Rampersad and David Roessell (New York: Vintage Classics, 1995), 385. Hereafter *CPLH*.

18. The album's cover art is an image of chains: slavery could be another explanation for the unknown identity of the original "Pa." The question, "Who's your daddy?" would apply in the opposite direction for Stevens. For an inquiry into Senegalese griotic patrimonies, see Keith Cartwright, *Reading Africa into American Literature* (Lexington: University Press of Kentucky, 2002).

19. Charles Mingus, *Beneath the Underdog: His World as Composed by Mingus*, ed. Nel King (New York: Random House, 1971), 69. Hereafter *BTU*.

20. Listen, for example, to a trio performance of Duke Ellington's "Money Jungle," where Mingus's battles with the quarter note assume a compelling, percussive violence (Blue Note CDP 7 46398 2; originally released in 1961). Although Ellington was Mingus's idol and the drummer Max Roach was his partner in crime at the Newport Anti-Festival, tensions were high at the sessions, producing an eccentric album where the clashes produced a hostility palpable to the ear. The album is a striking dramatization of Mingus's tensions with his precursor and peer, and does contain the definitive recording of the masterpiece "African Flower."

21. Eric Porter, *What Is this Thing Called Jazz?* (Berkeley: University of California Press, 2002), 102.

22. See *Triumph of the Underdog*. Directed by Don McGlynn, Shanachie Video, 1997.

23. Porter, *What Is this Thing Called Jazz?*, 104.

24. Wallace Thurman also skewers this world in his 1932 novel *Infants of the Spring* (New York: Simon and Schuster, 1996 [reprint]).

25. T. S. Eliot, *Selected Prose of T. S. Eliot* (New York: Harcourt, Brace, and Jovanovich, 1975), 60.

26. James Baldwin, *Collected Essays*, ed. Toni Morrison (New York: Library of America, 1998), 615. When Hughes adapted the twelve-bar blues to poetry, he cut it in half to six bars—a convenient shift for a poet being paid by the line, and one, unsurprisingly, emulated by future blues poets. For more on Hughes and blues poetry, see Steven C. Tracy, *Langston Hughes and the Blues* (Urbana: University of Illinois Press, 1988).

27. Jay Tolson, "The Duke and the Poet," *U.S. News and World Report*, July 8, 2002, 41.

28. Gene Santoro, *Myself When I am Real: The Life and Music of Charles Mingus* (New York: Oxford University Press, 2000), 140.

29. Gene Santoro, Personal correspondence, June 17, 2003.

30. Quoted in Arnold Rampersad, *The Life of Langston Hughes, Vol. II: 1941–1967, I Dream a World* (New York: Oxford University Press, 1988), 280.

31. Wallace Stevens, *The Palm at the End of the Mind*, ed. Holly Stevens (New York: Vintage Books, 1990), 77.

32. Stevens, *Palm at the End of the Mind*, 186–87.

33. Eleanor Cook, "Riddles, Charms, and Fictions," in *Wallace Stevens*, ed. Harold Bloom (New York: Chelsea House Publishers, 1985), 154.

34. Wallace Stevens, *Opus Posthumous* (New York: Alfred A. Knopf, 1989), 117.

35. Stevens, *Opus Posthumous*, 118.

36. Ibid.

37. Helen Vendler, "Ice and Fire and Solitude," *New York Review of Books*, December 4, 1997, 39–43.

38. For more on the Gwendolyn Brooks comment, see Joan Richardson, *Wallace Stevens: The Later Years* (New York: Beech Tree Books, 1988).

39. Tucker, *Duke Ellington Reader*, 172.

40. Tucker, *Duke Ellington Reader*, 208–9.

41. Stevens, *Palm at the End of the Mind*, 388.

42. For a more detailed account of the appearance of Ellington in *Murder at the Vanities*, see Krin Gabbard, *Jammin' at the Margins* (Chicago: University of Chicago Press, 1996).

43. Ralph Ellison, *Juneteenth* (New York: Random House, 1999), 23. Hereafter *JT*.

44. *The LeRoi Jones / Amiri Baraka Reader*, ed. William J. Harris (New York: Thunder's Mouth Press, 1991), 16.

45. Emily Bernard, ed., *Remember Me to Harlem: The Letters of Langston Hughes and Carl Van Vechten, 1925–1964* (New York: Alfred A. Knopf, 2001), 320.

46. Jones, *Black Music*, 14.

47. *Le Roi Jones / Amiri Baraka Reader*, 17.

48. Frank O'Hara, *The Collected Poems of Frank O'Hara*, ed. Donald Allen (Berkeley: University of California Press, 1995), 499.

49. Ibid.

50. For more on African derivations of the word "jazz," see Robert Farris Thompson, *Flash of the Spirit* (New York: Vintage Books, 1983).

51. Miles Davis, *Kind of Blue*. Columbia/Legacy, CK64935, 1997. Originally released in 1959.

52. For more on O'Hara and his context, see David Lehman, *The Last Avant-Garde*.

53. O'Hara, 325, *Collected Poems*.

54. Ibid., 325.

55. Jones, *Black Music*, 25.

56. Holiday, Billie. *Lady in Satin*. Columbia/Legacy, CK65144, 1997. Originally released in 1958.

57. In *The Portable Beat Reader*, ed. Ann Charters (New York: Penguin, 1992), 57.

58. Ibid., 57.

59. Ibid., 59.

60. Ibid., 54.

61. Ibid., 53–54.

62. Robert Kelly, "Jazz and Poetry: A Conversation (with Yusef Komunyakaa and William Matthews)," *Georgia Review* 46, no. 4 (Winter 1992): 645–46, 653–54.

63. Yusef Komunyakaa, *Blue Notes: Essays, Interviews, and Commentaries*, ed. Radiclani Clytus (Ann Arbor: University of Michigan Press), 6.

64. Ibid., 140–41.

65. Yusef Komunyakaa, *Neon Vernacular: New and Selected Poems* (Hanover, New Hampshire: Wesleyan University Press, 1993), 178.

66. Yusef Komunyakaa, "Twilight Seduction," in *The Second Set: The Jazz Poetry Volume 2*, 112.

67. Jayne Cortez, "If the Drum is a Woman," *Jazz Fan Looks Back* (Brooklyn: Hanging Loose Press, 2002), 27.

68. Komunyakaa, *Neon Vernacular*, 178.

69. Ibid., 72.

70. Scott DeVeaux, *The Birth of Bebop: A Social and Musical History* (Berkeley: University of California Press, 1997), 6.

NOTES TO CHAPTER FOUR

1. For more on Buddy Bolden, Storyville, and the criminalization of the red-light districts of New Orleans, see Al Rose, *Storyville, New Orleans: Being an Authentic, Illustrated Account of the Notorious Red-Light District* (Alabama: University of Alabama Press, 1974).

2. Morton was, in fact, a pimp, and his memoir, *Mister Jelly Roll*, is a fascinating example of an early jazz hustle. For a recent refutation of this account of jazz legends as playas and macks, see Wynton Marsalis's jointly authored memoir *Jazz in the Bittersweet Blues of Life.* (New York: Da Capo Press, 2001).

3. Robin D. G. Kelley, "Miles Davis: A Jazz Genius in the Guise of a Hustler," *New York Times*, May 13, 2001.

4. See John Szwed, *So What: The Life of Miles Davis* (New York: Simon and Schuster, 2002).

5. Billie Holiday and William Dufty, *Lady Sings the Blues* (New York: Doubleday, 1956), 14. Hereafter *LSB*.

6. See Ben L. Reitman, *The Second Oldest Profession: A Study of the Prostitute's "Business Manager"* (New York: Vanguard Press, 1931). The author, an erstwhile fellow traveler, hobo, and prison doctor, claims to be a native informant and author of the first extended study of the pimp.

7. "In truth, Billie could not write," writes Gary Giddins in the liner notes to *Lady Day: The Complete Columbia Recordings* (CXK 85 470).

8. For more on Holiday's childhood prostitution, see Farah Jasmine Griffin, *If You Can't Be Free, Be a Mystery* (New York: Free Press, 2001), 52–53.

9. Originally released as Clef 89096, currently available on *The Complete Billie Holiday on Verve* (517658-2).

10. Charles Schwartz, *Cole Porter: A Biography* (New York: Da Capo Press, 1979), 116.

11. Douglas Martin, "Elisabeth Welch, 99, Cabaret Hitmaker, Dies." *New York Times*, July 18, 2003.

12. Stuart Nicholson, *Billie Holiday* (Boston: Northeastern University Press, 1995), 233.

13. For more on Millstein's Carnegie Hall performance of Dufty's prose and Holiday's silent reaction, see Fred Moten, *In the Break* (Minneapolis: University of Minnesota Press, 2003), 103–8.

14. Leslie Gourse, ed., *The Billie Holiday Companion: Seven Decades of Commentary* (New York: Schirmer Books, 1997), 99.

15. Francis Davis, "Our Lady of Sorrows," *Atlantic Monthly*, November 2000, 104.

16. Quoted in Gary Giddins's lines notes to *Lady Day*, 20.

17. Nicholson, *Billie Holiday*, 172.

18. Holiday is using figurative language, of course, just as the Andrews Sisters sang "beat me up, daddy . . . beat me, daddy, eight to the bar." See Adam Gussow, *Seems Like Murder Here: Southern Violence and the Blues Tradition* (Chicago: University of Chicago Press, 2002).

19. Charles Mingus, *Beneath the Underdog: His World as Composed by Mingus*, ed. Nel King (New York: Random House, 1971), 355–56. Hereafter *BU.*

20. Janet Coleman and Al Young, *Mingus/Mingus: Two Memoirs* (Berkeley: Creative Arts, 1989), 8.

21. That eviction footage, like much of the self-mythmaking in *Beneath the Underdog*—indeed, like much of Mingus's music—is as brutal and disturbing as it is carefully orchestrated.

22. Miles Davis, with Quincy Troupe, *Miles: The Autobiography* (New York: Simon and Schuster, 1989), 66. Hereafter *MA*.

23. Kelley, "*A Jazz Genius*," 42.

24. There are some who will make the case that early 1970s fusion albums like *Agartha* and *Dark Magus* used the timbres of rock and roll, but to such dissonant and atonal effect, the results were anything but sell-outs. They are not easy on the ear, but have proven to be influential on various forms of electronica. For a defense of this period of Davis's work, see Paul Tingen, *Miles Beyond: The Electric Explorations of Miles Davis* (New York: Billboard Books, 2003).

25. There is such a disparity between those transcripts and the published book, though, that the transgressions might not necessarily have been Troupe's.

26. See Gayatri Chakravorty Spivak, "Can the Subaltern Speak?: Speculations on Widow Sacrifice," *Wedge* 7, no. 8 (Winter/Spring 1985): 120–30. For an actual subaltern who speaks while maintaining her sexual integrity, see Norma Miller's *Swingin' at the Savoy: The Memoir of a Jazz Dancer* (Philadelphia: Temple University Press, 1996).

27. For more on this story and its implications in the world of fashion and beyond, see Shane White and Graham White, *Stylin* (Ithaca: Cornell University Press, 1998).

28. Thomas Pynchon, *V.* (New York: Harper and Row, 1989), 366.

29. Ibid., 59.

30. John Litweiler, *Ornette Coleman: A Harmolodic Life* (New York: William Morrow, 1992), 82.

31. W. T. Lahmon, *Deliberate Speed: The Origins of a Cultural Style in the American 1950s* (Washington, D.C.: Smithsonian Institution Press, 1990), 236.

32. I transcribed these remarks from *Derrida*, dir. Kirby Dick, Zeitgeist Video, 2002.

33. Scott DeVeaux, *The Birth of Bebop: A Social and Musical History* (Berkeley: University of California Press, 1997), 189.

34. Thomas Pynchon, *Gravity's Rainbow* (New York: Penguin, 1973), 63.

35. *Celebrating Bird: The Triumph of Charlie Parker*, dir. Gary Giddins, Pioneer Video, 1987, DVD.

36. Rafi Zabor, *The Bear Comes Home* (New York: Norton, 1997), 13.

37. Ibid., 442.

38. See Michelle Mercer, *Footprints: The Life and Work of Wayne Shorter* (New York: Tarcher/ Penguin, 2004). Shorter also said this to me in an interview: David Yaffe, "Wayne Shorter's Roots," *Village Voice*, June 10, 1997.

BIBLIOGRAPHY

Adorno, Theodor. "Perennial Fashion—Jazz." In *Prisms*. Trans. Samuel and Shierry Weber. Cambridge, Mass.: MIT Press, 1981.

Albertson, Chris. *Bessie*. New York: Stein and Day, 1972. New Haven: Yale University Press, 2002 (revised edition).

Appel, Alfred. *Jazz Modernism: From Ellington and Armstrong to Matisse and Joyce*. New York: Alfred A. Knopf, 2002.

Baker, Houston. *Blues Ideology, and Afro-American Literature: A Vernacular Theory*. Chicago: University of Chicago Press, 1984.

Baldwin, James. "Sonny's Blues." In *Going to Meet the Man*. New York: Dial Press, 1965.

———. "The Black Boy Looks at the White Boy." In *Collected Essays*. Ed. Toni Morrison. New York: Library of America, 1998.

Baraka, Amiri (as LeRoi Jones). *Blues People: Negro Music in White America*. New York: Morrow, 1963.

———. *Black Music*. New York: Morrow, 1967.

———. *The LeRoi Jones/Amiri Baraka Reader*. Ed. William J. Harris. New York: Thunder's Mouth Press, 1991.

———. "Somebody Blew Up America." *Counterpunch*, October 3, 2002.

Barthelme, Donald. "The King of Jazz." In *Hot and Cool: Jazz Short Stories*. Ed. Marcela Breton. London: Bloomsbury, 1990.

Bergreen, Laurence. *Louis Armstrong: An Extravagant Life*. New York: Broadway, 1997.

Berliner, Paul. *Thinking in Jazz: The Infinite Art of Improvisation*. Chicago: University of Chicago Press, 1996.

Berman, Paul, Ed. *Blacks and Jews: Alliances and Arguments*. New York: Delacourte, 1992.

Bernard, Emily, Ed. *Remember Me to Harlem: The Letters of Langston Hughes and Carl Van Vechten, 1925–1964.* New York: Alfred A. Knopf, 2001.

Birkerts, Sven. "Harmonic Convergence." *The New Yorker*, January 13, 2003, 85–86.

Brazeau, Peter. *Parts of a World: Wallace Stevens Remembered.* New York: Random House, 1983.

Broyard, Anatole. "Keep Cool Man." *Commentary* 11, (April 1951): 361–62.

———. *Kafka Was the Rage.* New York: Vintage, 1997.

Carby, Hazel. "It Just Be's Dat Way Sometime: The Sexual Politics of Women's Blues." *Radical America* 20, no. 4 (June–July 1986).

Charters, Ann. *The Portable Beat Reader.* New York: Penguin Books, 1992.

Chinitz, David. "Dance, Little Lady: Poets, Flappers, and the Gendering of Jazz." In *Modernism, Gender, and Culture.* Ed. Lisa Rado. Garland, 1996, 319–35.

———. *T. S. Eliot and the Cultural Divide.* Chicago: University of Chicago Press, 2003.

Clarke, Donald. *Wishing on the Moon: The Life and Times of Billie Holiday.* New York: Viking Press, 1995.

Coleman, Janet, and Al Young. *Mingus/Mingus: Two Memoirs.* Berkeley: Creative Arts, 1989.

Collier, James Lincoln. *Benny Goodman and the Swing Era.* New York: Oxford University Press, 1989.

Cook, Eleanor. "Riddles, Charms, and Fictions." In *Wallace Stevens.* Ed. Harold Bloom. New York: Chelsea House, 1985.

Crane, Hart. *The Complete Poems and Selected Letters and Prose of Hart Crane.* Ed. Brom Weber. London: Oxford University Press, 1968.

———. *The Letters of Hart Crane, 1916–1932.* Ed. Brom Weber. New York: Hermitage House, 1952.

Crouch, Stanley. "Laughin' Louis." *Village Voice*, August 14, 1978.

———. *Notes of a Hanging Judge: Essays and Reviews, 1979–1988.* New York: Oxford University Press, 1988.

————. *Don't the Moon Look Lonesome: A Novel in Blues and Swing.* New York: Pantheon, 2000.

————. Personal communication. September, 2002.

Davis, Angela Y. *Blues Legacies and Black Feminism: Gertrude "Ma" Rainey, Bessie Smith, and Billie Holiday.* New York: Pantheon Books, 1998.

Davis, Francis. "Our Lady of Sorrows," *Atlantic Monthly*, November 2000, 104.

Davis, Miles, with Quincy Troupe. *Miles: The Autobiography.* New York: Simon and Schuster, 1989.

Dearborn, Mary V. *Mailer: A Biography.* New York: Houghton Mifflin, 1999.

DeVeaux, Scott. *The Birth of Bebop: A Social and Musical History.* Berkeley: University of California Press, 1997.

Dickstein, Morris. *Leopards in the Temple.* Cambridge, Mass.: Harvard University Press, 2001.

Douglas, Ann. *Terrible Honesty: Mongrel Manhattan in the 1920s.* New York: Noonday, 1995.

Eliot, T. S. *The Waste Land.* New York: Boni and Liveright, 1922.

————. *Inventions of the March Hare.* Ed. Christopher Ricks. New York: Harcort Brace, 1996.

————. *Selected Prose of T. S. Eliot.* Ed. Frank Kermode. New York: Harcourt Brace and Company, 1975.

Ellison, Ralph. *Invisible Man.* New York: Random House, 1952.

————. *Collected Essays.* New York: Modern Library, 1996.

————. *Juneteenth.* New York: Random House, 1989.

————. *Trading Twelves.* New York: Modern Library, 2000.

————. *Living With Music.* Ed. Robert O'Meally. New York: Modern Library, 2001.

Elledge, Jim. *Frank O'Hara: Be True to a City.* Ann Arbor: University of Michigan Press, 1990.

Feinstein, Sascha. *Jazz Poetry: From the 1920s to the Present.* Westport, Conn.: Greenwood Press, 1997.

Feinstein, Sascha, and Yusef Komunyakaa, eds. *The Jazz Poetry Anthology.* Bloomington: Indiana University Press, 1991.

———. *The Second Set.* Bloomington: Indiana University Press, 1996.

Ferguson, Otis. *The Otis Ferguson Reader.* Ed. Dorothy Chamberlain and Robert Wilson. Highland Park, Ill: December, 1982.

Finklestein, Sidney. *Jazz: A People's Music.* New York: International Publishers, 1948.

Fisher, Clive. *Hart Crane: A Life.* New Haven: Yale University Press, 2002.

Forrest, Leon. "A Solo Long-Song: For Lady Day." In *The Furious Voice for Freedom: Essays on Life.* Wakefield, R.I.: Asphodel, 1994.

Gabbard, Krin. *Jammin' at the Margins.* Chicago: University of Chicago Press, 1996.

———, ed. *Jazz Among the Discourses.* Durham, N.C. Duke University Press, 1995.

Gates, Henry Louis. *Thirteen Ways of Looking at a Black Man.* New York: Vintage, 1997.

Gillespie, Dizzy, with Al Fraser. *To Be or Not to Bop.* Garden City, N.Y.: Doubleday, 1979.

Giddins, Gary. *Satchmo.* New York: Doubleday, 1987.

Gooch, Brad. *City Poet: The Life and Times of Frank O'Hara.* New York: Alfred A. Knopf, 1993.

Gourse, Leslie. *Straight, No Chaser: The Life and Genius of Thelonious Monk.* New York: Schirmer Books, 1997.

———. *The Billie Holiday Companion: Seven Decades of Commentary.* New York: Schirmer, 1997.

Hajdu, David. *Positively Fourth Street.* New York: Farrar, Straus and Giroux, 2001.

Hammer, Langdon, and Brom Weber, eds. *O My Land, My Friends: The Selected Letters of Hart Crane.* New York: Four Walls, Eight Windows, 1997.

Hamilton, Ian. *In Search of J. D. Salinger.* New York: Random House, 1988.

Hammond, John. *John Hammond on Record.* New York: Summit Books, 1980.

Hartman, Saidiya V. *Scenes of Subjection: Terror, Slavery, and Self-Making in Nineteenth-Century America.* New York: Oxford University Press, 1997.

Holiday, Billie, and William Dufty. *Lady Sings the Blues*. New York: Doubleday, 1956.

Homans, John. "Voice Lesson." *New York Magazine* January 20, 2003, 85–86.

Howley, Kerry. "Cold Fusion." *Reason*, June 27, 2003.

Hughes, Langston. *The Collected Poems of Langston Hughes*. Ed. Arnold Rampersad. New York: Vintage, 1994.

———. *Weary Blues*. Verve, 841 660-2, 1990 (Originally released in 1958.)

Jackson, Lawrence. *Ralph Ellison: Emergence of a Genius*. New York: John Wiley and Sons, 2002.

Jazz. Directed by Ken Burns. 999 min. PBS Home Video, 2001. DVD.

"Jerry Jazz Musician," www.jerryjazzmusician.com/mainHTML.cfm?page=interviews.html.

Jemie, Onwuchekwa. *Langston Hughes: An Introduction to the Poetry*. New York: Columbia University Press, 1965.

Johnson, James Weldon. *Autobiography of an Ex-Coloured Man*. New York: Vintage, 1989.

Kelley, Robin D. G. "Miles Davis: A Jazz Genius in the Guise of a Hustler." *New York Times,* May 13, 2001.

Komunyakaa, Yusef. *Blue Notes: Essays, Interviews, and Commentaries*. Ed. Radiciani Ciytus. Ann Arbor: University of Michigan Press, 2003.

———. *Neon Vernacular: New and Selected Poems*. Hanover, N.H.: Wesleyan University Press, 1993.

Lahmon, W. T. *Deliberate Speed: The Origins of a Cultural Style in the American 1950s*. Washington, D.C.: Smithsonian Institution Press, 1990.

Leeming, David. *James Baldwin: A Biography*. New York: Henry Holt, 1995.

Lehman, David. *The Last Avant-Garde*. New York: Doubleday, 1998.

Litweiler, John. *Ornette Coleman: A Harmolodic Life*. New York: William Morrow, 1992.

Lott, Eric. *Love and Theft: Blackface Minstrelsy and the American Working Class*. New York: Oxford University Press, 1993.

————. "Double V, Double-time: Bebop's Politics of Style." In *Jazz Among the Discourses*. Ed. Krin Gabbard. Durham, N.C.: Duke University Press, 1995, 243–55.

Maggin, Donald L. *Stan Getz: A Life in Music*. New York: William Morrow, 1996.

Mailer, Norman. *Advertisements for Myself*. Cambridge, Mass.: Harvard University Press, 1992.

Mann, Thomas. *Doctor Faustus*. Trans. H. T. Lowe-Porter. New York: Random House, 1948.

Marsalis, Wynton. "What Jazz Is—and Isn't." In *Keeping Time: Readings in Jazz History*. Ed. Robert Walser. New York: Oxford University Press, 1999, 334–39 (originally published in *New York Times*, July 31, 1988).

Maynard, Joyce. *At Home in the World*. New York: Picador, 1998.

Melnick, Jeffrey. *A Right to Sing the Blues: African Americans, Jews, and American Popular Song*. Cambridge, Mass.: Harvard University Press, 1999.

Meltzer, David, Ed. *Reading Jazz*. San Francisco: Mercury House, 1993.

Mezzrow, Mezz, and Bernard Wolfe. *Really the Blues*. New York: Citadel Press, 1946.

Mingus, Charles. "Beneath the Underdog" manuscript [1964], Charles Mingus Collection, Library of Congress, Boxes 45–46.

————. *Beneath the Underdog: His World as Composed by Mingus*. Ed. Nel King. New York: Random House, 1971.

————. *More than a Fake Book*. New York: Hal Leonard, 1991.

Mingus, Sue. *Tonight at Noon: A Love Story*. New York: Pantheon, 2002.

Morgernstern, Dan. Liner notes to *Louis Armstrong: Portrait of an Artist as a Young Man* (Columbia/Legacy,1994).

Moten, Fred. *In the Break: The Aesthetics of the Black Radical Tradition*. Minneapolis: University of Minnesota Press, 2003.

Murray, Albert. *Stomping the Blues*. New York: McGraw Hill, 1976.

Nicholson, Stuart. *Billie Holiday*. Boston: Northeastern University Press, 1995.

Nielson, Aldon Lynn. *Black Chant: Languages of African-American Post-modernism*. New York: Cambridge University Press, 1997.

North, Michael. *The Dialect of Modernism*. New York: Oxford, 1994.

O'Hara, Frank. *The Collected Poems of Frank O'Hara*. Ed. Donald Allen. Berkeley: University of California Press, 1995.

O'Meally, Robert. *Lady Day: The Many Faces of Billie Holiday*. New York: Arcade Publishing, 1991.

———, ed. *The Jazz Cadence of American Culture*. New York: Columbia University Press, 1998.

Porter, Eric. *What Is This Thing Called Jazz?: African American Musicians as Artists, Critics, and Activists*. Berkeley: University of California Press, 2002.

Porter, Lewis. *John Coltrane: His Life and Music*. Ann Arbor: University of Michigan Press, 1998.

Posnock, Ross. *Color and Culture: Black Writers and the Making of the Modern Intellectual*. Cambridge, Mass.: Harvard University Press, 1998.

Powers, Richard. *The Time of Our Singing*. New York: Farrar, Straus, and Giroux, 2003.

Pynchon, Thomas. *Gravity's Rainbow*. New York: Penguin, 1973.

———. *Slow Learner: Early Stories*. New York: Little, Brown and Company, 1998.

———. *V.* New York: Harper and Row, 1989.

Rampersad, Arnold. *The Life of Langston Hughes, Vol. 1, 1902–1941: I, Too, Sing America*. New York: Oxford University Press, 1986.

———. *The Life of Langston Hughes, Vol. 2, 1941–1967: I Dream a World*. New York: Oxford University Press, 1988.

Rampersad, Arnold, and David Roessel, eds. *The Collected Poems of Langston Hughes*. New York: Knopf, 1998.

Richardson, Joan. *Wallace Stevens: The Later Years*. New York: Beech Tree Books, 1988.

Rosenberg, Deena. *Fascinating Rhythm: The Collaboration of George and Ira Gershwin*. New York: Dutton, 1991.

Rollyson, Carl. *The Lives of Norman Mailer*. New York: Paragon House, 1991.

Roth, Philip. The *Human Stain*. New York: Vintage, 2000.

Salinger, J. D. "Blue Melody," *Cosmopolitan*, September 1948.

―――. *The Catcher in the Rye*. Boston: Little, Brown and Company, 1951.

Santoro, Gene. *Myself When I Am Real: The Life and Music of Charles Mingus*. New York: Oxford University Press, 2000.

―――. Personal correspondence, June 17, 2003.

Saul, Scott. *Freedom is/Freedom Ain't: Jazz and the Making of the Sixties*. Cambridge, Mass.: Harvard University Press, 2003.

Savery, Pancho. "Baldwin, Bebop, and 'Sonny's Blues.'" In *Understanding Others: Cultural and Cross-Cultural Studies and the Teaching of Literature*. Ed. Joseph Trimmer et al. Urbana: NTCE, 1992.

Schuller, Gunther. *Early Jazz*. New York: Oxford University Press, 1968.

―――. *The Swing Era: The Development of Jazz, 1930–1945*. New York: Oxford University Press, 1989.

Schwartz, Charles. *Cole Porter: A Biography*. New York: Da Capo Press, 1979.

Searles, George J., ed. *Conversations with Philip Roth*. Jackson: University Press of Mississippi, 1992.

Sollors, Werner. *Amiri Baraka/LeRoi Jones: The Quest for a Populist Modernism*. New York: Columbia University Press, 1978.

Southern, Eileen. *The Music of Black Americans*. New York: Norton, 1997.

Spivak, Gayatri Chakravorty. "Can the Subaltern Speak?: Speculations on Widow Sacrifice." *Wedge* 7, no. 8 (Winter/Spring 1985): 120–30.

Standley, Fred L. et al. *Conversations with James Baldwin*. Jackson: University Press of Mississippi, 1989.

Stevens, Wallace. *The Collected Poems of Wallace Stevens*. New York: Alfred A Knopf, 1954.

―――. *Letters of Wallace Stevens*. Selected and edited by Holly Stevens. New York: Alfred A. Knopf, 1966.

―――. *Opus Posthumous: Poems, Plays, Prose by Wallace Stevens*. Ed. Samuel French Morse. New York: Alfred A. Knopf, 1957.

————. *The Palm at the End of the Mind: Selected Poems and a Play*. Ed. Holly Stevens. New York: Alfred A. Knopf, 1967.

Sudhalter, Richard M., "Composing the Words That Might Capture Jazz," *New York Times*, August 29, 1999.

Szwed, John F. *Jazz 101*. New York: Hyperion, 2000.

————. *So What: The Life of Miles Davis*. New York: Simon and Schuster, 2002.

————. "Really the (Typed-Out) Blues: Jazz Fiction in Search of Dr. Faustus," *Village Voice*, July 2, 1979, 72.

Tolson, Jay. "The Duke and the Poet." In *U.S. News and World Report*, July 8, 2002, 40–43.

Tracy, Steven C. *Langston Hughes & the Blues*. Urbana: University of Illinois Press, 1988.

Tucker, Mark. *The Duke Ellington Reader*. New York: Oxford University Press, 1993.

Unterecker, John. *Voyager: A Life of Hart Crane*. New York: Farrar, Straus, and Giroux, 1969.

Vendler, Helen. "Ice and Fire and Solitude." *New York Review of Books*, December 4, 1997.

Walser, Robert, Ed. *Keeping Time: Readings in Jazz History*. New York: Oxford University Press, 1999.

Weatherby, W. J. *Squaring Off: Mailer vs. Baldwin*. New York: Mason/ Charter, 1977.

Werner, Craig Hansen. *Playing the Changes: From Afro-Modernism to the Jazz Impulse*. Urbana: University of Illinois Press, 1994.

Woodward, Richard B. "A Rage Supreme: A Tale of Age, Rage, and Hash Brownies." *Village Voice*, August 9, 1994, 27–34.

Yaffe, David. "A Development in Depth." *Village Voice*, June 6, 2001.

————. "Ellison Unbound." *The Nation*, March 11, 2002.

Zabor, Rafi. *The Bear Comes Home*. New York: Norton, 1997.

INDEX